SHARE & BURR S.F.

PLAZA AND BARRACKS OF SONOMA.

HISTORICAL AND DESCRIPTIVE

SKETCHBOOK

OF

Napa, Sonoma, Lake and Mendocino,

COMPRISING SKETCHES OF

THEIR TOPOGRAPHY, PRODUCTIONS, HISTORY,

SCENERY, AND PECULIAR ATTRACTIONS.

BY C. A. MENEFEE.

NAPA CITY:

REPORTER PUBLISHING HOUSE

1873

James D. Stevenson, Ph.D.
Publisher
1500 Oliver Road Suite K-109   Fairfield, California 94533

iv

TO

The Pioneers of California,

THE BRAVE AND THE TRUE.

The purest Nobility, the Vanguard of Civilization,

THIS VOLUME IS

RESPECTFULLY DEDICATED

By the AUTHOR

Publisher's Foreword
to
1993 publication of
Campbell Augustus Menefee's

HISTORICAL AND DESCRIPTIVE SKETCHBOOK
OF
NAPA, SONOMA, LAKE, AND MENDOCINO
1873.

As residents and most visitors to the wine country know, this is an area with a colorful past. Mr. Menefee's history of the area has the special distinction of apparently being the first local history of its kind in California (see original Preface, page ix), and has been much quoted in subsequent histories of the Napa area. In its pages are some unforgettable stories. One such is a meeting of General Vallejo with an Indian of the area who was naked on a very cold day in the rainy season. (Chapter 1, Page 7). Historical events are reported, such as the Bear Flag Party which took possession of Sonoma. The Indians of the Napa area are described-they were at one time quite numerous. And in these pages we find the story of Agoston Haraszthy's contribution to the development of the internationally renowned California wine industry.

In order to make this significant historical work more useable, an index has been added, and the entire book set in a more readable Times New Roman 12 point typeface. This latter change was necessary because of the small print of the original edition. (In the 1970's a reprint reproduced the original typeface and size, however print quality is varied and some pages of that editon are virtually unreadable.)

To permit the reader to use the original table of contents in the present publication, page numbers of the original are placed in the text in parenthesis. The reader's attention will be drawn to these numbers which occur in the body of the text. The narrative is broken by the page number in the original work. For example in Chapter 1, page 2, the reader will find a (19) against the left margin to indicate the end of page 18 and start of page 19 in the original work. Here is that passage about the Indians which appears in the Napa section:

In 1843 there were from fifty to one hundred upon Bale Rancho, four hundred upon the Caymus Rancho, six hundred upon the Salvador Rancho, a large number upon the Juarez and the Higuera Ranchos, and a still larger number at Soscol. These were in some sense permanently fixed and residing constantly in one place. Besides these there were thousands of nomads, who roam-
(19)
ed the valleys and mountains as caprice or hunger dictated.

In the 1873 text the numbering system reserved numbers for blank pages and numbering started with an illustration which precedes the title page. Page (6) which occurred in the original preface was the first occurrence of a page number. In this publication, title, dedication, preface and other pages before Chapter 1 are given Roman numerals as is standard practice in modern book publishing.

Preservation of the original table of contents and paging described above allows one to use Mr. Menefee's numbering system to look for general topics. For more specific searches the index in the back of the book will be helpful. Page numbering for the index uses the present edition's paging system with the number next to an item in the index being the number at the top of a page, not the number in parenthesis from the original text.

As with any effort of this kind, errors creep in despite proofreader's best efforts. This will undoubtably occur in the present edition despite careful review. If an error is discovered which is believed to be attributable to the current work, the publisher will welcome a note describing an error. Reader corrections will be incorporated in future editions.

A note about errors which existed in the original work may be helpful. Virtually all occurrences of Mr. Menefee's typographic errors were reproduced as they were found. For example, in the table of Illustrations found on page xvi there were a number of page errors. For example R. T. Montgomery, A. J. Cox, and R. D. Hopkins were all listed as appearing on page (80). In fact Montgomery appears at page (64) in the original, A. J. Cox at page (72), with only R. D. Hopkins at the correct page. Correct page numbers for each illustration in this edition are placed adjacent to Mr. Menefee's entries.

Other materials of historical interest relating to the Wine Country of California may be ordered from *James Stevenson, Publisher*, 1500 Oliver Road, Suite K-109, Fairfield, California 94533. These include the story of <u>William B. Ide, The President of California</u>, and <u>McKenney's 1878-79 District Directory of Yolo, Solano, Napa, Lake, Marin, and Sonoma Counties, Including all Residents, with Sketch of Cities and Towns</u>. A booklist is available from the publisher, presently at no charge. Please send self addressed and stamped envelope to the address above.

James D. Stevenson, Ph.D.

Fairfield, California
May 1994

PREFACE. 1873

The author of this volume offers no other apology for his appearance in the *role* of book-maker than the desire to assist in the perpetuating in memory the scenes, the events, and the men of the past and present, who have acted so prominent a part in the formation and progress of our State and county; also the desire, fairly and honestly, to represent the beauties and attractions of the part of the State of which this volume treats. The merits of the subject are great, the endeavor to represent these merits fairly has been honest, and if the endeavor has failed, the failure is wholly attributable to the inability and want of judgment of the author. The work is purely local. It treats simply of local subjects, the early history, the pioneers, the progress of civilization, and the present condition and attractive features of these four counties. The labor that it has cost has been very great; yet looking upon the country of which it treats, as the garden spot of California, the task has been a labor of love. The work has been completed under the most annoying and discouraging circumstances. A more than due share of delays and disappointments has attended its compilation and its publication. This is the first local work of the kind ever published in California, and the first book that has ever been printed in the State that has been so illustrated, all the engravings of which were made by California artists.

(6)

The historical portion of Napa county chiefly compiled by Mr. R. T. Montgomery. He likewise arranged a few of the biographical sketches. He was engaged to finish the whole of this county, but circumstances prevented him, and the author was compelled to take up the half completed task, revise, re-compile, and complete.

The author here wishes to express his sincere thanks for the many courtesies that have been extended to him by numerous persons And especially has he cause for expressing his gratitude to Mr. J. L. Edwards of St. Helena, Mr. Tunis of Lakeport, and Mr. A. O. Carpenter of Ukiah, for valuable assistance rendered. Much of the interesting matter herein contained is due to the interest these gentlemen took in the work, and the material aid they rendered.

Great as the work has been, and strong as the desire to have it complete, the work is far, very from equaling what the author's ideal was when it was commenced. That it is imperfect he well knows; that many things of great moment, and many pioneers of note have been omitted, he freely acknowledges; but that it is the best that time and circumstances would admit, is claimed. It is so far from what he had intended, that it is with a feeling of mingled regret and disappointment that the author gives it to the reader. But, such is, with all its imperfections, it is placed before an appreciative public for their approval or condemnation.

x

CONTENTS.

NAPA COUNTY.

CHAPTER XI.

HISTORICAL AND BIOGRAPHICAL.

CHAPTER XII.

TOWNS AND WATERING PLACES.

CHAPTER XIII.

AGRICULTURAL RESOURCES.

CHAPTER XIV.

THE FUTURE OF NAPA.

LAKE COUNTY.

CHAPTER I

GENERAL DESCRIPTION

CHAPTER V.

GENERAL MISCELLANY.

MENDOCINO COUNTY.

GENERAL DESCRIPTION.

CHAPTER II.

GENERAL MISCELLANY.

ADDENDA.

BIOGRAPHIES AND STATISTICS.

ILLUSTRATIONS.

(First number is C. A. Menefee's original page number, followed by current number.)

ODE TO NAPA

BY R. M. S.

In the dark and sullen gloom
Of years long since gone by,
Once lay thy now happy homes
Uncarved, unmade, unknown.
The wild man trod thy rolling hills,
And bent his springing bow,
And sped his arrow at the game,
And lived as Nature taught him how.
Beaten trails among the brakes
And tangled ferns he made,
And in the clear and limpid streams
His swarthy limbs he bathed.

Silence reigned o'er hill and dale,
Save when his echoing whoop
Rang from crag to peak.
Then floated on the gale;
Save, too, the hawk's shrill scream,
Or the night bird's lonely cry,
Or the savage howl of cruel beast.
Naught but thy old oaks can tell,
Or the twinkling stars unfold
The changes wrought, and what befell,
Through those long years of Nature's rule,
Of earthquake, storms, and floods,
Of Summer suns, and Winter routs;
And yet, the Sage of Nature sees

Symbols in rocks and tongues in trees,
To him her hoary scars and shadowy signs
Speak wisdom, truth and eloquence.

A change came o'er thy mystic life,
Like the dawn of polar light
The dark and gloom began to break,
And flee away as if in fright.
One early morn the curling smoke
Of a stranger's camp fire rose,
And melted away in the mists of the morn
Like incense of the wild-thorn rose,
A signal of the red-man's doom.
Frought with a potency divine.
His power supreme so long endured.
Must swiftly, surely soon decline;
For e'er twelve moons shall wax and wane,

A thousand camps shall brightly burn;
And pale-faced bands with nerves like steel,
Though strangers in this Western land,
Shall make the red-man feel the might
And power of his conquering hand.
By magic all the scene is changed:
Where grew the lordly forest tree,
The plowshare turns the fallow lea,
The waving grain and rustling corn.
Hill and dale in times adorn;
And where the old adobe stood.
Its roof red-tiled and low,
A mansion now adorns the spot.
And dripping fountains flow;
Beneath the city's busy tread,
Lie the wigwams of yore,
And now high steeples mark the spot,
Where dusky maids in years before,
At the same wigwam door,
Sat thoughtless of their coming lot.

The steam-car rattles o'er the plains,
The light'ning speaks in words.
And where the light canoe
Athwart the stream they shot,
The paddled barge her course pursues,
With lungs of iron and breath of fire,
She stems the tide with giant strength,
The whirls and eddies heeding not;
And to thy mart like white winged birds,
In search o' bounteous fields,
The sailing fleets do gather here,

To take the golden yield,
The spoil of them who toil,
Who sow and reap on thy rich soil,
And sail away to other marts,
To furnish those who work the arts.
And when the evening chimes ring out,
And the faithful laborer's work is done,
The motherly matron spreads the board,
And happy children full of glee,
Haste to give their sire a kiss.
and when the holy Sabbath dawns,
Thy bells ring out, then pause,
The echoing answer hearing,
Peal on peal while ringing,
And the joyous throng while nearing,
Off'rings of faith are bringing.

No day e'er dawned with more apace,
No sun with more of splendor rose,
Than when the stranger came,
And smiled at Nature's repose;
The warm South wind but gently blew,
And meekly bowed the flowers,
While twittering birds their carols sang,

Half hid in leafy bowers;
The soft large moon looked mildly down.
The stars but twinkled in mirth,
The swaying boughs the chorus joined,
And praised the new day's birth.
Ring out ye bells, ring loud and clear,
The spell-bound years are gone,
New life and light are dawning here,
While plenty and peace abound.

NAPA SEMINARY.

NAPA COUNTY

AT THE RANCHERIA.

NAPA COUNTY:

AS IT WAS AND IS.

CHAPTER 1.

THE INDIAN TRIBES.

The Indians inhabiting the region now known as Napa County did not differ essentially from the other tribes-those found in Southern and Middle California. They presented the same physical characteristics, habits and customs. They were generally of small stature, broad shouldered, and possessed of great strength. They were of swarthy complexion, beardless, and had long, coarse and straight black hair. The shape of their heads indicated a low rank in the intellectual scale, and a predominance of all the propensities of the brute creation. Indeed they seemed to be rather an intermediate race or connecting link between man and the brutes, scarcely supe-
(18)
rior to the higher types of the latter, and only in a few points resembling the lowest class of the former. A few exceptions existed, but as a race, they were inferior to all the aboriginal tribes of this continent.

It is exceedingly difficult at this time to give an accurate account of these tribes. Their numbers were never exactly known, their habits being migratory, and their camps seldom permanent for any great length of time. It is not probable that the Indians knew their own number, or that they cared to know, and their rapid disappearance has left very few of whom even to make inquiry, and perhaps none who could give any definite information. We are therefore necessarily left to the alternative of estimating their numbers from the statements of early settlers and others who visited California at an early day.

Kit Carson says that in 1829, the valleys of California were full of Indians. He saw much of large and flourishing tribes that then existed. When he again visited the State in 1859, they had mostly disappeared, and the people who resided in the localities where he had seen them, declared that they had no knowledge of them whatever. They had disappeared and left no record of the cause which had led to their extermination. No estimate of their numbers appears to have been made until 1823, it was known that they had then greatly decreased.

Down to 1856 they thronged the streets of Napa City in great numbers, especially on Sundays, picking up odds and ends of castoff clothing, occasionally fighting, and always getting drunk if the means were procurable. Male and female, they encumbered the sidewalks, lounging or sleeping in the sun, half clad and squalid pictures of humanity in its lowest state of degradation. Now an Indian is rarely to be seen.

It was the custom of the Indians to establish their rancherias upon the grants of the early settlers, in order to gain a livelihood by occasional labor. In 1843 there were from fifty to one hundred upon Bale Rancho, four hundred upon the Caymus Rancho, six hundred upon the Salvador Rancho, a large number upon the Juarez and the Higuera Ranchos, and a still larger number at Soscol. These were in some sense permanently fixed and residing constantly in one place. Besides these there were thousands of nomads, who roam-

(19)

ed the valleys and mountains as caprice or hunger dictated. A few remain upon some of the ranchos named, but there are not one hundred altogether in the entire county.

George C. Yount, the first white settler in Napa Valley, (who arrived here in 1831) said that, in round numbers, there were from 10,000 to 12,000 Indians ranging the country between Napa and Clear Lake. Of this number he says there were at least 3,000 in Napa County, and perhaps twice that number. It is only certain that they were very numerous, and that they have mostly disappeared. As late as in 1856 they were quite numerous in the environs of Napa City, and were wont at certain times to make night hideous with their howlings among the willows along the banks of the river, with what purposes or motives we are left to conjecture.

At the time of Mr. Yount's arrival in the Valley, in 1831, there were six tribes of Indians in it, speaking different, although cognate dialects, and almost constantly at war with each other.

The Mayacomas tribe dwelt near the Hot Springs (Aguas Calientes) now Calistoga, at the upper end of this Valley, and the Callajomanas, on the lands now known as the Bale Rancho, near St. Helena. The Caymus tribe dwelt upon the Yount Grant, to which they gave their name. The Napa Indians occupied the Mexican grant of Entre Napa, that is, the lands between, Napa River and Napa Creek, to which they also gave their tribe name. The word Napa is said to signify "fish." The authority for this signification rests on the declaration of old pioneers, and is corroborated by the fact that in the cognate languages of the tribes on the northern coast, the word still bears the same signification. At least we have the information from one who was among the Gold Bluff adventurers, and who made a fish trade with an Indian, selling his shirt from off his back in exchange for a salmon. Doubtless the Indian word for fish must have been strongly impressed upon his memory by such a transaction.

The Ulucas dwelt on the East side of Napa River, near Napa City, and one of their words survives in the word Tulocay Ranch and Cemetery. The Soscol tribe occupied the Soscol Grant, on which are now situated the magnificent and extensive orchards of Messrs. Thompson, and of Morrissiana, the estate of Maj. Wm. Gouverneur Morris, U. S. Marshal. The languages of the various tribes on this coast appear to have

(20)

some words in common, and in the opinion of the missionary writers, were derived from one common stock, yet the dialects and idioms of the different tribes were so distinct and peculiar, as nearly to prevent verbal intercommunication among them.

The remnants of these tribes seem partially to have abandoned their native tongue since the occupation of the country by civilized men, and to have learned and adopted a large number of Spanish words, and more recently, some of our own language. These mixed with a goodly proportion of Indian, form a conglomerate "lingo," perhaps sufficiently expressive, but not remarkable for harmony or elegance.

The great numbers of these Indians is corroborated by the numerous circles of earth, stone and rubbish which mark the site of their rancherias, and by the remains of their inseparable "sweat-houses." They are found near springs or along the streams throughout Napa Valley and others adjacent. These perishable and perishing monuments tell us almost all that is to be known of a re-cently numerous, but almost extinct race. Of their wars and the causes of them we know nothing. Of their hopes, fears, joys and aspirations, we can form no conception. We only know that they were and are not-their poor remaining remnant being doomed to extinction as complete as that of the Narragansetts of New England, whose language, although preserved in print by the zealous missionary, Elliott, in his Indian Bible, can no longer be deciphered by a single human being.

All these Indians were in fact, as in name, "Diggers." A considerable portion of their food consisted of wild edible roots, among which was the *amole,* or soap-root. They could dig small animals out from their burrows, and when hard pressed would eat almost anything that had life even to earth worms. Of fish, they had at most seasons, an abundant supply. Grasshoppers were one of their favorite "dishes." They also made a kind of bread, sometimes from acorns, with which the valleys abounded, sometimes of pine-nuts, and at others from the crushed kernels of the buckeye, washed to eliminate their bitter and noxious qualities.

Incredible as it may seem, and loathesome even to think of, it is well authenticated that they carefully gathered certain large, fat and reddish spotted worms, found at some seasons of the year upon the

(21)

stalks of grasses and wild oats and used them as 'shortening" for their bread. The statement is made on the authority of a pioneer of unquestionable veracity, who was with a party of Indians, and who seeing one of them gathering every worm he met with and putting it in a pouch at his side, enquired what use was to be made of them. He had been eating of their bread, but it is hardly necessary to add that the stomach of even an old trapper, revolted from that hour against Indian cookery.

Their food corresponded well with their position in the scale of humanity, and this was well nigh the lowest. Of the building of permanent and comfortable habitations, they had no knowledge. They constructed for themselves in the rainy season, rude shelters with the boughs of trees, by no means impervious to rain or wind, and which, architecturally considered, were far inferior to the hut of the bear, or the lairs of the lower animals. In summer they encamped among the willows along the streams, or in the first thicket that promised even the semblance of protection from the elements. They deemed it unhealthy to sleep in a house, and indeed for *them* it probably was so. At least, when years afterwards, young Indians, male and female, were either captured or kidnapped, and made use of by white settlers as servants or slaves, as they were for several years, they seldom lived more than two or three years, being generally carried off by pulmonary diseases.

Before the period of the occupation of the country by Americans, the Mexicans tilled but a small portion of the soil, their chief pursuit being stock-raising. Immense herds of cattle roamed over the country, and many of the Indians, either by stealth, or by trifling labor for the owners of grants, could obtain a supply of beef and corn and beans to eke out a precarious support from other sources. The sudden influx of an American population put an end to this condition of things. The wild cattle gradually disappeared. Game grew shy and scarce. The holders of land grants were encroached upon by "squatters," who appropriated the soil without ceremony, so that they had no longer any use for the services of the Indians, and no motive, even if they had the power, for supplying their wants, except in rare instances. The valleys were fenced up and cultivated, and the right of private domain asserted and enforced on the banks of streams where the Diggers had fished from time im-

(22)

memorial. It became more and more difficult for the comparatively few that remained to subsist under the new *regime* so unexpectedly and so inexorably established.

It does not appear difficult to account for the rapid decrease in the number of these savages. We have already stated that the different tribes were almost continually at war. Besides this, the cholera broke out among them in the fall of 1833, and raged with terrible violence. So great was the mortality, they were unable either to bury or burn their dead, and the air was filled with the stench of putrefying bodies. A traveler who passed up the Sacramento Valley at this time, relates that on his way up he passed a place where about 300 Indians, with women and children, were encamped. When he returned, after an absence of three or four days, the ground was literally strewn with their bodies-all having died except one little Indian girl. She occupied the camp alone, while around her lay the festering bodies of her dead companions, and the air was rendered noxious by the horrid stench of decomposing dead bodies, which were found not alone in the camp, but for miles up and down the Valley. The disease does not appear to have been local, but general. As late as 1841, Mr. Charles Hopper, a most estimable citizen of this county, who is still living, in passing up the San Joaquin Valley, observed the skulls and other remains of great numbers of Indians lying in heaps, and was told by the Indians of that region, that a pestilence had swept away vast numbers only a few years before. Dwight Spencer, Esq., in 1851 also saw upon Grand Island, in Colusa county, the remains of more than 500 Indians.

It must be confessed that to all the causes, which we have assigned for the rapid disappearance of the Indians in this Valley, as elsewhere, we must add another, not creditable to civilization. The early Mexican settlers were not very chary of the lives of Indians, and their American successors have not unfrequently followed their example. While the Indians were yet comparatively numerous, their means of subsistence, at some seasons of the year, must have been very scant and precarious. The grant holders had abundance. Their cattle swarmed by tens of thousands over the country, and offered A constant temptation to the hungry Diggers. Theft was easy, and detection difficult. The settlers were annoyed by repeated losses. It was impossible to trace the offense to individuals. They only

(23)

knew in general that the Indians had stolen their cattle, and when possible, meted out to them cruel and indiscriminate punishment.

Only a few years before the American occupation, and within the memory of persons now living, a terrible instance of this kind occurred on the Bale Rancho, near Oakville. The settlers in Sonoma had lost great numbers of cattle, and traced their losses to the Callajomanas tribe. A party came over one night and surrounded the "sweat house," in which about 300 Indians were assembled. The whole number were slaughtered, man by man, as they passed out, and the tribe thus almost exterminated at a blow. A similar instance occurred in Trinity County in the Fall of 1850. The Americans surrounded the rancheria at night, and destroyed the whole tribe, excepting a few children.

In 1850 a party of Americans came over from Sonoma to avenge upon the Indians in general the murder of Kelsey in Lake county, in which the Indians of Napa had no hand. This party were on their way to Soscol to attack the Indians there, but were turned back by another party of white men at Napa, who prevented them from crossing the ferry. They then returned to Calistoga, and murdered in cold blood eleven innocent Indians, young and old, as they came out of their "sweat house," and then burned their "wickeyups," together with their bodies. The murderers (for they were nothing less) were arrested by authority of Governor Mason, and taken to San Francisco. However, the country was in such an unsettled and unorganized condition, that they were set free on *habeas corpus*, and never brought to trial.

The concurrent effects of savage warfare, pestilence, and such wholesale massacres as we have described, seem quite sufficient to account for the rapid decline of numbers among the Indians, long before the conquest.

In the excellent work of Mr. Cronise, entitled "The National Wealth of California," the influence of the Mission system is stated to be one of the causes of the degradation and consequent final extermination of the aboriginal inhabitants. The writer says: "There is no room to doubt that the degradation of the existing race is in some degree the result of the Mission system, which deprived them of the instincts that Nature had implanted: and left them no dependence but upon the will of the Fathers, which was impotent to save

(24)

them from extermination by the irresistible force of a higher civilization, in which they are unfitted to participate."

We are not inclined to the opinion that any such sinister influence was ever exerted upon the Indians of this region, or at least, to such an extent as to have changed them from manly, dignified, peaceable and intelligent people into the squalid and wretched creatures that were found here by the early American settlers. The nearest Mission was established at Sonoma, in 1820, and could not have done much towards the degradation of the Indians in this region. We think it pretty evident that the Napa tribes must have been a different race from those dwelling upon the coast, whose superiority seems to be fairly demonstrated. There must have been an original and radical difference between the Diggers and those tribes considered by Venegas as "equal to any race;"

described by Captain Roberts as "tall, robust, and straight as pine trees;" and said by the great navigator, Capt. Beachy to be "generally above the standard of Englishmen in height." Nor could they have been the same race of men seen at San Francisco in 1824, and described by Langsdorf, the surgeon of Admiral Kotzebue's ship, "who had "full, flowing beards," or of whom La Prouse says: "About one half of the males had such splendid beards that they would have made a figure in Turkey, or in the vicinity of Moscow." It is simply impossible that any amount of Missionary oppression could have wrought such a physical change as this. There must have been a vast original difference between the tribes inhabiting California. None of them dwelling in this county had beards, nor were they of great stature, and in point of skill and intelligence, it can only be said that very little evidence exists which indicates the possession of either, however much these attributes may have distinguished other tribes.

We have said that war and pestilence had thinned their ranks long before the conquest of the country, and it would seem that the presence of civilized society, with the great change of condition attending it, must necessarily have borne heavily upon them, and finally well-nigh completed the work of extermination. Indeed, no savage tribe thus far, has long survived the contact of civilization and its attendant vices. The California tribes will certainly not prove exceptions. Notwithstanding the eloquent plea which is made for the intelligence, benevolent disposition, and high physical develop-

(25)

ment of the Indian tribes on this coast, the savages in this region appear to have been lower in the scale of intelligence than any other upon the continent of America; so low, indeed, that since the secularization of the Missions, scarcely an attempt, by missionaries or others, has been made for their instruction or elevation. The heathen of other lands have had millions of dollars and years of toil expended upon them by every Protestant denomination of Christians, while the heathen tribes of California, have perished like brutes, in our midst, without even an attempt to provide for their spiritual welfare. Indeed, the most zealous Christian, the most sanguine philanthropist, acquainted with their mental and moral condition, would despair of making any lasting good impression upon a being so utterly stupid and stolid as the Digger Indian. No argument or authority could have made the least impression upon a being so low in the scale of intellect.

Even the truly benevolent efforts of the United States Government to improve at least the physical condition of the California Indians, have generally been singularly barren of good results. Wretched as their mode of life seems to us, there appears to be for them, a charm in it, since nothing short of compulsion or absolute hunger will induce them to remain upon a Reservation. In the opinion of the writer, much of the clamor against the Superintendents of Indian Reservations has been without cause. It is simply impossible for any man, however enlightened or benevolent, to truly civilize a Digger Indian. He may be taught to plow, reap, split rails, and perform many kinds of outdoor work. He may be fed to a goodly degree of fatness, and made to wash his face and wear decent clothing, but benevolence can go no farther. At the first impulse he returns to his vagabond life of idleness, his grasshopper diet and his wretched wigwam of boughs--the same untamed and untameable savage.

If they were superior to the wretched natives of Tasmania, we have overlooked the evidence of the fact. Certainly their dwellings, their modes of life, their weapons and utensils afford no such indications. A wretched shelter of boughs, a rude bow and arrow of little avail for killing game at a distance, a stone pestle and mortar, a feather head covering-these were all. Their arrows and lanceheads were made of obsidian, great quantities of which are found

(26)

near Uncle Sam Mountain, in Lake county, and their mortars and pestles of the hardest bowlders to be found in the streams. They are found in considerable numbers all over the country. R. M. Swain, Esq., Under Sheriff of this county, has collected numerous specimens, some of which exhibit considerable skill. To chip out such a brittle and refractory material as obsidian into arrows and lance heads must have required much time and labor, but of the former the Indians had abundance, while the sharp spur of necessity compelled them to submit to the latter. For a great portion of the year they wore no clothing, and even in winter were only half-clad in the skins of beasts.

True, the climate is so mild in this part of the State that, except in the rainy season, they scarcely needed clothing, so far as bodily comfort was concerned, and habit seems to have inured them to exposure to cold. A Digger, perfectly naked, once met General Vallejo on a very cold morning, at Sonoma. - "Are you not cold?" asked the General, "No," replied the Indian; "Is your face cold?"

"No," replied the General. "Well,' replied the Indian, ' *"I am all face!"* After the introduction of sheep by the early Mexican settlers, they were enabled to obtain a coarse wool, which they converted into blankets without loom or spindles. They twisted the threads with their fingers, and stretched the warp, attaching the ends to wooden pegs driven into the ground, and the filling was put in place by hand, a thread at a time. These blankets, no doubt, must have added greatly to the comfort of the few who could obtain them; but the great mass of the Diggers never attained to such a luxury.

Of navigation they were almost wholly ignorant. Their only method of crossing streams was by means of rafts constructed of bundles of tule bound together, somewhat similar, but far inferior to the *balsas* used by the Peruvian Indians upon Lake Titicaca, far up among the Andes.

Their knowledge of the proper treatment of disease was on a level with their attainments in all the arts of life. Roots and herbs were sometimes used as remedies, but the "sweat-house" was the principal reliance in desperate cases. This great sanitary institution, found in every rancheria, was a large circular excavation covered with a roof of boughs, plastered with mud, having a hole on one side for entrance, and another in the roof to serve as a chim-

(27)

ney. A fire having been lighted in the center, the sick were placed there to undergo a sweat bath for many hours, to be succeeded by a plunge in cold water. This treatment was their cure-all, and whether it killed or relieved the patient, depended upon the nature of his disease and the vigor of his constitution. A gentleman who was tempted, some years ago, to enter one of these sanitary institutions, gives the following story of his experience: "A sweat-house is of the shape of an inverted bowl. It is generally about forty feet in diameter at the bottom, and is built of strong poles and branches of trees, covered with earth, to prevent the escape of heat. There is a small hole near the ground, large enough for the Diggers to creep in one at a time; and another at the top of the house, to give vent to the smoke. When a dance is to occur, a large fire is kindled in the center of the edifice, the crowd assembles, the white spectators crawl in and seat themselves anywhere out of the way. The apertures both above and below are then closed, and the dancers take their positions.

"Four and twenty squaws, *en deshabille,* on one side of the fire; and as many hombres in *puris naturalibus* on the other. Simultaneous with the commencement of the dancing, which is a kind of shuffling hobble-de-hoy, the "music" bursts forth. Yes, music fit to raise the dead. A whole legion of devils broke loose. Such screaming, shrieking, yelling, and roaring was never before heard since the foundation of the world. A thousand cross-cut saws, filled by steam power-a multitude of tom-cats lashed together and flung over a clothes line-innumerable pigs under the gate, all combined, would produce a heavenly melody compared with it. Yet this uproar, deafening as it is, might possibly be endured; but another sense soon comes to be saluted. Talk of the thousand stinks of the City of Cologne! Here are at least forty thousand combined in one grand overwhelming stench; and yet every particular odor distinctly definable. Round about the roaring fire the Indians go capering, jumping, and screaming with the perspiration starting from every pore. The spectators look on until the air grows thick and heavy, and a sense of oppressing suffocation overcomes them; when they make a simultaneous rush at the door, for self-protection. Judge of their astonishment, terror and dismay, to find it fastened securely; bolted and barred on the outside. They rush frantically around the

(28)

walls in hope to discover some weak point through which they may find egress; but the house seems to have been constructed purposely to frustrate such attempts. More furious than caged lions, they rush bodily against the sides, but the stout poles resist every onset. Our army swore terribly in Flanders, but even My Uncle Toby himself would stand aghast were he here now.

"There is no alternative, but to sit down in hopes that the troop of naked fiends will soon cease, from sheer exhaustion. Vain expectation! The uproar but increases in fury, the fire waxes hotter and hotter, and they seem to be preparing for fresh-exhibitions of their powers. The combat deepens, on ye brave! See that wild Indian, a newly elected Captain, as with glaring eyes, blazing face and complexion like that of a boiled lobster, he tosses his arms wildly aloft, as in pursuit of imaginary devils, while rivers of perspiration roll down his naked frame. Was ever the human body thrown into such contortions before? Another effort of that kind, and his whole vertebral column must certainly come down with a crash. Another such a convulsion, and his limbs will assuredly be torn asunder, and the disjointed members fly to the four points of the compass. Can the human frame endure this much longer? The heat is equal to that of a bake oven. Temperature 500 degrees Fahrenheit. Pressure of steam 1,000 pounds to the square inch. The reeking atmosphere has become almost palpable, and the victimized audience are absolutely gasping for life. Millions for a cubic inch of fresh air; worlds for a drop of water to cool the parched tongue! This is terrible. To meet one's fate among the white caps of the Lake, in a swamped canoe, or to sink down on the Bald Mountain's brow, worn out by famine, fatigue and exposure, were glorious; but to die here, suffocating in a solution of human perspiration, carbonic acid gas and charcoal smoke, is horrible. The idea is absolutely appalling. But there is no avail. Assistance might as well be sought from a legion of unchained imps, as from a troop of Indians, maddened by excitement.

"Death shows his visage, not more than five minutes distant. The fire glimmers away leagues off. The uproar dies into the subdued rumble of a remote cataract, and respiration becomes lower and more labored. The whole system is sinking into utter insensibility, and all hope of relief has departed, when suddenly with a grand

(29)

triumphal crash, similar to that with which the ghosts closed their orgies, when they doused the lights, and started in pursuit of Tam O'Shanter and his old gray mare, the uproar ceases and the Indians vanish through an aperture, opened for the purpose. The half dead victims to their own curiosity, dash through it like an arrow, and, in a moment more, are drawing in whole buckets full of the cold, frosty air, every inhalation of which cuts the lungs like a knife, and thrills the system like an electric shock. They are in time to see the Indians plunge headlong into the ice cold waters of a neighboring stream, and crawl out and sink down on the banks, utterly exhausted. This is the last act of the drama, the grand climax, and the fandango is over."

The sweat house also served as a council chamber and banquet hall. In it the bodies of the dead were sometimes burned, amid the howlings of the survivors. Generally, however, the cremation of the dead took place in the open air. The body before burning, was bound closely together, the legs and arms folded, and forced by binding, into as small a compass as possible. It was then placed upon a funeral pile of wood, which was set on fire by the mother, wife, or some near relative of the deceased, and the mourners, with their faces daubed with pitch, set up a fearful howling and weeping, accompanied with the most frantic gesticulations. The body being consumed, the ashes were carefully collected.

A portion of these were mingled with pitch, with which they daubed their faces and went into mourning. During the progress of the cremation, the friends and relatives of the deceased thrust sharp sticks into the burning corpse, and cast into the fire the ornaments, feather headdresses, weapons, and everything known to have belonged to the departed. They had a superstitious dread of the consequences of keeping back any article pertaining to the defunct. An old Indian woman, whose husband was sick, was recently asked what ailed him. Her reply was that "he had kept some feathers belonging to a dead Indian that should have been burned with his body, and that he would be sick till he died."

The idea of a future state was universal among the California Indians, and they had a vague idea of rewards and punishments. As one expressed it: "Good Indian go big hill; bad Indian go bad place." Others thought if the deceased had been good in
(30)
his life-time, his spirit would travel west to where the earth and sky meet, and become a star; if bad, he would be changed into a grizzly, or his spirit-wanderings would be continued for an indefinite period. They expressed the idea of the change from this life to another, by saying that, "as the moon died and came to life again, so man came to life after death;" and they believed that "the hearts of good chiefs went up to the sky, and were changed into stars to keep watch over their tribes on earth." Although exceedingly superstitious, they were evidently not destitute of some religious conceptions. Certain rocks and mountains were regarded as sacred. Uncle Sam, in Lake county, was one of these sacred mountains, and no one except the priest or wizard of his tribe dared to ascend it. Two large bowlders between Napa City and Capel Valley, were also sacred, and no Indian would approach them. They also held the grizzly in superstitious awe, and nothing could induce them to eat its flesh.

The Diggers, too, had their sorcerers, male and female, who had great influence over them. They pretended to foresee future events and to exercise supernatural control over their bodies and to cure diseases by curious incantations and ceremonies. Four times a year each tribe united in a great dance, having some religious purpose and signification. One of these was held by night at the Caymus Rancho, in 1841, about the time of the vernal equinox and was terminated by a

strange, inexplicable pantomime, accompanied with wild gestures and screams, the object of which the Indians said was "to scare the devil away from their rancherias." An old gentleman who witnessed the performance, says he has no doubt that their object must have been attained if the devil had the slightest ear for music. Superstition enveloped and wrapped these savages like a cloud, from which they never emerged. The phenomena of nature on every hand, indeed, taught them that there was some unseen cause of all things-some power which they could neither comprehend nor resist. The volcano and the earthquake taught them this, and many accounts of these in past ages are preserved in their traditions. But farther than this their minds could not penetrate. It does not appear that under the Mission system, they made the slightest advance in moral or religious culture, in spite of the most zealous efforts of the Fathers. They were taught to go through the forms of Christian worship, and did so, but without the least com-
(31)
prehension of their significance. The whole subject of religion was beyond the reach of their untutored intellects, and it maybe doubted whether a trace of their early teachings now remains in the mind of a single Indian in California. Heathen they were from the beginning, and heathen they will remain to the end.

Forming our judgment of their mode of life from our standpoint, as civilized men, we are apt to conclude that the Diggers were a most unhappy race, and they were so, according to all our ideas of happiness. But it is probably true, nevertheless, that they enjoyed life as well as the most civilized nations. They knew no other kind of life, and aspired to nothing better. Habit inured them to hardships, exposures, and privations, which they considered as necessary and normal conditions of their existence. A kind Providence has so ordered that in whatsoever condition a man may find himself, not one can be found who would willingly exchange places with any other. Many might wish to change conditions in certain respects, but not one would lose his identity in another for any earthly consideration. The Esquimaux who dwell in the midst of the ice fields of the Polar regions, regard their country and their mode of life as preferable to any other, and after having visited civil countries, return to their old haunts and rude life with joyful alacrity. Just so was it, doubtless, with the Digger Indians. They were as happy after their fashion as their civilized successors and exterminators, and would have so remained, but for the advent of a superior race. Probably the sum of human happiness was as great before as after the settlement of the country by the whites. It was simply a substitution of one race for another-of so many tame men for so many wild ones. In such changes might gives right, and will gives law, and the result was inevitable; but *for the savages,* savage life was unquestionably the happiest of which they were capable.
(32)

CHAPTER II.

NAPA COUNTY-GENERAL DESCRIPTION.

This county is relatively small, but one of the most salubrious and fertile in the State. Its total area is about 450,000 acres, (828 square miles before the recent addition of territory from Lake County) large portion of which consists of mountains, worthless for the purposes of agriculture. Many of the mountains and hills are however, of some value for grazing purposes, while a few barren. The Assessor's returns show that in 1871, there were 107,650 acres enclosed, and in 1872, 48,000 acres under cultivation, of which 31,500 were in wheat and 3,725 in barley. The county at the time of the conquest, formed part of the Northern Military Department, under the Mexican Government, of which the headquarters were at Sonoma. It was organized and its boundaries fixed by the Legislature, April 25th, 1851. The boundaries were afterwards changed by an act approved April 4th, 1855. A considerable portion of its area was cut off by an act approved May 20th, 18th, 1861,

(33)

(amended Feb. 29, 1864) and became a portion of Lake county. At the last session of the Legislature a further change was made, changing, its northern line, and giving a portion of Lake county to Napa. Lake county still bounds Napa on the north, but the dividing line cannot yet be given, as no map is yet made which exhibits the changes made by legislation. It is bounded on the west by Sonoma, on the south by Solano, and on the east by Solano and Yolo counties. It is divided, for all legal purposes, into three town ships-Napa, Yount, and Hot Springs. A good general idea of the topography of Napa county may be obtained by considering it as consisting of three nearly parallel series of valleys (like the spaces between the four fingers of the hand) running, in a north-westerly and south-easterly direction, and approximately parallel with the trend of the Pacific coast. These valleys are separated by ranges of mountains and hills, with innumerable spurs, at varying angles, which, although they detract somewhat from the agricultural value of our lands, add greatly to the beauty of the scenery of Napa. The main dividing ranges consist of mountains from 500 to 2,500 feet high. The Mayacama mountains separate into two branches in the county of Sonoma, one of which forms the boundary between Napa and Sonoma, and are united by various spurs with the general coast range, which with a few interruptions, extends southeasterly, the entire length of the state. The other branch bounds the valley of Napa on the east. It is exceedingly difficult and perhaps impossible, by any mere written description, to convey any adequate idea of the mountains of California. If we say, in general terms, that any two ranges are parallel, we do not tell the exact truth, for these ranges are in many places united with each other by mountains running in all directions, some of which are as high as those which form the ranges themselves. It would perhaps be as near the truth to say that our mountains form a stupendous network, irregularly woven, with occasional threads running in nearly parallel lines.

The mountain range which bounds Napa on the east, contains several peaks of considerable elevation, the highest being Mount St. Helena, supposed to be an extinct volcano, 4,343 feet high. North of the same, twelve miles, is Pine Mountain, nearly as high as St. Helena. Directly east of Napa City, at a distance of three miles is "Bald Mountain, a lofty peak in the general chain which forms the eastern boun-

(34)

dary of the county. There are many other peaks to which local names have been given, but their altitudes have not been measured. This range every where shows evidence of volcanic action. In some places the rocks, generally a species of whitish sandstone, stand nearly in a vertical position, showing that the original crust has been broken up by internal convulsions. In others the surface is formed of volcanic ashes, or of rocks bearing evidence of the action of fire. Portions of this range are rocky and bare, but most of them are clothed to the summit with chemisal, "grease-wood" and other small shrubs of great beauty, whose dark green hides the deformities of the shattered rocks from which they spring. Here, as all over the State, the peculiar vegetation upon the mountains gives them a beauty not found in mountains at the east. On their lower portions the pine, redwood, manzanita and madrona attain a vigorous growth. The same trees are also found occasionally, although dwarfed, upon the highest peaks.

The evidence of mighty internal convulsions in past ages, are visible all over Napa and Lake counties. The topographical character of this region must, at some time, have undergone a complete change. Many of the mountains were volcanoes, as is proved by the existence of old craters, volcanic ashes, melted scoriae, obsidian and pumice stone. Some of the hills and mountains must once have been below the level of the sea. At Knoxville, within a mile of the Redington mine, 40 miles from the ocean, and at least 1,200 feet above its level, there is a large tract of limestone rock almost entirely composed of fossil sea shells. Oysters, clams, muscles, cockles, and many other kinds of shell fish, are found in vast quantities, and as perfect in form as when they were living in their native element. The petrified forests near Calistoga also give evidence of volcanic changes. All the valleys were unquestionably once submerged. Below the alluvial surface soil is a bed of clay, varying in depth, and then a bed of rounded, water-worn pebbles and small bowlders, in horizontal strata, which may be seen in many localities along, the banks of the present water courses. No other agency than that of running, water could have rounded these pebbles and spread them out in regular strata over so great an area. No one who has attentively examined this region can doubt that sometime in the remote past, our hills and mountains were islands, whose shore-lines

(35)

were far above the present level of the streams, and that fishes once sported where men now cultivate their fields and erect their habitations. Nothing else than some great convulsion of nature could have wrought such a change, and it may well be that the tradition current among the Indians, that the Golden Gate was opened by an earthquake, may commemorate it. The existence of almost countless mineral and hot springs, the abundance of sulphur impregnating the rocks and soil in many localities, and the proximity of this county to the Geysers in Sonoma, and the Sulphur banks and gas springs of Lake county, show that we are within the scope of the great subterranean agencies that have changed, and may again, the whole face of the country.

The great central valley between the two branches of mountains named, is about thirty-five miles long and widens gradually towards its southern extremity to about five miles. The upper portion beyond St. Helena, is quite narrow-in some places less than a mile wide. Its general course is about N. 30⁰ W. It is traversed through its whole extent by Napa River, which gives its name to the county. This stream is quite tortuous, especially in the southern portions, where it passes through a large tract of level tule land. It runs generally close to the foot hills on the east side of the valley.

All the valleys in the county are approximately level, but with a gradual descent towards the southwest.

All are intersected by water courses, whose sinuous banks are fringed with trees and shrubs. Laurel, live oaks, buckeyes, manzanitas, alders, willows and the ash, are the principal trees. Of shrubbery there is a great variety, among which we name the ceanothus or California lilac, elder, bay, and hazel nut. There are also in many places, large tracts covered with a species of dwarf holly, bearing beautiful red berries in heavy clusters. Wild grape vines abound along every stream, and used to afford the grizzly a considerable portion of his provisions during the fall.

Except in the mountains there is no heavy timbered land in the county. The land when fenced is all ready for the plow. Away from the water courses, every valley is dotted over with majestic oaks of several varieties, with occasional gigantic madronas, whose bright green leaves and reddish bark give them, at a distance, the appearance of orange trees. In the northern portions of the coun-
(36)
ty, besides the trees named, are found firs, pines, cedars and redwoods. Very few of the latter, however, are found north of Howell Mountain, east of St. Helena. Upon this mountain sugar pines are found six feet in diameter, and of enormous height. The "bull pine," is found in all parts of the county, but is almost worthless except for timber, and very inferior, even for that. Indeed, we may here properly remark that we have very little "hard wood" timber, that is of much value except for fuel. All kind of oaks that grow here are brittle and worthless. The ash is rare and inferior, and almost all our supplies of oak, ash and hickory are brought from the East. The laurel is a beautiful wood for furniture, but of little value for other purposes.

Where man has not changed the natural condition of things, the surface of all our valleys is densely covered for several months of the year with clover, wild oats, and flowers of great beauty, which afford food and cover to great numbers of quail, hare and rabbits. The larger valleys are in some parts quite narrow, where the foothills project at a large angle. Their surface is also diversified by isolated hills, which stand like green islands in an ocean of level verdure.

WEST SIDE OF THE VALLEY.

The mountains on the westerly side of Napa Valley put forth various spurs and foothills, forming several minor valleys. Among these, on the southerly slope, are Carneros and Huichica Valleys, and on the eastern, near Napa City, Brown's Valley, one of the most fertile and picturesque in the State. On the eastern declivity rises a small stream called Napa Creek, which empties into Napa River at Napa City. This creek, like all the water-courses in California, carries a large volume of water in the rainy season, but is insignificant in summer, although never wholly dry.

In early spring, during the spawning season, salmon of large size, are often caught in these streams, many miles from tide water. The writer has caught several that weighed from 7 to 10 pounds, in the Carneros, five miles from its mouth, where the water was not a foot deep. Many are stranded upon the shoals when the water falls, upon the cessation of the rains.
(37)
Gold has been found in small quantities in Huichica Creek, but none has ever been found in Napa county in paying quantities.

Another creek rising in the same range, called Sulphur Creek, and passing through the cañon upon which the celebrated White Sulphur Springs are situated, two miles west from St. Helena, runs eastward into Napa River. Cinnabar has been found in these mountains, and several claims are now being worked, further notice of which will be found in the chapter on mines and minerals. Redwood timber was formerly abundant upon the lower portion of this range, but it is now rapidly disappearing. The demand for building purposes and fencing has increased so rapidly that our supplies are now mostly obtained from Mendocino and Humboldt.

EAST SIDE OF THE VALLEY.

The range of mountains bounding Napa Valley on the East, are generally somewhat higher than those on the West, and of the same geological character. Seen from the valley, these mountains present a most picturesque and varied outline. Indeed, in our wonderfully clear Summer atmosphere, every mountain seems where meeting the sky, sharp cut as a cameo, exhibiting its dark green foliage in vivid contrast with the cloudless blue of the heavens.

The passes through this range to the series of valleys Eastward, are generally steep and difficult in their present condition, although heavy sums have been expended in improving them. None, however, are beyond the skill of the engineer, with an adequate outlay. The principal road at present in use through this range is the one leading from Napa City to Monticello in Berryessa Valley, and thence to Knoxville and Lower Lake. Knoxville is the seat of the celebrated Redington Mines, and was named after Mr. Knox, the first lessee of the mines, of which we shall have occasion to speak hereafter. This road was built partly by a subscription of $4,000, and partly by contributions from the General Road Fund, and the Road Funds of the Districts through which it passes. Its original cost was about $12,000, and a large amount has since been expended upon it. Two roads cross the range from St. Helena by way of Howell Mountain to Pope Valley. The "old road" is now

(38)

little used. The new grade, surveyed by T. J. Dewoody, formerly County Surveyor, is one of the best mountain roads in the State. The steepest grade in it is one foot in eight. Another road passes from Calistoga, over the South side of Mt. St. Helena to Lake County, another Southwestward to Santa Rosa, the County Seat of Sonoma, and another Westward to Russian River Valley and Healdsburg.

In the range separating Pope Valley from Napa are numerous Quicksilver mines, which are now being successfully worked, attracting a considerable immigration, and affording a home market for many farm products. Cinnabar is found in this range for a distance of twenty miles North of the Pope Valley Mines. Another road passes from Napa Valley through Conn Valley and cañon, into Chiles Valley, which is connected with Pope, only a low "divide" intervening. This road presented to the engineers most formidable difficulties, the cañon through which the road passes for some five or six miles, being very steep on both sides, and so narrow as to afford only room for a small stream called Conn Creek. This creek when suddenly swollen by rains often rises to a great height within a few hours, sweeping every thing before it. The road formerly passed along its bed, but of course, in the rainy season it was useless as a highway. The grade has been raised and greatly improved, being protected for long distances by substantial stone walls. Portions of it, however, are still very steep and narrow, and a large sum will be necessary to make it a good road even for Summer travel. To place it beyond the reach of floods would probably require a much higher grade and a reconstruction of the whole road.

THE MINOR VALLEYS.

The valleys East of the mountains separating Napa Valley from Pope are comparatively narrow and short, and are connected by roads passing over moderate elevations. Beginning with Coyote Valley in Lake County, on the North we pass into Pope Valley over a very steep hill, high enough

to pass for a mountain in England. The latter valley is about ten miles long, and in some places three miles wide. It is dotted over with fine oaks, with occasional pines
(39)
and madronas. A large portion of it is excellent grain land; other parts being gravelly and sandy, would be better adapted to fruit or vines. It is still very sparsely settled, except immediately about the quicksilver mines, and the price of land is very moderate. This valley is connected with Chiles by a road which passes over a low "divide." Chiles Valley is about five miles long, and is very fertile.

In a southerly direction are Gordon Valley, about five miles long, and Wooden Valley, of still less dimensions. Connected with the valleys thus far named, and at various angles on both sides of the mountains, where the main range is broken into branches extending easterly or westerly, are numerous smaller valleys, each having a communication more or less direct with all the rest. Thus Foss, Wild Horse, Wooden, Gordon and Conn Valleys connect directly with the main valley of Napa.

The valleys of Lake county are also connected with each other and with those of Napa, forming a chain of valleys, large and small, each of which his its own peculiar beauty. Among them are many only large enough for a single farm, but all possess similar characteristics of soil and climate. Some of them are apparently encircled wholly by mountains as is a jewel by its setting, beautiful in themselves, yet almost completely isolated. About twelve miles Northeast from Napa City on the east side of the dividing ridge, is the small but beautiful Capel Valley, apparently shut out from all the world, but connected with Napa City by a mountain road, and with Berryessa Valley by a cañon six miles long. Coal has been found here, but little is known of its extent or value.

East of Pope Valley is another range of mountains, some of which are very lofty and precipitous. Commencing at the Redington Mines, which are near the Northerly boundary of the County, the traveler passes Southeastwardly through Sulphur Cañon. This canon is very steep and narrow, but occasionally widening out so as to afford a limited area of arable land. It is about twelve miles long, and is traversed by a small creek, with high and steep banks, very crooked, and crossing the road many times, making a difficult thoroughfare for the traveler.

This cañon opens into Berryessa Valley, which is about fourteen miles long, and from one to three miles wide, next in size to Napa Valley, and scarcely second to it in beauty and productiveness. It
(40)
has been settled within the past four years, and yields a very large amount of wheat of the best quality. The new town of Monticello is in this valley, about twenty-five miles from Napa City.

An almost continuous wall of exceedingly steep and lofty mountains separates Sulphur Cañon and Berryessa Valley on the east from the level lands of Yolo and the Sacramento plains. The northern part of this range has, from its perpendicular western side and level, horizontal outline, received the local name of "Table Mountain."

Berryessa Valley is watered by Putah Creek, which at its foot takes an easterly direction, cutting off the continuity of the mountain chain, and passing for six miles through a most rugged, rocky and difficult cañon, and emerging into the level plain at Wolfskill's, on the northern boundary of Solano county. Until the building of the Putah Creek bridge and Berryessa road leading to Napa City, the productions of Berryessa Valley could only reach a market at Sacramento by traversing this cañon, or at Suisun by travelling Rag Cañon, almost equally bad, and thence by way of Gordon and Green Valleys. But neither of these routes, bad as they were, could be taken in winter, when the Putah was swollen, and the plains beyond Wolfskill's were under water. The few inhabitants of the valley four years ago, could only leave it by swimming their horses, and crossing the mountains to Pope Valley, from which communication to other points was practicable. The construction of the Putah Creek bridge and the opening of the road from Monticello to Napa have removed this difficulty, and the whole valley having been purchased four or five years since by Messrs. John Lawley, J. H. Bostwick and Wm. Hamilton, and cut up into small farms, Berryessa lands have risen in price 500 per cent, and are considered equal to any in the State for every agricultural purpose.

(41)

CHAPTER III.

CLIMATE OF NAPA COUNTY.

The climate in all parts of the county is mild and semi-tropical, but varies considerably in different localities. Those portions which are partially sheltered by mountains from the prevailing winds have the most equable temperature, and those far from tide water have the greatest extremes of heat and cold. In no part, however, are these extremes so great as in the northern counties of the State. The contrast between the climate of San Francisco and other towns on or near the ocean and that of the interior is remarkable. The change is as great in traveling from San Francisco to Napa, distant only fifty miles, as from New York to Florida. When the lightest summer clothing is worn in Napa, heavy overcoats are generally quite comfortable near the ocean. San Francisco has a more equable temperature than the interior, and is free from frosts throughout the year, but it is always many degrees colder, and exposed, during a portion of the year, to a harsh sea breeze and heavy fogs, which

(42)

are unpleasant to strangers. The lower end of Napa Valley is open to the breeze, which passes northeasterly throughout its entire length, about forty-five miles, and keeps down the extremes of heat and cold to a remarkable degree. The lower part of the valley, south of Napa City, being level, is exposed to its direct action, but not to so great an extent as to be disagreeable. The wind is greatly modified in its force and temperature in passing over the warm surface of the land, and its effects are felt less and less as it penetrates inland. Probably the pleasantest climate is found in and near Napa City. The sea breeze, by passing over a long stretch of level land, loses its roughness, and yet keeps down the heat of summer, and renders the winters mild. The farther north, in the valley, the greater the extremes of temperature. About Napa City the thermometer scarcely ever gets beyond 80^0, although it has been, in rare instances, as high as 105^0. In winter ice is sometimes formed at night half an inch thick upon standing water, but it disappears the next morning before the heat of the sun. Snow is a great rarity in this part of the valley. None has fallen about Napa City, except in three instances, during the past twenty years, and then to the depth of only half an inch. The surrounding mountains sometimes put on a snowy mantle for a few hours, but it soon disappears. The towns further North have a little more snow, being on higher ground and further from tide water, but never sufficient to cover the ground more than a few hours. Mount St. Helena, however, sometimes wears its diadem of snow for several weeks. The smaller valleys, being shut out from the sea breeze, are hotter and colder than the valley of Napa, but there is no part of the county where outdoor work is unpleasant in the coldest part of the year. In many business houses no fires are lighted from January to December. In regard to temperature, the climate is not unlike that of Savannah, Georgia. Many of the more hardy plants and vegetables grow throughout the year. Most varieties of roses never lose their leaves, and flowers are plucked in December. Cabbages, beets, and many other garden vegetables grow during the winter, and hardy vegetables of several kinds are often sown as early as the first of January.

The first rains generally fall in October, and continue at intervals until May, and by the middle of December the whole county is as green as the Eastern States are in May, and beautiful beyond des-
(43)
cription. Strangers are apt to suppose that the "rainy season" is one of continuous rain, and exceedingly unpleasant. It is, however, excepting a few days, the pleasantest part of the year, with a bright sun and almost cloudless skies. Indeed the month of February is generally the most delightful in the whole year.

No shelter is required for cattle during the rainy months. Domestic animals thrive with little attention during the coldest portion of the year. There is, however, a short period between the springing of the grass and its growth, when they require a small supply of food. In the dry season, when the grass has withered, they still find abundant nourishment. There being no rains in summer, the grass, wild oats, and various kinds of clover, are changed into hay where they grew, retaining all their nutritious qualities. The seeds also falling to the around, are eagerly devoured by cattle. This remark does not apply to Napa county alone, but to most parts of California. The farmer here has little need of barns or sheds for any purpose. In summer he can leave his grain in the field unthreshed or in sacks. He can leave his hay in stacks without protection for months, and is never obliged to obey the proverb about "making hay while the sun shines," being perfectly sure that, not a drop of rain will fall before the latter part of September or the first of October. However, during the early part of the haying season light showers occasionally fall. Sometimes these Spring showers are sufficient to give the farmer considerable trouble about his hay, but it is rare that they do much damage.

We have described the practice of our early farmers. It was rough and rude enough. Many cattle were lost yearly from exposure and lack of food . The later comers from the East have brought their ideas with them, and it is now pretty well understood that adequate shelter for cattle is a good thing economically considered. A better supply of food than the open range afforded, is now one of the things towards which the intelligent stock-raiser directs his attention. Under the old system, cattle could generally live, but when the question of profit came in, it was found best to resort to the old and sure practice of Winter feed and shelter. As our lands become more and more subdivided, a new system will take place of the old, and probably, our old plan of stock-raising may give place to another, which affords a certainty of the con-
(44)
tinued health of animals in the worst weather, and a good article of beef for market at all times of the year.

The mean temperature in the shade, at Napa City, will be found at the end of the volume.
(45)

SCENE FROM THE WHITE SULPHURS, NAPA COUNTY.

CHAPTER IV.

PROGRESS OF THE CITY AND COUNTY.

Twenty-five years have wrought a wonderful change in this county, in common with others. In 1847 there was not a house in the county, excepting a few adobe buildings, occupied by Mexicans. There was not a store, hotel, saloon, church, or school within its borders. There were neither roads, bridges nor fences, excepting a few small enclosures, one of which was on the Rancho of Cayetano Juarez, east of the river, opposite Napa City. With these exceptions, the whole county was open. Wild cattle and horses roamed over the county at will. The universal mode of traveling was on horseback, and horses were so plentiful and cheap that a rider never hesitated, when his steed became tired, to turn him loose and lasso the first fresh one that came to hand. In 1849 a rude bridge was built across Napa Creek near the line of Brown street, which fell in the autumn of 1851, under the weight of a load of wheat belong-
(46)
ing to J. W. Osborn, killing two horses. Another, in its place, was built on Main street, which was carried away by a freshet in the winter of 1852-3, and the drift and debris lodging against the trees, threw back the waters and flooded the town. Another bridge was built on First street the same year.

The agriculture of the Mexicans was on the most limited scale. They had no market for agricultural products, even if they had had the desire to extend their operations. A little wheat and corn, a few beans, watermelons, onions, and Chile pepper, for home consumption-these were all they produced in this garden spot of the world. Even in 1850, when onions and eggs commanded 50 cents a piece, and watermelons from $2.50 to $5.00, the Mexicans were too indolent to supply the market, and when the Americans took possession, they soon monopolized the business of furnishing vegetables and almost everything else that was needed by the emigrants. In general, the Mexicans made little use of vegetables, their chief reliance being upon beef. They were stock-raisers, not farmers. The Vallejo rancho, (Entre' Napa) the largest in the county, had in cultivation only a narrow strip along the river, three or four miles Long, and some twenty rods wide. Even this was unfenced. The Indians, of whom there were several hundreds on the rancho, built their "wickey-ups" or wigwams at intervals along the line of the tract cultivated, and the women and children kept watch of the cattle by day. At night mounted Indians rode up and down the line, driving away intruders. This was a "live fence" in the literal sense of the term. Occasionally, in damp ground, they supplemented this with closely planted lines of willow. The Mexicans, in general, considered most of the valley land as of little value except for stockraising purposes, and supposed it impossible to raise anything without irrigation. For this reason they always built their adobes near a stream of water, where they could raise the few articles of vegetable food to which they were accustomed. It was not until after the advent of the Americans that they learned to appreciate the agricultural value of their lands.

Hides and tallow were the only articles which they could exchange for the products of other parts of the world. A fat cow was considered worth $8-$6 for the tallow and $2 for the hide. For these they received payment from the "droghers" along the coast, in

(47)

clothing, articles of hardware and trinkets at an enormous price. When they stood in need of supplies from the outside world, they collected together and slaughtered hundreds of cattle, leaving the flesh to putrefy or be devoured by wild animals, buzzards, or Indians. The slaughter grounds are said by early pioneers to have been the most disgusting places imaginable.

D. M. Howard (afterwards Howard & Mellus), of San Francisco, represented the "Boston Hide Company," and two of their clerks, Teschemaker and J. P. Thompson used to come up the river with launches to deliver goods and receive hides and tallow in return. This mode of doing business continued as late as 1850. Such was commerce in California, and Napa was in the same condition as the rest of the State.

The first mention in a newspaper, of what is now Napa City, is in an article in the *Californian,* published by Brannan & Kemble, in 1848, in which it is stated that the ship *Malek Adhel* had passed up the Napa River and found plenty of water to a certain point, and that beyond that was the *Embarcadero de Napa.* There were no buildings near the town site, excepting two *adobe* dwellings, one occupied by Nicholas Higuera and the other by Cayetano Juarez. The site of the original city was a field of beans in 1847, and contained only a few acres, bounded East by the river, west by the line of Brown street, and extending six hundred yards from the creek to the present steamboat landing.

In consequence of the enormous prices of lumber and labor, buildings were often imported from Norway and the Eastern States ready framed, and some of them are still standing. Three of these united in one formed Gregg & Seawell's store, and now constitute a portion of the German Hotel on the corner of Brown and First streets. The store lately occupied by A. Y. Easterby & Co., and the store opposite (burned several years since), a portion of the old Court House, the Napa Stable, the first building erected at Oak Knoll, a small store erected for Lawrence & Kimball, and the present residence of Geo. N. Cornwell, Esq., on First street, were among these imported buildings. As an example of prices in those days, we give this illustration. In 1849 Vallejo & Frisbie (Don Mariano de Vallejo and John C. Frisbie) had three stores, one in Napa, one at Benicia, and another at Sonoma, in which Geo. N.

(48)

Cornwell, Esq., was also interested, and acted as superintendent. He states that the lumber for the Napa store cost delivered at Bodega Mills, $300 per thousand feet. The freight by wagons by way of Sonoma was $80. and it was thence shipped to Napa upon boats belonging to the firm. Mr. Cornwell also paid to John Wooden in 1849, for two string-pieces for a bridge sixty feet long, $100 each! The same year he fenced forty acres of barley on what is now called "Cornwell's Addition," with rails that cost *one dollar* each. He paid $400 for threshing the barley in Mexican style, $400 for a fanning mill, and $125 each for, old fashioned cradles. However, he had the satisfaction of getting his money back, as he raised sixty or seventy bushels of barley to the acre, and sold it at from eight to fifteen cents per pound.

Early in May, 1848, the first building was erected in Napa City. It was a story and a half high, and in size 18x24 feet, and was built by Harrison Pierce for a saloon. The building is still standing and in good condition. It is near the river on the South side of Third street, and in the same enclosure with the "Shade House." The lumber for this building was sawn by Ralph Kilburn, Harrison Pierce, and Wm. H. Nash, at Bale & Kilburn's mill, two miles above St. Helena, and was hauled to Napa by Wm. H. Nash. Six buildings were framed the previous Winter at these mills, and shipped to Benicia and San Francisco. Lumber was then worth only $40 per thousand. The town site had been recently surveyed, and nothing but lines of stakes showed the locations of streets and lots, and even these were not easily found, being well nigh concealed by a luxuriant growth of wild oats. Most of the]and now covered by the town was mowed in 1848 by John Trubody, who had a contract for supplying hay to the Government. The pioneer building was first put together, all excepting the rafters, and located, by mistake, in the middle of Main street. Nicholas Higuera and Harrison Pierce discovered the mistake, and the frame was pushed back to its present position and completed. On the 8th of May gold was discovered, and the building left unoccupied. On the 20th of May, the owner, Harrison Pierce, Wm. H. Nash, Ralph Kilburn, John Kelley, Frank Kellogg, William McDonald, Hiram Acres, and Benj. Duell, (together with an old Indian, Guadalupe and his wife, who had been brought from Mexico by Wm. Gordon and Pope), left Napa for the

(49)

newly discovered gold fields. Returning in the Fall the new building was opened by Pearce as the "Empire Saloon." The following Summer it afforded accommodations in the shape of lodgings, and "square meals" of beef, hard bread and coffee at $1.00 each. The first election in Napa County was held in this building in 1847. It was subsequently occupied by various persons, among others by the author, as a dwelling house. The old sign "Empire Saloon," was still visible in 1857. Other buildings, small, temporary structures, half canvas, half redwood shakes, "were erected in the Fall and Winter Of 1848-9, and a ferry established by William Russell and a partner, at a point near the foot of Third street. There was a ford near this point, passable at low tide. At high water men swam their horses previous to the establishment of the ferry. In 1851 a toll bridge was built just above the site of the Vernon Mills, by J. B. Horrell, who obtained a franchise for the same from the Court of Sessions.

The first store was opened in 1848 by J. P. Thompson in a building erected at the foot of Main street, on the site of the Star Warehouse. Vallejo & Frisbie's, on the point at the junction of Napa Creek and River was the next. In the winter of 1848-9, the town was almost entirely deserted by its male population, none remaining except Geo. N. Cornwell, J.P. Thompson, and a few old men. There was another store erected by Capt. Brackett and R. L. Kilburn on Main street, below the American Hotel, (occupied by Montgomery and Cox in 1856 as a printing office) and within the next two years several others, among which was Hart & McGarry's, on Main street, near the site of Messrs. Goodman's Bank. It was originally used as a dwelling, and was built by Arch. Jesse. Jacob Higgins built a store on the Southwest Corner of Brown and First streets, now forming a part of German Musical Hall. On the Northwest corner was the store of Seawell & Gregg, a one story frame building owned and kept by J. Mount and another, subsequently by Angus Boggs, and afterwards J. H. Howland. The shop now occupied by M. Haller on Second street, was occupied as a dwelling. There were two other stores on Main street, one on the Southwest corner of Main and Second streets, and another on the Northwest corner occupied by Penwell & Walker. The McCombs'

(50)

building on the Northeast corner of Main and First streets, now occupied by Zubrick & Kiefer, was occupied as a butcher stall by R. M. Hill, and for years afterwards as a saloon. On the Southeast corner was Guthries' blacksmith shop. Excepting a few dwellings on Coomb street, there were few buildings down to 1854, except mere shanties, West of the Court House. The first of any considerable size was the dwelling of Maj. John H. Seawell, which has since been remodeled and is now one of the buildings connected with Miss McDonald's Ladies' Seminary. South of this street was an open common with here and there a shanty, down as far as the residence of Col. W. S. Jacks at Jacks' Point. The first warehouse was erected on the South side of First street, at the then steamboat landing, but was carried off by a flood the Winter following. Another warehouse, was put up in 1850 by John Trubody, near the foot of Main street, on what is known as Short street, and nearly in rear of the lumber yard of J. A. Jackson & Co., directly upon the river bank, and was occupied successively as a warehouse, store, saloon, post office, church, magistrate's office and boarding house. It was still standing in 1871, a relic and remembrancer of early days. Another warehouse was erected by Angus L. Boggs in the Spring of 1851, a block North on the same street.

The first steamer which ran between Napa and San Francisco was the *Dolphin,* Capt. Turner G. Baxter. She commenced running in 1850. She was very small, not much larger than a whaleboat, and her engine similar to that of a locomotive. Her few passengers had to "trim ship" very carefully to keep her from upsetting. It is said that when coming up the river, the Captain (who is very tall) came in sight long before the smoke stack. Col. W. S. Jacks still preserves the bell of the *Dolphin* as a relic. The next steamer was the *Jack Hayes,* Capt. Chadwick, who was afterwards lost on the *Brother Jonathan.*

In 1851, the bark *Josephine,* which had been in Morehead's Expedition to the Gila, was purchased by Geo. N. Cornwell, and sailed up the river by Capt. Chadwick for $100. Having been dismantled and housed over, she was anchored to the bank of the river, near the point of confluence of the river and creek, East of the First street bridge, and used for several years as a wharf-boat and store-

(51)

ship. She was ultimately sold to Wm. A. Fisher, who rented it for the same purposes, and finally removed it on the change of the landing place to the present steamboat landing.

The population in 1848 was made up of a motley collection of all the nations under the sun. The New England Yankee elbowed the "Sydney duck," and the Chinaman and Negro stood cheek by jowl with the Digger Indian. Napa was a favorite resort for the miners in Winter, whether "flush" or "dead broke." The chief places of business were the saloons. A store or two made its appearance, and gold scales were upon every counter. Very little United States coin was in circulation. Down to 1856 the medium of exchange was either gold dust, foreign coin or a substitute for coin issued by the Assay office of Kellogg & Humbert in San Francisco. They issued gold pieces of the value of $5, $10, $20 and $50, which were of full weight and equal in fineness to the Government standard, and these were everywhere accepted as legal coin. Without them it would have been impossible to transact business. The French franc and English shilling passed freely at 25 cents, and the five franc piece for a dollar. No silver was used smaller than a "bit," or dime. The prices of everything, especially of labor, were enormous. Money was the only thing that was plenty. Gambling was the most fashionable pursuit, and men of all classes engaged in it. San Francisco saw itself repeated on a smaller scale in our nascent city. A more rollicking and reckless set of men was never seen. Fights were hourly occurrences, and practical jokes of all sorts were the order of the day. There were neither churches nor schools, and practically there was no law. Each man was "a law unto himself." Very few had settled habitations. Rents even for the meanest structures were enormous. The mass of the people had no family ties to hold them in check, and there were no places of public resort excepting the barrooms, saloons and gambling houses. It is not strange that very many of the early pioneers contracted ruinous habits, causing the premature death of many, and a life-long regret to those that survive. They lived in a fever of excitement, careless of the morrow, and determined to enjoy the present, at all hazards, to the full.

With the organization of the county in 1851, came the necessity

(52)

of a Court House. The first one was erected on the corner of Coombs and Second streets-a small two-story structure innocent of plastering, with Court Room below and Clerk's office above. Persons sentenced for long terms were confined in the *adobe* jail of Sonoma county, Petty offenders were confined in the upper story of the Court House. This was occasionally occupied on Sundays as a place of worship, but oftener as a hall for itinerant lecturers. We have a vivid remembrance of having seen a Professor Somebody, who lectured upon "Biology" (whatever that may be), describe a double sommersault through the back window into a hogshead of water. This feat must have been miraculous, for the "boys" declared unanimously that they had no hand in it. The old Court House was removed on the erection in 1856 of the present structure, and is now used as a tailor's shop on Main street.

The corner stone of the present Court House was laid in the Summer of 1856, with Masonic ceremonies. The jail occupied about half the first story. It has since been entirely re-modelled-a new jail erected in rear of the building-a fire-proof vault constructed for the offices of the Clerk and Recorder, rooms fitted up for the Supervisors, Judges, and other county officers, and the position of the cupola changed. Indeed, it is probable that money enough has been expended in altering and adding to the original building to erect a new one. It is evident that with the rapid increase of population the Court House building and jail will be inadequate, making the erection of new and larger buildings an absolute necessity.

The Court House Plaza was occupied by Lawley & Lefferts as a lumber yard in 1855. It had long been a vacant lot covered knee deep in tar weed. After the erection of the county buildings, the Supervisors contracted with John H. Waterson, (afterwards for many years Deputy Sheriff), to build a fence around it for $572. In 1857, A. D. Pryal took the contract for grading the grounds and planting shrubbery. The expense was met partly by an appropriation of $200. by the Supervisors, and partly by private subscription.

Napa City was laid off as a town by Hon. Nathan Coombs in the Spring of 1848. The original limits of the town included only the land included between Brown street and the river, and ex-
(53)
tending 600 yards from Napa Creek to the steamboat landing. Captain John Grigsby and Mr. Coombs built a building for Nicholas Higuera and took this tract of land in payment, shortly after Capt. Grigsby sold out his interest to Mr. Coombs. They had taken a bond for a deed, but when the conveyance was finally made, Mr. Coombs purchased and had included in it, an additional tract, including the land now known as "the Commons."

Several other "additions " to the original town plat have since been made, by various owners of lands adjoining it. Among them are Thompson's, Briggs & Russell's, Hills', Hartson's, Cornwell's, and Lawley's Additions, all which are now considered for all legal purposes, as portions of Napa City.

The town was formerly divided into " Napa *Alta*" and " Napa *Abajo* " -upper and lower Napa, the latter constituting, Thompson's Addition of over 100 acres, and these names are sometimes still used in descriptions of land. The *Embarcadero,* or landing, at the head of navigation, and the ford just above it, determined the location of the town. There being no bridges in those days, gave the ford much importance.

From 1849 to 1854, the population both of city and county had increased largely. Most of the valley lands were taken up by American immigrants, fenced and put under cultivation, yet large tracts remained untouched. The Spanish Grants, which covered all the best lands in the county, for a long time, checked immigration, as no valid title could be secured. A large portion of the immigrants therefore became "squatters," to the great annoyance of the Grant holders, who had to pay the taxes upon their lands, while the squatters had the free use of them, and bade them defiance. But for this fact doubtless the population of the county would be double what it is to-day.

Still, the soil and climate are so very inviting that even at this early day they attracted people from abroad, and there was a constant increase of business and population. In 1854 Napa City could boast of a population of 300 or 400 people, and about forty buildings, mostly of a temporary character. The American Hotel was erected in 1850 by Nathan Coombs, Lyman Chapman and Samuel Starr; and the Napa Hotel, by James Harbin the year following.
(54)
Several lodging houses and restaurants had previously been opened, as apendages to saloons. In addition to the American and Napa Hotels, there were in 1854 a blacksmith shop on First Street, near the corner of Main; a butcher shop on the corner, kept by R. M. Hill; a restaurant just below it, kept by Sanderson; a saloon just below it, kept by J. M. Dudley, and a store kept by J. C.

Penwell and A. B. Walker, on the present site of the Bank of Napa. On the east side of Main Street were Charles Hoit's store, the Shade House, and a few temporary buildings, mostly occupied as saloons, or restaurants. Arch Jesse built a dwelling, afterwards used by Hunt & McGregory as a store, where Goodman & Co.'s banking house now stands.

In the fall of 1855, the first brick building was erected by John S. Robinson. It is a small dwelling house, now occupied by John Simmons, gardener. The same year the first church edifice (Presbyterian) and the first school house were erected. The church has since been remodeled and improved, so that it bears little resemblance to the original edifice. In 1856 Wm. H. James, in connection with Thomas Earl, erected a brick block, on the corner of Main and First Streets. Adjoining it on the west, A. W. Norton soon afterwards built a brick blacksmith shop. These now form a part of Edgington's block. The numerous other structures since erected need not here be noted.

On the 4th of July, 1856, appeared the first newspaper published in Napa City-the NAPA COUNTY REPORTER, by A. J. Cox. The writer of this chapter was the first subscriber, and has the subscription book still in his possession. Further reference to this subject will be found in another chapter.

As late as 1856, very little effort had been made to improve the streets or highways. Both were almost impassable in the rainy season. There were only two places in Main Street where a pedestrian could cross, one opposite the American Hotel, and the other nearly opposite the Napa House. The crossings were made of bundles of straw thrown into the mud till the bottom was found. Woe to the unlucky wight who got belated, or who had too much "tanglefoot" aboard. A single misstep would send him in mud up to the middle, to flounder out as best he might. The streets in wet weath-

(55)

er resembled mud canals rather than thoroughfares for men or horses. In summer they dried up and became solid enough, but were full of undulations, and not very gentle or regular ones. They soon became, owing to much travel and the passage of heavy teams, cut up into deep ruts, and canopied with intolerable clouds of dust, through which people floundered over a strange mosaic of rubbish, cast-off clothing, empty bottles and sardine boxes. These were the days in which every man wore heavy boots over his pantaloons, and, in the winter time, was covered to the knees with mud, while in summer he choked in a cloud of dust; and every one laughed at these annoyances, knowing that they were common to all, and the necessary concomitants of a new settlement in a wild unoccupied country.

From 1856 the town increased steadily, though not rapidly, in business and population. The statistical tables at the end of this volume will afford much interesting data in regard to the progress of this beautiful young city.

The first bank was established by J. H. Goodman & Co., September 1st, 1858. It proved of great public utility, and is still in successful operation.

A telegraph line was built to Vallejo the same year. It was built by a company of twelve citizens of Napa, of whom the writer was one, who subscribed $100 each, the number of shares being twenty-five. The remaining shares were taken by Mr. Lambert, who put up the Wires and superintended everything. It was not erected for profit but for public convenience, and never paid the stockholders for their original investment. Indeed, it was impossible that it should, as the rates were well nigh prohibitory. A message of ten words cost fifty cents. Then it passed over another line to Benicia at the same cost, and finally over a third line to San Francisco for fifty cents additional, making $1.50 for sending a message of ten words fifty miles!

Another line from Napa City to Calistoga was built in 1867. Both lines have since been transferred to the Western Union Telegraph Company.

(56)

THE NAPA VALLEY RAILROAD.

The Napa Valley Railroad Company was chartered by the Legislature of 1864-5, and a clause inserted leaving the question to the people whether or not to vote a subsidy of $5,000. per mile from Napa City to Calistoga, and $10,000 per mile from Napa City to Soscol, payable in bonds of the County bearing ten per cent interest and payable in twenty years. The subsidy was voted by a large majority, and the road was built from Napa to Soscol immediately. In the Spring of 1867 it was extended to Calistoga, its present terminus. Under a special Act of the following Legislature the Board of Supervisors were authorized to issue County bonds for the further sum of $30,000 to reimburse the Directors for advances made to procure the necessary rolling stock. After some litigation the bonds were issued. The indebtedness of the County was thus heavily increased, to pay the interest on which her citizens were to pay thirty cents on the $100 in the shape of taxes. Under the former assessment taxes as high as sixty and one-half cents was paid. The County received in exchange for her own bonds those of the railroad, and default having been made in the payment of the interest, outside holders of the bonds foreclosed, and the road passed into the hands of the California Pacific Railroad Company, and subsequently into those of the Central Pacific. The County thus lost her interest in the road altogether.

Looking at the facts thus far presented, it would seem that the County had made a very bad bargain. But in fact, the County has been evidently a great gainer. An impetus has been given to every branch of business, and both County and City have awaked as if from a long slumber. The value of land in the upper half of the County has been enhanced from 100 to 300 per cent., and this advance alone would repay the subsidy four-fold. The railroad, by giving us the means of rapid communication with San Francisco, and all parts of the State, and the East, has called attention to our town and valley, and caused a heavy immigration of the best class of citizens. If the railroad were to be removed, a million of dollars would not cover the loss. It is not here intended to defend or

(57)

apologize for the management, or heavy rates of fare and freight charged on this road, but merely to state the general proposition, that nothing yet has done so much to call forth the latent resources of the County, and increase her wealth and population, as the railroad. The upper portions of the valley have been specially benefitted. St. Helena and Calistoga have risen into thriving towns, and lands in their vicinity are dotted over with vineyards and villas, where nothing of the kind before existed. Within five years it will double the population and wealth of this county, and the market value of every acre.

The progress of the town has never been rapid until within the past two years. Still it has been constant and sure.

From 1854 to 1858 there was a period of stagnation all over the State, and Napa made comparatively small progress. There was little immigration. The Harry Meigs frauds were followed by heavy bank failures, and the organization of the Vigilance Committee in San

Francisco produced many disastrous results in city and country alike. Still, more and more attention was given to agriculture. Some small exportations of wheat were made, and individuals here and there commenced the planting of vineyards. The discovery of the Frazer River Mines in 1858, for a while depleted the population of California, and rendered real estate almost unsaleable.

In 1862 the discovery of rich mines in Washoe, poured immense wealth into the State, and city and county received a fresh impulse. In spite of the war between the States, business and population increased, and Napa shared in the general advancement.

Instead of having no churches and no schools as in 1858, we have now seven churches, several of them fine edifices, a Collegiate Institute, a flourishing Ladies' Seminary, two public school houses and several private schools.

The "Town of Napa City" was incorporated and the provisions of a special Act of the Legislature, passed at the session of 1871-2, and the first officers were elected under its provisions on the 6th of May, 1872. John Even, J. A. Jackson, T. F. Raney, Henry Fowler and Louis Bruck constituted the first Board of Trustees. E. Biggs was elected Marshal, and C. E. Comstock Treasurer; S. E. Smith Clerk of the Board.
(58)

The town had long needed a separate and independent organization for the protection of its citizens and for securing a better local government than could be well furnished by a Board of Supervisors. The municipal regulations established thus far appear to work advantageously and economically. No public debt has been thus far created, and it is safe to say that our citizens will never consent to the election of a Board of Trustees that will create any city indebtedness. The income of the corporation is small, and its expenses small in proportion, yet the beneficial efforts of a city organization are already manifest on every hand.

A constant improvement in streets, sidewalks and buildings has gone forward with the increase of population and wealth. The principal streets, formerly almost bottomless in Winter, are filled with gravel or stone, and the buildings are generally of a better class than are commonly found in a place of the size of Napa City. Many of the private residences are elegant and substantial structures. The town is mostly built of wood, excepting its principal business houses, the grain warehouses, banks, and the Collegiate Institute. Thousands of shade trees and shrubs have been planted within a few years, adding greatly to the beauty of the town, which now ranks as one of the most pleasant and prosperous in the State. In general, each citizen owns his own house and lot, and the evidences of good taste and thrift are seen on every hand.

The towns of St. Helena, Yountville and Calistoga have improved quite as rapidly as Napa City. St. Helena, in particular, has grown into a place of importance. It is one of the most beautiful villages in the State, and is the center of the vineyard district, which produces an immense amount of wine and brandy for exportation. All the quicksilver from the Redington, Manhattan, California, and Pope Valley Mines is transferred to the cars at St. Helena on its way to Napa City. From present indications it is probable that Yountville may eventually dispute the palm with her in the export of wines. Calistoga is also growing into a considerable inland business center, being the Northern terminus of the valley railroad, and a center of trade for the people of Lake County. Monticello, in Berryessa Valley, is a new town, not five years old. It is improving year by year, and has now 300 or 400 inhabitants. Several stores,
(59)

a fine hotel, and most kinds of mechanics' shops, accommodate the inhabitants of this great wheat region. Knoxville (now again a part of Napa County), has grown up since the discovery of the Redington Quicksilver Mines eleven years ago, into an important business place. Ten years ago its site was called the "Buck-Horn Ranch," with only a single house upon it.

The great outlines of valley and mountain remain as in early days, but the filling up of the picture is entirely different. Three elegant and substantial stone bridges span Napa River and creek at the County Seat.

The roads are everywhere greatly improved throughout the county. The principal one-that from Napa City to Calistoga being heavily gravelled for eighteen miles to St. Helena. Beyond that point the soil is such as to require little more. This is also true of the valley road East of the river. Many more and important roads have been opened, and substantial bridges built wherever needed for public convenience.

We have now many beautiful drives, comparatively free from dust, most of the heavy teams having left the highways, and the freighting business having been transferred to the railroad. Population is increasing all along the line of the road, and new buildings, many of them elegant mansions, are becoming numerous, where room existed before the advent of the iron horse. The great ranches of other days have been, and are being constantly subdivided and cultivated. The result is better and more thorough cultivation, increased production, the multiplication of schools and churches, and the general improvement of the county.

There are very few spots on the earth's surface more beautiful than Napa Valley, especially in Spring-time. The magnificent mountain scenery on both sides, the rich verdure of grain-fields, vineyards and orchards, the scattered oaks in foliage, and the cosy dwellings embossed in flowers and shrubbery, form a picture of surpassing loveliness, which thousands of travellers and tourists have already learned to appreciate. Every year increases their number, as the valley increases its attractions. If it is lovely now, with only twenty-two years of cultivation and improvement, what will it be twenty years hence, when taste and wealth shall have completed its adornment?
(60)

But it is not alone the beauty of this county that commends it. The soil and climate of Napa are almost unrivalled. We have neither extreme heat nor extreme cold. The land is remarkably fertile, even far up among the foot-hills. There has never been a failure of crops since its settlement by Americans, an assertion that can be truly made by few other counties in the State.

The means of communication and transportation are ample from almost all parts of the county. The cross-roads of the main valley and those leading to the minor valleys all serve as feeders to the valley railroad. There are two daily lines up and down from Calistoga, passing through St. Helena, Oakville, Yountville, and Napa City to Vallejo, and connecting at that point with steamers for San Francisco, so that a resident of almost any part of the county can visit the Metropolis and return within twenty-four hours, while from most parts of the valley the same journey can be made in twelve hours. A tri-weekly steamer also runs between Napa City and San Francisco, and a large freighting business is done by means of schooners.

There are six feet of water at Napa City at high tide, in the dryest season. Many vessels of one hundred tons are constantly employed in river transportation. Napa, is moreover, directly connected by rail, express and telegraph with all the lines in California and the Atlantic States. Thus connected with all points, and possessing within itself so many elements of attraction, it is evident that Napa must always be a favorite resort of tourists, and a section of the State to which immigrants from the East will be sure to turn their attention.

SCHOOLS.

The first school house in Napa County was built by Wm. H. Nash, near Tucker Creek, above St. Helena, in 1849. In it a private school was taught by Mrs. Forbes, whose husband perished with the Donner party in 1846.

(61)

In no respect has the county made greater progress than in the facilities provided for education. Down to 1854 there was not a public school in Napa County. Two or three private schools were opened previous to that time. In 1855 a public school house was erected by subscription in Napa City, which is still occupied as a school for colored pupils.

In 1857 there were only 911 children in the county (this including Lake) between the ages of four and eighteen years, and only thirteen teachers. In 1858 the official returns show that less than half the children between four and eighteen attended school. Labor was so dear that parents generally could not well afford to send their boys to school more than a short time during the Winter, and many did not care to send them at all. A large proportion of the population then consisted of hardy and worthy frontiersmen who had little appreciation of the value of book-learning, and who considered it more important to teach their sons how to ride a wild mustang and handle a rifle with skill, than to fathom the mysteries of grammar or arithmetic.

It is gratifying to note the great change in public sentiment which has since taken place with regard to the importance of education. Probably no county in the State of like population is now better supplied with facilities for education than Napa. Besides the Collegiate Institute and Ladies' Seminary at Napa City, both institutes of high merit, the county has now thirty-five public schools. Many of the school houses are neat and commodious edifices, such as would compare well with those of the Eastern States.

The present public school house in Napa City was erected in 1868-9, upon a lot 240 feet square, at a cost of about $17,000, the cost being defrayed by a special tax upon the inhabitants of the District. It is an elegant and commodious building, and accommodates 300 pupils. Very commodious and elegant school houses have also been erected at St. Helena, Calistoga, Yountville and Soscol, and many others of smaller dimensions at various points throughout the county.

By the Report of the Superintendent it appears that there were on the 30th day of January, 1872, 2,071 children in these districts between the ages of five and fifteen, and 1,011 under the age of five

(62)

years. Of these, from five to fifteen, 1,011 were boys and 999 girls. Number attending public schools, 1,533; private schools, 100; attending no schools, 446. The total expenses of these schools for the year was $26,136.50, of which $23,460 was for buildings and apparatus; $23,092.51 for teachers' salaries ; $142.34 for libraries, and $2,314.35 for rents, repairs, and contingent expenses. Number of school houses of wood, thirty-six, of concrete, 1. Male teachers, 21; females, 23; average wages of male teachers, $77.58; female, $67.10.

It is most gratifying to record such a progress in school matters. Few portions of the New England or Middle States are better supplied with the facilities for a good Common School education than Napa County. The schools are generally well attended, and are accomplishing much good for the great success of the rising generation. Of course they can, here as elsewhere, only furnish the rudiments of a thorough education, but even these are of incalculable value. For those who desire to study higher branches, the Collegiate Institute and the Young Ladies' Seminary in our own county furnish ample facilities. In addition to these two excellent institutions, Prof. C.W. Blake has lately opened a high school for boys, at which a limited number can be accommodated, and instructions given in all the higher branches, including the Classics. Also, in connection with the Public School of St. Helena, one of the finest Public Schools of the county, there has for several years been a department especially designed for giving instruction in the higher branches. The State University and Normal School also furnish to the youth of California the means of persuing a course of study as thorough and comprehensive as in the best institutions of older States. For the present flourishing condition of our schools, the thanks of the public are due especially to Rev. Mr. Higbie, Rev. E. J. Gillespie, and the present Superintendent, Rev. G. W. Ford. They have done their utmost to secure the cooperation of our citizens in elevating the standard of instruction, in promoting the building of proper school edifices, the purchase of libraries, and in securing teachers of sound attainments and character. Excepting San Francisco, there is probably no county in the State that has a more efficient corps of teachers, or that can boast a higher standard among pupils.
(63)

CHAPTER V.

HISTORICAL MISCELLANY.

In the earlier records there appears considerable confusion; apparently it took some time for the people to understand whether they were under Mexican or American rule. The first deed recorded in this county is dated April 3d, 1850, from Nicholas Higuera "of the County of Napa and State of California" to John C. Brown, and acknowledged before M. H. N. Kendig, Recorder. Many of the records are in the Spanish language.

The second is dated February 15th, 1850, from Nathan Coombs, and Isabella his wife, to Joseph Brackett and J. W. Brackett "of Napa Valley, District of Sonoma, in the Northern Department of California." The property conveyed was lot 3 in Block 5, Napa City," acknowledged before "R. L. Kilburn, Alcalde."

The next deed recorded is dated November 29th, 1848, from Nicholas Higuera to Joseph P. Thompson, acknowledged before "L. W. Boggs, Alcalde of Sonoma."
(64)

Another early deed is dated October 18th, 1845, from George Roch to Jacob P. Leese, conveying the grant called "Guenoc." It is in the Spanish language and acknowledged before "Jose de la Rosa, Seventh Constitutional Alcalde of Sonoma."

As illustrative of the value of money at an early day we mention a mortgage dated October 20th, 1850, from Jose S. Berryessa to W. R. Basshaw, for $1,000 at 10 per cent interest per month! Strange to say, the money was paid within a few months.

So far as it is now possible to ascertain from the records of Napa County there must have been an election for county officers previous to July, 1850. The date of the first entry in book "A." of the Records of the Court of Sessions bears date August 4th, 1851, but there is no record extant of such an election. The first proceedings of the Court of Sessions are not recorded, but filed on separate sheets of paper. The earliest of these bears date July 30th, 1850.

John S. Stark was Judge, and M. D. Ritchie and S. H. Sellers were Associate Judges; M. W. McKimmey, Sheriff, and G. N. Cornwell Deputy; H. H. Lawrence was Clerk, and P. D. Bailer Deputy Clerk; District Attorney, Bristol. Contract was let at the December Term for building a Court House 20x30 feet, "to be erected of good substantial materials, with a corridor the whole length six feet wide, covered overhead by an extension of the roof, the stairs to be in said corridor, outside; the second store to be divided by a hall four feet wide running through the center, and into four rooms 13x10 feet each; all rooms to be ceiled, both walls and overhead; seven doors, fifteen windows, a plain desk and railing for the bar, and six benches eight feet long."

A right to establish a ferry across Napa River was granted to N. McKimmey. Following are the rates of ferriage:

Wagon and 4 animals	$3.50.
" 3 "	2.50.
" 2 "	2.00.
Carriage of every kind	1.00.
Each horse or mule attached to carriage	50.
Horse or mule, and rider,	1.00.
" " without rider	50.
Footman	25.
Each head of cattle	50.

R. T. MONTGOMERY

(65)

Sheep and hogs per head . . . . 20.

Money was plenty in 1850, but not more plenty than was necessary to pay such charges for crossing a small river, which every citizen can wade across at numerous points free of expense. In the proceedings of the October Term, 1850, the name of C. Hartson first appears as District Attorney.

It used to cost something to take care of prisoners in those days. At the May Term, 1851, the following items were allowed:

To N. McKimmey for taking charge of prisoner,

N. McCauley, charged with the murder of Sellers,

a Justice of the Peace $126.75

To B. F. Weed for services as guard 280.00

E. H. Cage, ... 121.00

J. R. McCombs, ... 44.00

Charles Leach, ... 74.00

W. W. Stillwagon, ... 44.00

Wm. Streets, ... 26.00

H. H. Lawrence, room rent for prisoners, ... 62.50

James N. Edmondson, guard, ... 112.00

L. Miller, ... 36.00

James M. Watson, ... 2.00

Erastus Pond, ... 94.00

Jason Smith, ... 44.00

———————

$1176.25

McCauley was tried and convicted at the March Term, (records of which are missing.) J. D. Bristol, District Attorney, was ordered paid $120 for his services.

McCauley was confined in the upper story of the building on the southwest corner of Main and Second streets, the first story of which was occupied by Lawrence, Kendig & Kilburn, and subsequently by Pauli & Schultze, Muller & Schultze, and by A. Y. Easterby & Co., as a store. Great efforts were made by his friends to obtain a reprieve from Governor McDougal, and were finally successful. On the day appointed for execution, one report states that Stephen Cooper, now of Colusa, arrived from Benicia with the reprieve, but was refused a passage across Napa River at the Ferry, and compelled by parties inimical to the prisoner to proceed up the river to the "Trancas," some three miles North of the town in or-

(66)

der to cross. While he was making this brief journey, the people took the law into their own hands, imprisoned the Sheriff and hanged the prisoner in the room, where he was confined, in spite of the reprieve, which they well knew was in the hands of Mr. Cooper.

At this distance of time we cannot give any details, except as they are given to us by the pioneers of those days. All accounts agree that McCauley, was illegally hanged, but the circumstances are differently related. Mr. Wm. H. Nash, who was subsequently one of the

Coroner's jury in the case, slept on the night of the hanging, in the building on Brown street, then occupied by Angus L. Boggs, as a store, and states that about two o'clock in the morning officers from Benicia came to the door and asked Mr. Boggs if he thought it would cause any public excitement if they attempted to serve the notice of reprieve upon the Sheriff. Mr. Boggs thought it would not. They returned at daylight and told Mr. Boggs that they had visited the building where McCauley, was confined, before coming to his house, and that they had found a rope extending out of the door of the upper story, and fastened to the railing of the outer stair. From this they were satisfied that the prisoner had been hanged before their arrival. Whoever his executioners were, they were never discovered. They first broke the padlock to his fetters and hanged him by one of the collar beams of the building. The evidence was that he was hanged by "persons unknown."

At the same term John B. Howell received a charter for a Toll Bridge across Napa River, (near Vernon Mills), for twelve years. Tariff of charges: 4 horse team, $1.00; 2 horse team, 75 cents; 50 cents for horse and buggy; 28 cents for horse and rider, and 12 1/2 cents for footmen.

County Order No. 1 was issued to the Assessor for $258, for his services.

At the June Term, Judges Johnson Horrell and M. D. Ritchie presiding, the first licenses were issued, as follows:

To Hart & McGarry to sell foreign and domestic goods one year, and to retail liquors six months. Joseph Mount to sell foreign and domestic goods one year, and liquors three months at "Our House," also to sell liquors at his public house. Also, licenses to
(67)
sell liquors granted to James G. Baxter, Stephen Broadhurst and L. Miller.

$150. allowed H. H. Lawrence for rent of room six months for offices of Recorder, Treasurer, and County Clerk.

At a special session held in July, 1851, the Court examined the new Court House.

Hon. E. W. McKinstry was in 1851 a practising lawyer in this county.

At the August Term it appears that fifty cents on $100. was levied for general county purposes, and twenty-five cents on $100. to pay for the Court House. Edward H. Cage and E. G. Phelps were allowed for guarding the body of Hamilton McCauley $64 each. Joel P. Walker $200. for services as Assessor, and J. D. Bristol $200. for services as District Attorney.

At the October Term Hon. Johnson Horrell was presiding Judge and Matthew D. Ritchie, associate. License to Soscol Ferry renewed to M. G. Vallejo and M. Brookerman on payment of $200. Rates of ferriage: 4 horses and wagon, $1.50; two horses and wagon, $1.; horse and buggy, 75 cents ; horse and rider, 50 cents footman, 25 cents.

At the April Term, 1852, Hon. Johnson Horrell presided, M.D. Ritchie and David H. Steele were associate Justices. N. McKimmey, Sheriff; C. Hartson, District Attorney, and John H. Seawell, Clerk. Edward McGarry resigned the office of Treasurer, to which he had been elected at the general election on the 3d day of September, 1851. Of this election no record can be found. Joseph D. Bristol was appointed Treasurer, *Vice* McGarry resigned.

E. A. d'Hemecourt was at this date County Surveyor. At the May Term, 1852, Jesse C. Penwell was appointed Assessor in place of Wm. H. Nash, resigned.

VALUE OF LANDS IN 1852.

At the July Term the Salvador Ranch assessed at $5, was raised to $10. L. W. Boggs, 600 acres, raised from $5 to $8. John Grigsby's land assessed at $6, was raised to $8 per acre. Lands of (68) J. S. Stark, Wm. H. Nash, M. D. Ritchie, R. L. Kilburn, F. E. Kellogg, Fowler & Hargrave, Henry Owsley, Enoch Cyrus, and J. York, raised from $3 to $5 per acre. Nicholas Higuera, 1,200 acres at $4, raised to $7. Ingle & Cook, 2,560 acres, raised from $1.50 to $3. Cayetano Juarez, 8,000 acres, raised from $3 to $5. A. Pierpont & Baxter, 64 acres, raised from $1.50 to $4. Peter D. Bailey, 370 acres, raised from $8 to $10. Sisto Berryessa, 26,640 acres, assessed at $1.50, raised to $3. James Capel, 444 acres, raised from $1. to $2. Estate of Pope, 8,880 acres, raised from $1.50 to $3. A. A. Ritchie, 39,960 acres, raised from 40 cents to 50 cents. Many other assessments on land were raised from 25 to 60 per cent.

These facts are given as illustrations of the prices of land in this county twenty years ago. Much of the land named, will now command from $70 to $100 per acre, and probably none of it could be purchased for less than $18, except such tracts as are situated in the mountains.

At the October Term, 1852, the County was divided into three Townships, Yount, Hot Springs, and Napa, as it is still divided.

At this Term W. W. Culver was one of the Associate justices.

At a Special Term held October 20th, a contract for repairing the bridges was awarded to Paisley Thompson at $1,190. The Court at this Term made choice by ballot of Wm. Culver and Geo. F. Fulsom as Associate Justices.

At a Special Term, held October 23d, 1853, Judge Johnson Horrell, presiding, J. H. Hatch and Wm. D. Deering, Associates, J. M. Dudley was appointed Supervisor, *vice* F. E. Kellogg, resigned, and Jotham H. Howland was appointed Police Administrator. December 9th, 1853, Henry Edgerton was admitted an attorney and counsellor at law.

April Term, 1854, Hon. Chancellor Hartson, presiding; Associate Justices Wm. D. Deering and W. H. Hatch; A. J. Watson, Clerk; N. McKimmey, Sheriff.

At this time Gen. John F. Miller was a practicing attorney in this county.

April 6th, 1852, Board of Supervisors met. John M. Hamilton, F. E. Kellogg and Jesse W. Whitton constituting the Board.
(69)

The indebtedness of Napa County was ordered to be ascertained by the Board of Supervisors December 6th, 1852, and found to be $12,000, against which were claims against the State amounting to $3,824.40, and the Treasurer was ordered to retain any moneys in his hands belonging to the State until such indebtedness be paid or liquidated.

May 3d, 1858, Sheriff McKimmey, was found to be indebted to the county $1,465.01.

October 17th, 1853, Board met, consisting of James McNeil, Richard C. Haile, and F. E. Kellogg. Proposal of Wm. A. Fisher to build a bridge for $1,600 across Napa Creek at the head of Main street, accepted.

December 16th, 1853, the East room over the court room ordered to be appropriated as a jail.

December 19th, 1853, Edward McGarry and others authorized to build a bridge on First street at a cost of $400.

Special Term, May 5th, 1855. John S. Robinson resigned, and the Court appointed Archer C. Jesse to fill the office for the unexpired term.

August Term, 1855, Hon. Chancellor Hartson, presiding, Wm. A. Haskin and S. Jesse, Associate Justices; R. R. Pierpoint, District Attorney, H. Johnson, Sheriff, and A. J. Watson, Clerk.

December Term, 1855, Hon. C. Hartson Judge, A. B. Walker and W. L. Webster, Associate Judges; Henry Edgerton, District Attorney, J. S. Stark, Sheriff, and A. J. Watson, Clerk. Supervisors, October 2d, 1854, R. C. Haile, Wm. Baldridge and Jesse Grigsby.

April 3d, 1855, tax levy ordered as follows: General county purposes, 45 cents on $100; 5 cents for public schools; 60 cents for State purposes, and Poll Tax $3.

May 5th, 1855, Robert Crouch was appointed Sheriff, *vice* John S. Robinson, resigned.

August 7th, 1855, lands were classified for assessment as follows:
All valley land between Napa City and Dry Creek, $15 per acre; all valley land between Dry Creek and Yount's North line, $10 per acre; all valley land between Yount's North line to head of valley, $7 per acre.

Special Term, May 5th, 1855.
(70)

This shows something of the value of real estate at this date. A great portion of this same land, under its present highly cultivated condition, could not be purchased short of from $100 to $200 per acre. Many of the wealthy people in the valley have become so chiefly by this great rise in the value of real estate. If values continue increasing as they have done in the past, it is hard to estimate what they will be a few years hence. The valley lands are continually being divided and subdivided, and beautiful - and pleasant homes going up on each. Every such improvement adds largely to the value of the land.

On page 83, Book "A" of Supervisors Transactions, under date of September 17th, 1853, appears the first entry of election returns, as follows:

For Assembly, Richard C. Haile ; County Clerk, A. J. Watson; Sheriff, John S. Stark; County Treasurer, Wm. H. James; District Attorney, Henry Edgerton; County Surveyor, A. L. Haven; County Assessor, G. W. Dennison; Superintendent Common Schools, Wm. E. Taylor; Public Administrator, J. B. Smith; Coroner, I. Ritchie; Justices Napa Township, A. B. Walker and Pulaski Jacks; Justices Yount Township, W. L. Webster and Jesse W. Whitton; Justices Hot Springs' Township, J. H. McCord and R. H. Lawrence.

John H. Waterson received the appointment of Under Sheriff November 29th, 1855.

Ordered that $1,000 be paid Charles E. Hart for a bill of sale of the toll bridge in Napa City. January 8th, 1856, $205.25 ordered paid to W. H. James for a safe for the use of the county.

May 28th, 1856, contract entered into with A. C. Latson for construction of Court House and jail for the sum of $19,990. Besides this sum, $350 was subsequently allowed for making box frames with weights for windows, and $750 for a cupola.

Cornelius Coyl appointed January 27th, 1856, superintendent of the work,
(71)

COUNTY ELECTION RETURNS, 1856.

Assembly, Thos. H. Anderson; County Surveyor, N. L. Squibb; Public Administrator, John Lawley; Justices Napa Township, Pulaski Jacks and John Gage; Justices Yount Township, P. F. Harris and R. H. Walker; Justices Hot Springs Township, J. H. McCord and J. Stafford; Justices Lake Township, R. B. Houghton and A. Brown.

COUNTY INDEBTEDNESS.

Board of Supervisors, Edward Evey, J. W. Whitton and I. N. Larrimer. February 5th, 1857, the financial condition of the county was reported as follows:

Amount funded to January 31st, 1857	$28,797.03
Probable amount to be funded	2,500.00
Court House debt	11,855.41
Indigent sick debt	542.49
	$41,194.93

Amount in treasury January 31st, 1857 ....$5,889.92
Revenue for 1856 uncollected 9,712.82

Of which about $5,000 may be available, leaving actual debt $30,505.01. August 31st, 1857, old Court House ordered sold to highest bidder.

COUNTY OFFICERS ELECTED SEPTEMBER 2, 1857.

Representative, Thos. H. Anderson; County Judge, Pulaski Jacks; Clerk, Robert Crouch; Sheriff, John S. Stark; District Attorney,
(72)
Robt. R. Pierpont; Treasurer, Wm. H. James; Assessor, A. S. Roney; Coroner, John Lawley; Surveyor, N. L. Squibb; Superintendent Schools, J. C. Herron; Public Administrator, Riley Gregg. Justices Napa Township, J. C. Penwell and Henry Hensley; Justices Yount Township, M. R. James and P. F. Harris; Justices Hot Springs Township, J. H. McCord and John Newman; Justices Clear Lake Township, J. Bowers and W. Crawford.

Supervisors elect, Charles H. Allen, A. F. Grigsby, W. A. Haskin.

———

TAXES LEVIED FOR 1858.

State, 70 cents on one hundred; County, 50 cents; Court House, 40 cents; Schools, 5 cents; Sinking fund, 25 cents; Road fund, 5 cents; Special Hospital, 8 cents; Special road fund, 25 cents. Total, $2.28.

———

COUNTY OFFICERS ELECTED SEPT. 1ST, 1858.

Assembly, Wm. R. Mathews. Justices of Napa Township, Wm. N. Seawell, J. C. Penwell; Justices Yount Township, J. J. May, A. W. Childers; Justices Hot Springs, James H. McCord, Jonathan Ball; Justices Lake Township, J. F. Houx, W. W. Meredith. Supervisors, C. H. Allen, Jesse W. Whitton, Lansing T. Musick.

April 4th, 1859, contract for constructing Chiles Cañon road awarded to James W. Warren at $4,999. A further sum of $245 was allowed him on one section of said road. Also $500 for making "turn-outs."

At the June Term of the District Court 1858, John H. Smith was tried and found guilty of the murder of B. F. Taylor at Lower Lake, Aug. 3d, 1857. Sentenced to be hanged on the 6th of August, 1858.

June 25th, 1859, the contract for building a jail and jailyard was awarded to Benjamin & Sandford at $7,000.

———

COUNTY OFFICERS ELECTED SEPT. 7TH, 1859.

Assembly, Nathan Coombs; Sheriff, John S. Stark; Treasurer, John S. Woods; District Attorney, R. D. Hopkins; Assessor, T.

A. J. COX.

(73)
Frank Raney; Public Administrator, Jo nathan Bell; Superintendent of Schools, John M. Hamilton; County Surveyor, T. J. Dewoody; Coroner, Francis Schultze; Justices Napa Township, G. W. Towle, S. S. Tucker; Justices Yount Township, A. A. Hunnewell, W. A. Childers; Justices Hot Springs Township, Albert Knapp, John Nusman; Justices Lake Township, J. F. Houx, G. A. Lyon. Supervisors, Jesse W. Whitton, Geo. N. Cornwell, L. T. Musick.

TAXES LEVIED FOR 1860.

For county purposes, 50 cents; sinking fund, 25 cents; special road fund, 25 cents; general road fund, 5 cents; school fund, 5 cents; hospital fund, 8 cents; Court House, 22 cents. Total, $1.40.

$70 allowed G. F. & H. T. Barker for furnishing and planting eighty trees and shrubs in Court House Square.

Contract awarded to Williston & Murphy for building stone bride on Main street, 40 feet span, at $5,397.

Contract awarded to same parties for stone bridge in continuation of First street, 111 feet span; at $11,890.

Contract awarded to Gillam, Barron & Warren for bridge across Napa River near St. Helena, at $1,050.

September 28, 1860, T. Frank Raney was allowed $85.32 for enrolling 1,422 persons subject to military duty.

TAXES LEVIED FOR 1861.

For State purposes, 60 cents; for general county purposes, 50 cents; for sinking fund, 25 cents; for special road fund, 25 cents; for general road fund, 25 cents; for hospital fund, 5 cents; for school fund, 5 cents. Total, $1.95 on $100.

COUNTY OFFICERS ELECTED SEPTEMBER 4TH, 1861.

Assembly, Edward Evey; County Judge, Pulaski Jacks; County Clerk, Robert Crouch; Sheriff, Charles H. Allen; County Treasurer, Geo. E. Goodman; District Attorney, G. W. Towle; Assessor, A. B. Walker; Coroner, E. N. Boynton; County Surveyor,
(74)
T. J. Dewoody; Superintendent of Schools, Wm. Jacobs; Public Administrator, Thomas Earl. Justices Napa Township, John H. Waterson, A. A. Hunnewell; Justices Yount Township, J. J. May, Marston Jarvis. Supervisor 2d District, W. A. Elgin. Justices Hot Springs Township, T. H. Anderson, W. A. Haskin.

TAXES LEVIED FOR 1862.

For State purposes, 62 cents; for county purposes, 50 cents; general road fund, 20 cents; hospital fund, 5 cents; school fund, 5 cents. Total, $1.42.

Napa Guard allowed $56, February 11th, 1862, for two months rent of Armory.

Alfred Higbie appointed February, 11th, to fill vacancy in the office of Superintendent of Common Schools.

April 15th, 1862, Wm. N. Seawell appointed Supervisor of Second District, *vice* J. W. Whitton, resigned.

July 9th, 1862, contract awarded to James M. Warren for building stone bridge on First street at $9,318. Subsequently allowed $1,451 for extra work.

COUNTY OFFICERS ELECTED SEPTEMBER, 1862.

Assembly, C. Hartson; Superintendent of Schools, Alfred Higbie; Supervisors, Thos. H. Thompson, Silas Ritchie, Peter Burtnett; Justices Napa Township, A. A. Hunnewell, Elijah True; Justices Yount Township, W. A. Childers, Stephen Mead; Justices Hot Springs, W. A. Haskin, Henry Owsley. Number of votes cast, 1,329.

October 13th, 1862, the amount of public debt was $26,428.57. Indebtedness of General County Fund over revenue for ensuing year, $492.49. Indebtedness of Road Fund over revenue, $3,017.35.

OFFICERS ELECTED SEPTEMBER, 1863.

Senator 18th District, Chancellor Hartson; Assembly, Napa and Lake, W. B. H. Dodson; Sheriff, A. B. Walker; County Clerk, J. M. Carter; Treasurer, G. E. Goodman; Recorder, J. H. How-
(75)
land; District Attorney, J. E. Pond; Assessor, B. W. Arnold; Surveyor, T. J. Dewoody; Coroner, Jonathan Bell; Public Administrator, Thomas Earl; Superintendent of Schools, Alfred Higbie; Supervisor, Silas Ritchie. Total vote, 1,566.

At the Judicial election held October 21st, 1863, the following persons were elected: Robert Crouch, County Judge; Alexander Coles and Sam'l Heald, Justices for Napa Township; W. A. Childers and M. K. McCorkle for Yount Township; W. A. Haskin and Henry Owsley for Hot Springs Township.

TAXES LEVIED FOR 1864.

For State purposes, 92 cents; for county purposes, 52 cents; for road fund, 25 cents; for school fund, 10 cents; for hospital purposes, 10 cents; Napa and Clear Lake Road fund, 1 cent; Napa Valley and Clear Lake road fund, 10 cents. Total, $2.90; to which was added the State tax of 30 cents. Total, $3.20.

April 18th, 1864, contract awarded to Bart. R. Sheehan for grading Clear Lake and Napa Valley Road at $4,604, and with "turnouts," $4,896. Contract for bridge at Yount's mill was awarded to E. M. Benjamin at $800. To the same for building stone wall along the Chiles cañon road, section first, $10.60 per rod lineal measure; section 2, $11.80; section 3, $10.80, and with excavating per cubic yard $5.50, amounting to $9,860.57. To the same for constructing fire-proof vault in Clerk's and Recorder's office $ 1,900.

In the District Court, June Term, 1863, Charles Britton was found guilty of the murder of Joseph W. Osborn at Oak Knoll on the 18th of April previous, and executed on the 18th of August.

A special election authorized by the Legislature was held May 11th, 1864, to determine whether the county should subscribe $10,000 per mile to the capital stock of the railroad, from Napa to Soscol, and $5,000 per mile from Napa to Calistoga. Total vote 659; majority for the subscription 318. Cars first ran to Calistoga, in the Spring of 1867.

October 11th, 1864, rates of toll established for the Lakeport Turnpike Road Company.
(76)
November 12th, 1864, $50 for rent of Armory allowed to Napa Rangers, "$750 for 3 months' allowance from August 1st to November 1st, to Washington Artillery Company."

November 7th, 1864, Peter Burtnett was elected Supervisor.

November 14th, 1864, contract for bridge in Chiles Cañon awarded to J. B. Chiles at $250.

February 11th, 1865, purchase of 150 feet of hose authorized for Pioneer Engine Company No. 1.

TAXES FOR 1865.

For State purposes, $1.15; for county purposes, 55 cents; for road purposes, 25 cents; for school purposes, 15 cents; for hospital purposes, 8 cents; Napa City and Clear Lake Road, 10 cents. Napa Valley and Clear Lake Road, 10 cents. Total, $2.38.

March 14th, 1865, additional levy of 25 cents to provide for payment of railroad subscription. Total, $2.63. Poll tax, $2.

March 16th, 1865, $750 allowed Washington Artillery for three months.

March 16th, 1865, contract for Soscol bridge awarded to George Ward at $730.

At the February Term of the District Court, J. Gilbert Jenkins was found guilty of the murder of Patrick O'Brien, and executed March 18th. His published confession showed that he was guilty of nineteen murders.

June 5th, 1865, contract awarded to George Wood for building fire cisterns at corner of Brown and First streets and in Court House Square, at $1,279 each.

Same date contract awarded to Jones & Co., for painting Court House, brick and wood work, re-glazing windows at $750.

Same date contract awarded to E. M. Benjamin for building a bridge across the slough near Chas. Thompson's, in Yountville, at $600.

July 3d, 1865, the railroad from Napa to Soscol being completed, county bonds amounting to $41,000, were issued to the Company.

ELECTION OF SEPTEMBER 6TH, 1865.

Assembly, John M. Coghlan; Clerk, C. B. Seeley; Sheriff, R. (77) Ellis; Treasurer, George E. Goodman; District Attorney, W. W. Pendegast; Assessor, B. W. Arnold; Recorder, J. H. Howland; Surveyor, W. A. Pierce; Coroner, R. H. Olmstead; Public Administrator, Matthias Dorr; Superintendent Schools, A. Higbie; Supervisor, 1st District, T. H. Thompson; Supervisor, 2d District, Joseph Mecklenberg.

Judicial Election, October 18th, 1865--Justices Napa Township, A. A. Hunnewell, A. M. Poe; Justices Yount Township, H. N. Utting, A. Beauchamp; Justices Hot Springs Township, W. A. Haskin, J. W. Clark.

TAX LEVY FOR 1866.

For State purposes, $1.13; general county purposes, 55 cents for road purposes, 25 cents for school purposes, 25 cents; for hospital purposes, 5; Napa City and Clear Lake Road, 10 cents; Napa Valley and Clear Lake Road, 10 cents; Napa Valley Railroad, 25 cents; Napa City Improvement Fund, 50 cents; District Road Fund, 50 cents. Total, $3.68.

February 12th, 1866, construction of wharf at the foot of Brown street by the California Steam Navigation Company, duly authorized by the Board.

February 26th, 1866, canvass of vote at election held February 21st, on the proposition to subscribe a further sum of $5,000 per mile to the stock of the Napa Valley Railroad from Napa City to Calistoga. Total vote, 1,307. For subscription, 415. Against, 892. Majority against subscription, 477.

May 11th, 1866, purchase authorized of 250 feet of hose for Pioneer Engine Company No. 1.

September 5th, 1866, a special election was held to decide upon the question of constructing a McAdamized road, and the question whether to donate to the Napa Valley Railroad the county's interest therein. On the first proposition the vote was "No" 402; "Yes" 82. On the second, "No" 243; "Yes" 241.

At a special election held January 23d, 1867, Smith Brown was elected Supervisor to serve the unexpired term of Thos. H. Thompson, resigned; and Wm. A. Trubody the unexpired term of Albert G. Boggs, resigned.

(78)

·Exclusive privilege granted to William Smith and others, (Napa City Gas Light Company), to lay down gas pipes and supply Napa City and its additions with gas for fifteen years. Price of gas limited to $7.50 per 1000 feet. The county to take all the gas required for public purposes and street lamps at rates to be adjusted at the end of three years from commencing, and every five years thereafter. The charge for the first five years to be thirty cents per street lamp per night. The first lamp was lighted August 28th, 1867. The price of gas was fixed at $7.50 per 1000 feet.

May 9th, 1867, contract for building Engine House on Brown street awarded to Wm. Richmond at $5,450.

A levy of ten cents additional to the school tax authorized.

ELECTION RETURNS SEPTEMBER 4TH, 1867.

Senator 18th District, W. W. Pendegast; Representative Napa and Lake, John C. Crigler; Sheriff, A. B. Walker; Recorder, J. H. Howland; Treasurer, A. G. Boggs; Clerk, C. B. Seeley; District Attorney, R. N. Steere; Superintendent of Schools, E. J. Gillespie; Public Administrator, I. N. Larrimer; Surveyor, E. A. d'Hemecourt; Coroner, M. B. Pond; Supervisor 3rd District, J. Mecklenberg; Assessor, J. M. Mayfield.

September 10th, 1867, bonds for $10,000 conveyed to Napa Valley Railroad Company.

October 16th, 1867, Judicial Election at which Robert Crouch was elected County Judge; F. M. Hackett and A. A. Hunnewell Justices for Napa; A. J. Ford and R. C. Gillaspy, for Yount; Edward Evey and J. W. Clark for Hot Springs Township.

December 10th, 1867, contract entered into with Napa City Gas Light Company to put up twelve street lamps at $9 per month each for five years.

At the election held November 3rd, 1868, Ralph Ellis was elected Supervisor for the 1st District.

November 30, 1868, Napa Wood Company authorized to build a wharf at Soscol and collect tolls thereon for ten years.

December 18th, 1868, eight more lamp posts authorized to be put up by Napa City Gas Light Company.

(79)

$22,500 bonds ordered issued to Napa Valley Railroad Company. January 14th, 1869, in view of the prevalence of small pox, Dr. B. S. Young, Dr. R. Garnett, Dr. J. S. Adams, and Dr. A. Fouch were appointed to attend to vaccinations, and authorized to procure buildings in their several districts as pest-houses. $1,000 bonds issued to Railroad Company.

February 8th, 1869, purchase from C. Hartson of twelve acres of land for $1,500 authorized, for the site of a County Infirmary.

March 11th, 1869, contract awarded to B. Robinson for building Infirmary at $8,218.55, and $759.13 allowed for extra work.

May 31, 1869, contract for building bridge in Road District No. 1 and 2, awarded to B. Robinson & Son at $4,995.

ELECTION OF SEPTEMBER 1ST, 1869.

Representatives of Napa and Lake, John C. Crigler; Sheriff, A. B. Walker; Clerk, C. B. Seeley; Recorder, L. M. Corwin; Treasurer, A. G. Boggs; District Attorney, T. J. Tucker; Assessor, B. W. Arnold; County Surveyor, T. J. Dewoody; Superintendent of Public Instruction, G. W. Ford; Supervisor 1st District, E. N. Boynton; Supervisor 2d District, John Finnell; Public Administrator, J. D. Blanchar; Coroner, C. T. Overton.

Judicial Election October 20th, 1869. Judge of Seventh Judicial District, W. C. Wallace; Justices of Peace for Napa Township, G. W. Towle, E. D. Sawyer; Justices for Yount Township, R. C. Gillaspy, A. C. McDonell; Justices for Hot Springs Township, L. N. Duvall, J. H. Allison.

TAXES LEVIED FOR 1870.

For State purposes, 97 cents; for general county purposes, 40 cents; infirmary fund, 15 cents school fund, 25 cents; road district fund, 25 cents; railroad interest, 60 cents; general road fund, 25 cents; Napa City improvement fund, 30 cents. Total, $3.17.

June 14th, 1870, $1,150 ordered paid to E. M. Benjamin for building bridges, from Rutherford's station across the Napa River.

August 2d, 1870, contract awarded to E. M. Benjamin for building bridge across Putah Creek at $8,350. $1,264 allowed for extra work and material.

(80)

September 7th, 1870, at a special election Joseph Mecklenberg was elected Supervisor of the 3d District.

March 6th, 1871, contract for building road over Howell Mountain awarded to B. Robinson at $8,749. June 13th a further allowance of $1,779.90 was made for extra work.

The sum of $1,151 ordered paid to J. C. Brush for building fence around the Court House Square.

TAXES LEVIED FOR 1871.

For State purposes, 86 1/2 cents; for county purposes, 54 cents for school fund, 25 cents; railroad interest, 60 1/2 cents; general road fund, 25 cents; district road fund, 25 cents; Putah Creek bridge, 19 cents; Napa City improvement fund, 30 cents; infirmary fund, 15 cents. Total, $3.40. Road Poll Tax, $3.

March 8th, 1871, the sum of $779.18 ordered paid to J. H. Griswold for constructing side-walks around Court House Square.

ELECTION RETURNS OF SEPTEMBER 6TH, 1871.

Member of Congress, John M. Coghlan; Senator 18th District, W. W. Pendegast; Representative, W. W. Stillwagon; County Clerk, C. B. Seeley; County Recorder, L. M. Corwin; District Attorney, R. Burnell; Sheriff, John F. Zollner; County, Treasurer, A. G. Boggs; County Assessor, B. W. Arnold; Superintendent of Schools, G. W. Ford; County Surveyor, W. A. Pierce; Public Administrator, A. S. Knapp; Coroner, R. D. Pond; Supervisor, first District, Robert Brownlee. For amendment of the Constitution, 1,021 majority. To re-fund the debt, 114 majority.

Judicial Election October 18th, 1871. County Judge, Thomas P. Stoney; Justices for Napa Township, R. M. Swain, G. W. Towle; Justices for Yount Township, A. C. McDonell, D. O. Williams; Justices Hot Springs Township, J. H. McCord, A. C. Palmer.

R. M. Swain, Esq., was subsequently appointed Under Sheriff, having resigned the office of Justice of the Peace.

November 6th, 1871, the Spencer Creek Water Company was authorized to lay down water pipes in Napa City and its additions. Works to be completed in one year.

(81)

R. D. HOPKINS.

November 6th, 1871, two additional street lamps ordered. The town of Napa City was incorporated by an Act of the Legislature approved March 23d, 1872.

May 11th, 1872, the town of Napa City was set apart by the Board of Supervisors from Road District No. 2, in pursuance of said Act, and the road taxes therein ordered collected and paid over to the County Treasurer until the indebtedness of said District ($13,440.07) and interest shall be liquidated. The Board also released to the city all control and interest in the Engine House, Engine and equipments, and the fire-cisterns outside the Court House block.

Contract with the Napa City Gas Light Company was annulled and declared terminated.

August 12th, 1872, the time for supplying street lamps was extended to July 31st, and $567 allowed for the same.

October 8th, 1872, the Board authorized the construction of a draw-bridge across Napa River at the foot of Third street, the cost not to exceed $10,000. Also a bridge across Napa River in Yount Township, where the road petitioned for by J. R. Garner and others crosses said river, and also a bridge crossing the slough on said highway. Cost not to exceed $1,800.

————

TAXES LEVIED FOR 1872-3.

For State purposes, 50 cents; for county purposes, 41 cents; for school purposes, 5 cents; railroad interest, 30 cents; general road fund, 5 cents; for road district, 25 cents; infirmary fund,

11 cents; bounty fund, 3 cents; Napa City improvement fund, 20 cents; Napa City, 10 cents. Total, $2.30. This levy was made upon property at its actual cash value, under the new law regulating assessments, and amounted to $8,235,587. The percentage would have been about twice as large upon each $100 under the old system, of assessments.
(82)

CHAPTER VI.

HISTORY OF NEWSPAPERS IN NAPA COUNTY.

The *Napa Reporter* was the first newspaper published in Napa county. The first number was issued on the 4th of July, 1856, by Alexander J. Cox, editor and proprietor. R. T. Montgomery became joint proprietor in December of the same year, and in February following new material was procured and the paper enlarged and improved. When first established, Napa had neither business nor population adequate to the support of a newspaper. The *Reporter* consequently maintained but a sickly existence for the first six months. It was issued irregularly, sometimes once a week, and at others once in two or three weeks, according to circumstances.
(83)
was a small sheet of four columns to the page, and one-fourth the size of the *Alta California,* with two of its pages constantly filled with dead advertisements. The subscription list up to 1857 did not contain the names of twenty paying subscribers, and its advertisements were mostly such as were required by law to be published. It paid nothing because it was worth nothing.

The office was in a rickety old shanty about eighteen feet square, next below the American Hotel on Main street. It was neither ceiled, plastered nor papered, and the floor was of rough lumber, through which were cracks an inch wide. In the roof was a large hole, apparently left for a flue or chimney, through which the rain descended in torrents. There were no windows, except a couple of sashes nailed directly to the wall. It was with great difficulty in winter (even when wood was obtainable) that the place could be kept warm enough to work in, and it often happened that wood could not be had at any price, in consequence of the horrible condition of the roads. In the winter of 1856-7, the publisher paid $5 for as much as filled the box of a buggy. It was hauled less than 20 rods, and the seller got "stalled" on Main street, buggy and horse sinking in the mud, and it cost in "treats" more than the cost of the wood to pry the team out and place it upon *terrafirma*. The editorial lodging room was in the garret. An iron camp-bedstead and a few blankets comprised its entire furniture.

THE PIONEER PRESS.

The material of the office was on a level with the building in which it was contained. It consisted, all told, of a Washington Press (foolscap size), with platen 14 by 17 inches, on which the paper was printed a page at a time, and a small font of second-hand minion and another of long-primer. There was no jobbing material whatever. The press is now in possession of the Sonoma Pioneers. It was brought to San Francisco from Mexico at the close of the war, and taken by Mr. Cox to Sonoma, where it was used some three years in printing the Sonoma *Bulletin.* He then removed it to Vallejo, and in the Fall of 1855, in connection with Dr. E. B. Eaton, published for a few weeks the Vallejo *Bulletin*. In June, 1856, he

(84)

brought it to Napa, where the *Reporter* was printed upon it (a page at a time) until February, 1857, when a new press and material were purchased by Montgomery & Cox, and the office removed to the corner of Main and Third streets, where Hartson's brick building now stands. On the 6th of September, 1858, Mr. Cox left the *Reporter*, and in the division of the material the old press fell to his share, and was used for three months by Cox and Farrell in publishing the Napa *Semi-Weekly Sun*. Shortly after, Mr. Cox removed his office to Healdsburg, and used the same press in printing the Healdsburg *Review*. Thence the press went to Lakeport, Lake county, and did service in printing one or two small political papers, each of which died a natural death. Probably its labors are now at an end, as in the hands of the Pioneer Association it will be kept as a relic of the olden times. The writer has earned many a thousand dollars and performed many a hard day's work upon it in the days of high prices, when very common cards and bill-heads were $3 per 100, and small sheet handbills $30 per 100.

The *Reporter* could hardly be called an established newspaper until Montgomery & Cox, in February, 1857, purchased new material, enlarged the paper, and began to publish it regularly on the appointed day. From that time, through all the changes of proprietorship, it has never failed to appear punctually. The office began from that time to be a paying institution, and to command a respectable subscription and influence. For two years the paper took no part in politics; but finally, when the great split occurred in the Democratic on the Kansas question, became the advocate of the principles of Stephen A. Douglas.

Mr. Montgomery, in connection with M. D. Brownson, A. M. Parry and J. I. Horrell, continued to publish the paper down to October, 1863, when the establishment passed into the hands of Miner & Higgins, and finally into the hands of Lank Higgins alone. The political character of the paper was changed, and it became a vehement opponent of Lincoln's Administration. In the winter of 1870 it was sold to W. F. Henning, who still continued it as a Democratic organ. In October, 1871, R. T. Montgomery purchased the establishment. Soon after C. A. Menefee became a partner, and in Aug. 1872, purchased the whole establishment. Shortly after a half in-

(85)

terest was sold to A. A. R. Utting, and the paper is still published by these gentlemen under the firm of C. A. Menefee & Co. From the date of Mr. Montgomery's purchase great additions have been made to the material of the office, and it has gradually grown up from a small beginning to be one of the most complete in the country. The *Reporter* is now published as an independent paper, and is in a flourishing condition. In November, 1872, it was enlarged, and printed on a new Taylor & Co.'s cylinder press. An engine has since been purchased, and all the machinery of the establishment is now run by steam power.

———

THE NAPA REGISTER.

The Napa *Register* was started by Horrell & Strong, August 10th, 1863. On the 14th of November following, Mr. Strong died suddenly of apoplexy, and on the same day R. T. Montgomery took the editorial charge of the *Register*, which he retained until January 1st, 1864, when Mr. Horrell sold a half interest to Mr. N. E. White. Mr. Montgomery still continued to contribute to its columns, and at the end of a month purchased Mr. Horrell's interest. The paper was continued by Montgomery & White until January 1st, 1866, when Mr. White purchased the establishment. On the first of May following, Mr. Montgomery became sole proprietor, and so continued down to October 23d, 1869, excepting only a period of six months ending July 1st, 1868, during which Mr. White was publisher and proprietor. October 23d, 1869, the establishment was sold by Mr. Montgomery to R. D. Hopkins & Co., who some months afterwards sold a half interest to G. M. Francis, the firm becoming Hopkins & Francis. In the winter of 1872, Mr. Hopkins sold out his interest to G. W. Henning, one of the present publishers. The *Register* has an excellent office, and has always been a successful newspaper. In politics it has always been an advocate of the principles of the Republican party.

In 1858 the Napa City *Herald* first made its appearance. It was owned by a joint stock company comprising the most influential

(86)

Democrats in the county. It was a strong advocate of the measures of Buchanan's Administration, and of the Southern view of the slavery question. J. D. Lillard, Esq., a young lawyer from Kentucky, was its first editor, and was succeeded by Wm. H. Towns and Thos. J. Tucker. The paper, however, proved unsuccessful, and stopped within a few months. The establishment soon after came into the hands of Farrell & Higgins (Frank Farrell and J. Wallace Higgins), and a new paper of the same character appeared in 1859, under the head of the Napa *Times.* This paper also died in a few months for lack of support. The office shortly afterwards was purchased by Montgomery & Brownson of The *Reporter*.

July 20th, 1861, Alexander Montgomery commenced the publication of the Napa *Echo,* which violently opposed the Administration of President Lincoln and every measure taken to subdue the Southern rebellion. Its circulation and patronage were limited, and in a pecuniary point of view it was never successful. Still it kept on until April, 1865, when it suspended publication on the morning of the announcement of Mr. Lincoln's assassination.

DAILY PAPERS.

The Napa *Daily Advertiser* appeared September 22, 1866, but was suspended after a few issues, as it was found that the undertaking would not pay. It was edited and published by R. T. Montgomery. The Napa *Daily Reporter* was published in 1866 by Higgins & Leach, and after a few months by Higgins & Gregg, when it was discontinued for lack of support.

In the Spring of 1870, W. J. Bowman commenced another paper styled the Napa *Daily Gazette,* which was only published about three months.

In December, 1872, the first number of the *Daily Register* appeared. It is published by Messrs. Francis & Henning, and the same matter used in making up their weekly edition.

It will be seen that since 1856 Napa City has had no less than nine newspapers-only three of which survive. It cannot be doubted, whatever their imperfections may have been, that each has contribu-

(87)

ted something to the welfare and advancement of the county. The *Reporter* and *Register,* having been longest in the field, have unquestionably earned the thanks of the people of Napa.

The Calistoga *Tribune* was first issued June 15, 1871, by Thomas McGeorge, and takes a respectable rank among the local papers of the State.
(88)

CALISTOGA SPRINGS, LOOKING WEST.

CHAPTER VII.

MINES AND MINERAL PRODUCTIONS.

Our little county enjoys most of the luxuries afforded by other parts of the State, but in some of them she has shared only to an infinitesimal extent. While Washoe, Gold Bluff, Kern River, and other kindred localities have supped full of enormous "strikes" and astonishing developments, Napa, being only a "cow county," dropped behind in the general current of excitement, and was never, but once, aroused from her customary impassivity as to the enormous mineral resources of this region. However, the good old county could not altogether escape.

In the Winter of 1858-9 there arose an excitement really worthy of the "good times" in the mineral districts. All at once, no-
(89)
body could very well tell why, a grand silver excitement arose, which permeated the whole community. It was found by various parties that the mountains on the East side of the valley were full of the ores of silver, of untold, because unknown richness. Simultaneous with this grand discovery, every unemployed man from Soscol to Calistoga turned prospector. Blankets and bacon, beans and hard bread rose to a premium, and the hills were lighted up at night with hundreds of camp-fires. Hammers and picks were in great demand, and there is ocular evidence even to this day that not a bowlder or projecting rock escaped the notice of the prospectors. There was silver in Washoe, why not in Napa? It was a question of probabilities which were bound soon

to harden into certainties. Indeed, it was only a short time before silver prospects were possessed of a defined value. Claims were opened, companies formed. and stock issued on the most liberal scale. Everything wore the *couleur de rose.* As usual, upon similar occasions, there was great strife about claims. Some were "jumped " on the ground of some informality twice in twenty-four hours. Heavy prices were paid for "choice" ground, and it is quite safe to say that our mountain sides and summits have never since borne such an enormous valuation. It seemed as though the whole community had been bitten by the mining tarantula. One man, whose name we withhold, in his perambulations in the profound cañons about Mount St. Helena, in company with his son, discovered a ledge of *solid silver.* As neither had brought either blankets or "grub," the old gentleman concluded to stand guard over the precious discovery during the night, armed with a shot-gun, while the son went down into the valley for those indispensable supplies. When the morning broke, the old man was still at his post, shot-gun in hand, but tired, sleepy and hungry. The son, laden with food and other inner comforts, "toiled up the sloping steep" with the *de quoi manger* strapped to his back, and both father and son sat down in the gray of the morning, by a hastily lighted fire, to discuss their rude breakfast and the limitless wealth before them. It would not do to leave such an enormous property unguarded. It would be "jumped" in ten minutes. So the shot-gun was transferred to the son, while the father, with an old pair of saddle-bags stuffed to repletion with " sil-

(90)

ver," descended the mountain. His mule soon brought him to Napa, the denizens of which town he was shortly to astonish with his great discovery. He walked up into the *Reporter* office, saddle-bags in hand, opened the fastenings with an exultant smile but a trembling hand, when out fell some brilliant specimens of *iron pyrites.* Alas, that it should be told, but such was the scope and extent of his great silver discovery. But the opinions of the unskilled were of no value. A regular assayer would, of course, tell a different story. And, we suppose, on the principle that the "supply always equals the demand," there were discovered in San Francisco large numbers of "assay offices," at which, for the moderate price of $15, a certificate of quantitative analysis of anything from a brick-bat to a lump of obsidian could be had, showing silver anywhere between $20 and $500 per ton! We were shown numbers of these certificates, and probably gave them all the credence to which they were entitled. There were a few individuals here who had understood from the beginning the character of the whole excitement. One of these, G. N. C., was the recipient of a sample of a very dark pulverized ore of *something*, and, being fond of a joke, dissolved a two-bit piece in nitric acid, and added the resultant to the powdered ore. When the assayer's certificate got back, there was an enormous excitement. The specimen forwarded had yielded $428 to the ton! Of course, when the joke had been duly enjoyed, the secret was revealed, to the great disgust of the lucky proprietors.

Judge S., formerly Sheriff of the county, had been up the valley on business in the muddiest part of the winter, and on his way back met a chap on his way to the "mines." "Have you been to the mines?" said the fellow. "Yes," answered the Sheriff, "but everything is pretty nearly taken up-at least, all the best claims." "But d--n it," said the would-be proprietor, "isn't there anything left?" "Oh, yes," returned the Sheriff, "you *might* perhaps, get in on some outside claim." Without waiting to make any reply, the fellow clapped spurs to his Rosinante, headed up the valley, and, as the Sheriff declared, "in less than two minutes *you couldn't see him for the mud he raised.*

(91)

The excitement lasted for several weeks, and grew better and better. Scores of men laden with specimens thronged the hotels and saloons, and nothing was talked of but "big strikes" and "astounding developments." A local assay office was started, for the miners could not wait the slow process of sending to San Francisco. It is probable that this local assayer, Mr. Frank McMahon, a very honest and capable man (since engaged about the Knoxville mines), did more than any one man towards pricking the great bubbles of the time. His assays were far less favorable than the imported article, and it came to pass that his customers were dissatisfied with the results of his experiments. Finally, as these threw a shadow of doubt over the value of the argentive discoveries, some of the heavy operators concluded to consult some of the most skillful and well-known assayists of the city-men whose decisions were beyond the reach of suspicion, and whose reputation was above cavil or doubt. Several specimens, considered to be of the highest value, were forwarded. The general disgust of claim owners may be conceived when the formal certificates of assay were returned. Most specimens contained *no silver at all,* and the very best only *"a trace."* Nothing of value had been discovered. Thereupon ensued a sudden hegira of prospectors to the valley. The millionaires of to-day left their rude camps in the mountains, and, with ragged breeches and boots out at the toes, subsided at once into despondency and less exciting employments. The hotel and saloon keepers, saying nothing of the editors, proceeded to disencumber their premises of accumulated tons of specimens of all kinds of "shiny rocks" to be found within an area of thirty miles square-making quite a contribution, to the paving material of the streets of Napa City. Thus subsided the great mining excitement. The result was that a few were a little poorer, but many hundreds a great deal wiser than they hoped to be.

Thus far no mines have been worked in this county, except those of cinnabar. Some discoveries of copper and iron have been made, but so far as tested, nothing of practical value has been developed. Indications of coal have been found in several localities, but it is still a matter of doubt whether any true coal veins exist in the county. Geologically considered, the prospect must be regarded as un-

(92)

favorable. Of gold we have none, and it is quite doubtful whether we have any ore of silver worth working. From explorations thus far it is probable that quicksilver will be, for a long time to come, the only metal found in Napa that can be profitably obtained. The principal ore of this metal, cinnabar, is very widely diffused in the mountains on both sides of the valley of Napa, and numerous "claims" have been recorded. Many companies have been incorporated for working them, and several have proved successful.

It is now established beyond doubt that Napa County possesses vast mineral wealth, but it is confined to this one mineral, cinnabar. There appears to be a wide belt of country rich in this ore, extending along the whole Northwestern, Northern, and Northeastern sections of the county. New discoveries have been made in the mountains West of St. Helena, and in the Northern part of the county towards the Geysers, and the surface ore is flattering as that of any of the mines already developed. We can but look upon the mineral resources of the county as only awaiting development to be one among our chief sources of wealth.

In order to give an idea of the progress thus far made, we give the following list of incorporated Quicksilver Companies, together with a sketch of the condition and prospects of each, up to the present time.

Quicksilver Mining Companies organized under the Act of April, 1853, to form corporations for certain purposes.

———

PHOENIX MINING COMPANY.

Location, Pope Valley. Certificate filed November 15th, 1861. Term of existence 50 years. Names of original Trustees, C. B. Sharp, A. H. Botts, John Waterson, John Newman, J. A. Butler. Capital Stock, $19,200. Shares 192 of $100 each. Original locators, John Newman, R. P. Tucker, F. B. Gilmore, J. A. Butler, J. H. Waterson, J. W. Tucker, Wm. H. James, James Lefferts, M. J. Church, G. W. Morris, A. H. Butts, S. A. Morris, G. W. Amesbury, C. B. Sharp, Jacob Ellsbury, C. H. Holmes, E. Boukofsky. Capital stock increased January 13th, 1868, to $955,000. Most of (93)
the stock of this Company is now held in Napa City. More extensive excavations have been made in this mine than any other in the Pope Valley district, and it has yielded a much larger amount of metal.

The following particulars concerning the Phoenix line have been kindly furnished by George Fellows, Esq., Superintendent. The communication of Mr. Fellows is dated December, 1872:

The Phoenix Mine is situated on the side of a steep mountain sloping to the Northeast. It is twelve hundred feet in breadth, and includes the main portion of a well defined mineral belt, commencing at an altitude of four hundred feet above the valley, and extending back four thousand feet to the top of the mountain. The ore is in true fissure veins, running diagonally through the belt, and crossing the mountain in a Southeast and Northwest direction.

The first discovery of cinnabar was made in September, 1861, by John Newman. A Company was organized soon after and some prospecting done, when a considerable quantity of ore was found scattered over the surface of the ground at the extreme lower end of the claim, having apparently broken off and rolled down from the numerous ledges above.

Some time in the Winter of 1862, the mine was leased to James Hamilton, who worked it for about one year, but failed to make it pay, (as tradition has it), through bad management and inexperience in mining. After the Hamilton Company suspended operations there was no more work done at the mine for three years, and most of the owners disposed of their interests at a low price. In the Summer of 1867 work was again resumed, and in the Spring of 1868 a new bench of retorts was put up, the work being carried on under the management of Daniel Patten, but again without meeting with financial success, and during the succeeding Winter work was wholly suspended. In the Spring of 1870, having been appointed Superintendent of the mine, I commenced work the 12th of April, with six men. In May following, three of the old retorts were fixed up, and we commenced reducing ore. Working altogether in the mine and at the retorts only sixteen men during April, May, and June, and producing sufficient quicksilver, (sold at the market price) to put $10,000 in the treasury of the Company over all expenses.
(94)
In August a new bench of six retorts was put up, together with a crushing mill for breaking the ore, and a circular saw for cutting the wood. A steam boiler was put up at the mouth of the tunnel, a steam pump put into the mine and a steam engine attached to the boiler on the outside for driving the crushing mill at the retorts. Commenced reducing ore again the first of September, run until

January, 1871, and closed down for the Winter, having produced during the season 960 flasks, or 73,440 pounds of quicksilver, which amounted to $50,673.

Continued to work eight men in the mine during the Winter, and commenced reducing ore again the first of April, 1871, and run until the last of October, when we stopped and commenced building furnace. Worked twenty-five men during the Summer, and produced 764 flasks of quicksilver, or 58,446 pounds, which amounted to $40,326. Commenced erecting furnace October, 1871, and completed it January, 1872, but did not get it to working right until the first of July. Have kept forty-five men employed this Summer, and have produced up to the present time, October 1st, 670 flasks, or 51,255 pounds. We are now making 60 flasks a week. Since April, 1870, there has been a double shaft put down 150 feet, and 2,200 feet of tunneling down, besides taking out the ore that has supplied the reduction works. The richest ore worked this season has been taken from the lower level, and there is now a sufficient quantity cut to keep the furnace running for two years.

The improvements consist of one furnace of the Knox & Osborn patent, capable of reducing 600 tons of ore a month, costing, with fixtures, some $30,000; building over furnace, 30x30 feet square, and 40 feet high; building over condensers, 65 feet long by 30 feet wide, and 16 feet high; wood house 120 feet long by 30 feet wide and 16 feet high; draw shed 30 feet long by 16 feet wide and 14 feet high; one large house for assorted ore 110 feet long by 30 feet wide, and 14 feet high; two sorting sheds, each 60 feet long by 30 feet wide, 12 feet high; boiler house and blacksmith shop 45 feet long by 32 feet wide, 12 feet high; wood shed adjoining boiler house 80 feet long by 30 feet wide and 14 feet high; boarding house and office, main building, 32 feet long by 18 feet wide, two stories; L part for dining room, 60 feet long by 16 feet wide, one
(95)
story; L part for kitchen and store-room 50 feet long by 16 feet wide, one story; two lodging houses each 30 feet long by 18 feet wide, one story; one lodging house 36 feet long by 22 feet wide, one story; one house for reading room 24 by 24 feet square, one story; 5 family houses 22 by 24 feet one story; one barn 40 by 50 feet. There are a number of miners' cabins interspersed among the other buildings, which, together with the family houses along the side of the mountain, give the place an appearance of a small town.

The machinery consists of one 25-horse power boiler set in stone masonry, with a Blake pump for feeding; one 12-horse power hoisting engine at the top of the shaft in main tunnel; one No. 8 steam pump in shaft capable of throwing 30,000 gallons of water an hour; also No. 6 steam pump in shop to use in sinking air shaft; one 12-horse power engine with boiler set in brick masonry, for driving blower and soot pan at the furnace.

What has been done in opening the mine so far, can only be called prospecting, although the working has about paid for all the improvements, besides some dividends to the stock-holders.

The Phoenix Mining Company was incorporated in 1868, with a capital stock of $96,000. Principal office in Napa City.

At the last annual meeting the following Trustees were elected John Lawley, C. Hartson, C. B. Seeley, J. F. Lamdin and George Fellows. At a subsequent meeting of the Trustees George Fellows was elected President and Superintendent, C. B. Seeley, Secretary, Robert Crouch, Treasurer.

George Porter is underground Foreman in the mine; Wm. P. Cook, Engineer at main shaft; Jos. Hartshorn, Foreman at the furnace; J. H. Cowan, Bookkeeper.

The mine is now in good working order. By another year it can be made to pay handsome dividends; and there is but little doubt it will be, at no distant day, one of the richest mines in the State.

––––––––

X. L. C. R. MINING COMPANY, NOW THE REDINGTON.

Location Sulphur Cañon, North of Berryessa Valley. Certificate filed December 16th, 1861. Capital Stock $420,000, in 420 shares
(96)
of $1,000 each. Original Trustees, George N. Cornwell, R. T. Montgomery and George E. Goodman. Locators, George N. Cornwell, R. T. Montgomery, A. Y. Easterby, James Lefferts, P. Hunsinger, John B. Phippin, Seth Dunham, Isaac Day, W. H. H. Holdermann, Francis A. Sage, W. W. Stillwagon, George E. Goodman, M. G. Ritchie, L. D. Jones, J. S. Stark.

This Company leased their mine in 1862, to Knox & Osborn, who after working it for a year, found it to be one of the richest in the State, and second only to the New Almaden. Most of the stock had been meanwhile purchased by Redington & Co., of San Francisco, who are still the principal owners. The monthly production is about 1,000 flasks of quicksilver.

Considering the immense value of this mine, some account of its discovery may be worthy of notice. The writer, having been one of the original locators, is familiar with the circumstances. In 1860 a company of twelve was formed in Napa City for the purpose of prospecting for mines and minerals, and two old pioneer prospectors, Seth Dunham and L. D. Jones, were sent out to examine Napa and the adjacent counties. What might be found was matter of doubt, but the Company, informally organized, concluded to pay a small monthly assessment of $2.50 per month each, in order to find out what might be the resources of the land. The prospectors were wont to bring in, about once a month, the results of their labors. The prevalent idea then was that silver abounded in the mountains of the county, and accordingly all eyes were directed to the discovery of the ores of that metal. The Company individually, and the prospectors as well were well nigh equally ignorant of mineralogy, and the "specimens" brought in ranged from iron pyrites to bituminous shale, all of which were supposed to contain silver. Every newspaper office and hotel bar were replete with these samples of the wealth and value of the mineral resources of the county, all of which, economically considered, were only inferior specimens of macadamizing stone, glistening, but valueless. At last, Messrs. Jones and Dunham, in their perambulations among the hills, struck a new road, then recently built between Berryessa Valley to Lower Lake, and on ascending a hill at the head of Sulphur Cañon, just above the "Elk Horn Ranch;"
(97)
where the soil and rock had been removed to permit the passage of teams, discovered on the upper side of the road, at the turning point, that the rocky point, partly removed by the road-makers, was of a peculiar color and texture. Fragments broken off were very heavy and of a liver-color. They were brought to town, and by the experts of those times pronounced cinnabar. And such they proved. This first discovery led to the opening of the rich mine of which it was but an indication. The ignorant workmen who had constructed the road, had rolled down into the cañon below many tons of cinnabar, which would have yielded 50 or 60 per cent. of metal. This discovery led to the

opening, of this splendid mine, which is now probably only second to the far-famed New Almaden.

POPE VALLEY MINING COMPANY.

Location Pope Valley. Certificate filed February 15th, 1868. Capital stock $300,000, divided into 3,000 shares of $100 each. Original Trustees, A. Y. Easterby, T. J. Dewoody, G. W. Towle. Locators, A. Y. Easterby, T. J. Dewoody, G. W. Towle, R. Burnell, T. J. Tucker. No work as yet has been done upon this claim beyond preliminary prospecting.

WASHINGTON MINING COMPANY.

Location Pope Valley, adjoining the Phoenix. U. S. Patent secured. Certificate filed December 2d, 1862. Original Trustees, C. B. Sharp, D. D. Wickliff, R. F. Miles, J. M. Hamilton, W. W. Stillwagon. Locators, J. M. Hamilton, W. W. Stillwagon, Wm. Brigham, D. D. Wickliff, C. O. Billings, R. F. Miles, Jacob Elsbury, Joseph Clayes. Capital stock increased from $50,000 to $500,000, with 50,000 shares of $10 each.

About one-half the stock in this Company has since changed hands, and is now held principally in Napa City. Dr. W. W. Stillwagon owns a controlling interest. The mine was prospected to some extent in 1865-6, but nothing found of importance. Within the last year, however, it has been under lease to Messrs. Stillwagon & Patten, and reduction works erected. The surface ore has been (98) found sufficiently rich to pay an average profit of $1,000 with the labor of six men, which it still continues to do.

A recent discovery has been made of a mass or ledge of good ore, (some of which is of the highest grade), and which extends nearly horizontally into the hill to a distance of 200 feet, and of unknown depth. It is sufficient, even as far as already developed, to supply a 10-ton furnace for two years. This ledge will yield probably five per cent. of quicksilver on an average, although some portions will yield as high as 60 per cent. Work on this ledge is still in progress, and no signs of its giving out are yet seen. On the contrary, the ore improves with every foot of progress. It seems now beyond question that the Washington will prove highly valuable property. The Company have a U. S. Patent for their mine, and for 160 acres adjoining, making altogether 274 acres. Present officers: W. W. Stillwagon, President; E. N. Boynton, Secretary; A. Y. Easterby, Treasurer. These three gentlemen, with J. F. Lamdin and Jacob Ellsbury constitute the Board of Directors.

HAMILTON QUICKSILVER COMPANY.

Certificate filed June 30, 1862. Capital stock $28,800. Number of shares, 144, of $200 each. Original Trustees, J. M. Hamilton, I. N. Larrimer, T. B. McClure, H. H. Coster and W. P. Hammond comprising all the corporators. This Company was formed to work the ores of the

Phoenix mine, and did so for several months, but in a pecuniary point of view, unsuccessfully. Insufficient works and lack of experience, brought its affairs to a stop within a year after its organization.

———————

VALLEY MINING COMPANY.

Certificate filed May 16th, 1867. Location, Pope Valley. Capital Stock $30,000 in shares of $50 each. Original Trustees, John Newman, Ezra Carpenter, R. T. Montgomery, H. F. Swarts, Joseph L. Duchay, Jesse Barnett. Capital Stock increased April 21st, 1871, to $300,000 in 60,000 shares of $5 each. The mine worked
(99)
by this Company is situated directly in Pope Valley, in level ground. It was leased by Col. J. W. Colt soon after the organization of the Company, and reduction works erected of his own invention. These, however, proved a complete failure, and his lease was abandoned, the mine reverting to its original owners. Extensive works have been since erected, and are producing 50 flasks of quicksilver per month. The works upon this mine are of a costly and substantial character, and the indications are that the property will become quite valuable. To all appearances the supply of ore is inexhaustible, although thus far it has been of low grade. The mine being located in the valley itself, and in ground approximately level, some trouble has been experienced in getting rid of the water in the lower excavations. A powerful steam pump is in constant operation, and the prospects are so favorable of a higher grade of ore, that the Company do not hesitate to incur the expense of artificial drainage. Mr. Edward Clark, the Superintendent, has full faith in the success of the mine.

———————

THE SUMMIT MINE

Was originally located by members of the Whitton family, of Yountville, and patiently prospected by them for several years. It is situated three miles from Rutherford Station, upon the very summit of the Mayacamas Mountains dividing Sonoma from Napa county. The reduction works are a mile further to the east. Mr. J. Pershbaker has within a few months become the sole proprietor, having purchased the property for $45,000. The claim is very extensive, and there are attached to it 160 acres of timber land. The Summit is one of the most promising, Quicksilver claims in the county. The surface prospect is very extensive. The surface ore is found on the west side of the mountain for a distance of over 1,000 feet, and can from its favorable position be obtained to a great depth, at moderate expense, without tunneling or blasting. The underground work consists of three main tunnels with seven branches. The main working tunnel is 400 feet in length. The mine is worked upon two levels connected by a shaft. There is a substantial railway track in the main tunnel and chutes from the upper to the lower level, by
(100)
which ore is passed to the main tunnel and railway. Below the lower level is a shaft 50 feet deep in which is situated a steam engine and force pump to keep the works free from water. The lowest workings are 165 feet below the surface, and the quality of the ore improves constantly from the

surface downwards. The surface ore averages about one per cent. That from the tunnels and shafts will, without selection, pay from 1 1/2 to 2 1/2 per cent.

Work upon this mine upon a large scale was commenced in August last. The former proprietors, Messrs. Whitton Brothers, up to that time transported the ore upon the backs of mules to their furnace, which was a small affair of the capacity of one and a half tons per day, situated upon the site of the present reduction works. The profits of the mine, worked even upon that scale, were very great, considering the capital invested. After the purchase by Mr. Pershbaker, a fine mountain road was constructed from the mine to the reduction works, which were greatly enlarged. The capacity of the present furnace is 24 tons per day. New buildings have been erected, very complete and convenient for ore sheds, boarding houses, and other purposes. The furnace is of a new and improved construction, and can be fed and discharged hourly, thus capable of being kept in constant operation. The chimney is some 80 yards from the furnace, and the condensers are so perfect in their operation that no particle of mercury escapes. A draft is created by a fan moved by water power.

No accurate estimate can yet be formed as to the annual product of this mine, as it has been only a few months in operation; but it is evident that the Summit must prove very valuable property. Its contiguity to a market must add greatly to its value. The mine and works are under the charge of Mr. James D. Ewen, a practical miner Of 25 years experience. The present working force is 22 white men and 8 Chinamen. A change will be made in the road during the present Spring, by which the ore can be supplied directly from the mine to the furnace by means of chutes and cars, saving about a mile of transportation, and bringing the furnaces and fuel supply into close proximity.
(101)

_____

OAKVILLE QUICKSILVER MINING COMPANY.

Location west side of Napa Valley above Oakville. Certificate filed January 22, 1868. Capital stock, $300,000 in 3,000 shares of $100. Original Trustees: E. N. Boynton, S. Hutchinson and O. P. Southwell. Locators: W. W. Stillwagon, E. N. Boynton, S. Hutchinson, R. Burnell and O. P. Southwell. The capital stock of this company has wholly changed hands, having been bought by San Francisco parties at $5 per foot or $30,000 for the whole mine. Substantial works have been erected, and the mine promises to be valuable.

Since the purchase of these mines about a year since, very extensive explorations have been made, and works on quite an extensive scale erected. The first furnace erected was of the capacity of ten tons for each 24 hours, and the yield of quicksilver from 75 to 102 flasks per month. A furnace of the capacity of 15 tons for 24 hours was completed last December. This will give a reducing capacity to the works of 25 tons per day, and more than double the present product of quicksilver. Much of the ore at present used is from the surface, being fine carmine-colored cinnabar mixed with yellow clay. This is made into rude adobes, in order to allow the passage of the furnace flames through the mass, and the yield of this class of ore is about one per cent. The excavations already made in following up the cinnabar are now a mile in extent. They consist of working tunnels, shafts, inclines, and perforations at all imaginable angles, upwards, downwards, right and left. The ore from the excavations thus far yields about 2 3/4 per cent., and its value increases as a lower depth is attained. The mine is already worked at a fair profit, with every prospect of still better results in the future. John A. McQuaid is President of the Company and W. H. Mott is Secretary. Mr. Luckard is General Superintendent and general overseer of the works. At present there are 16 white men and 30 Chinamen employed. The close proximity of the Oakville mine to the railroad and to tide-water, gives it great advantages over mines at points farther inland.

In February, 1873, the company sold out to the Napa Mining Company. The new owners intend doubling the capacity of the works, and putting on a larger force of workmen.
(102)

NEW BURLINGTON QUICKSILVER MINING COMPANY.

Location near Oakville, Napa county. Certificate filed May 17, 1871. Capital stock, $300,000; shares 3,000 of $100 each. Original Trustees: David Doak, Wm. Baldridge, Wm. A. Lewis, Henry H. Harris and John Steckter. Locators: John Philpott, H. H. Harris, John White, Wm. A. Lewis, Wm. Baldridge, B. F. White, David Doak, John Steckter. No work done except prospecting.

RED HILL QUICKSILVER MINING COMPANY.

Location, Pope Valley. Certificate filed March 2, 1871. Capital stock, $480,000, in 4,800 shares of $100 each. Original Trustees: W. W. Stillwagon, A. Y. Easterby, Daniel Patten, J. H. Howland and R. Burnell. Same parties locators. This is a very promising claim, but as yet not fully explored. Prospecting now in progress.

SILVER BOW MINING COMPANY.

Location, Pope Valley Mining District. Certificate filed October 2, 1871. Capital stock, $180,000, in 1,800 shares of $100. Original Trustees, J. H. Kester, P. Van Bever, A. W. Norton, Joseph N. Reynolds and C. E. Comstock. Locators: Jesse Barnett, Henry Mygatt, J. N. Reynolds, J. Israelsky, P. E. Perl, A. W. Norton, P. Van Bever, D. B. Parks, J. H. Kester, C. E. Comstock. Considerable work has been done upon the Red Hill mine, and it now supplies a portion of the ore reduced in the works of the Valley mine.

OVERLAND QUICKSILVER MINING COMPANY.

Location, Summit Mining District, Napa county. Certificate filed October 6, 1871. Capital stock, $300,000, in 3,000 shares of $100. Original Trustees: G. N. Cornwell, E. J. Smith, E. N. Boynton. Locators: E. N. Boynton, W. W. Pendegast, John T. Smith and H. H. Clark. This claim is now being prospected, and gives evidence of being valuable. The claim is adjacent to the Summit mine and probably upon the same lead.
(103)

———

MUTUAL QUICKSILVER MINING COMPANY.

Location, adjoining Oakville mine in Napa Mining District. Certificate filed March 1, 1872. Capital stock $300,000; 3,000 shares of $100 each. Original Trustees: R. H. Sterling, T. H. Thompson, Henry Fowler, W. W. Thompson, J. F. Lamdin. Locators: R. H. Sterling, Henry Fowler, W. C. Watson, W. W. Thompson, J. F. Lamdin. Nothing yet done except prospecting.

———

MAMMOTH MINING COMPANY.

Object to own, occupy and work mines of cinnabar and to extract quicksilver and other metals from the ores of said mines, and to carry on the business of quicksilver mining generally in Napa and Lake counties. Certificate filed Sept. 22, 1871. Original Trustees: John Lawley, John Pershbaker, T. P. Stoney, M. B. Pond and Sylvester E. Smith. Capital stock, $4,000,000, in 40,000 shares of $100 each. No work done yet except prospecting.

Many other certificates of incorporation have been filed and companies formed for working gold and silver claims in Nevada, and petroleum claims in this county and Humboldt, but none of them have succeeded in developing anything of value. The petroleum companies whose claims were in Humboldt county found plenty of oil, but the rock strata overlying its sources were found to be so broken up that it could not be obtained in wells as in Pennsylvania. The oil oozes out of the ground through innumerable fissures in the rocks over a large tract of country, showing itself upon every spring and water-course near the Mattole river, and even covering the ocean with a film for a long distance at its mouth; but all the claims are abandoned. The inhabitants of the oil region easily collect enough for home consumption, but none is obtained for commercial purposes. The great excitement of 1865-6 has completely subsided.
(104)

COAL COMPANIES.

———

PACIFIC COAL MINING COMPANY.

The organization of these companies is mentioned here as a fact of local history, although nothing has been done by any of them beyond preliminary prospecting of their several claims. A few, small seams of good coal have been discovered in Capel Valley, but nothing yet, thus far, of commercial value. Farther prospecting may give better results.

Certificate filed May, 17th, 1871. Object, "to mine for coal beds or strata." Capital Stock, $2,000,000 in 20,000 shares of $100 each. Original corporators and Trustees, E. Huguenin, Henry Mygatt, W. W. Stillwagon, J. H. Kester and W. A. S. Holt.

Certificate filed February 1st, 1871. Object to "purchase and own coal lands in the State of California and open coal beds and veins thereon, and remove the coal for the purpose of commerce." Capital 3,000,000 in 30,000 shares of $100 each. Original Trustees, W. C. S. Smith, George N. Cornwell, W. R. Brown, E. N. Boynton and John Mudgett, being the corporators.

————

CLARK COAL MINING COMPANY.

Certificate filed March 7th, 1871, to mine coal on lands owned by George W. Clark in Napa County, and to purchase and sell coal lands. Capital Stock, $2,000,000 in 20,000 shares of $100 each. Trustees and corporators, W. W. Stillwagon, Henry Mygatt, Ralph Ellis, E. Huguenin, Robert Crouch.

————

ATLANTIC COAL COMPANY.

Certificate filed May 17th, 1871. Object to work coal beds or shale. Capital Stock $2,000,000 in 20,000 shares of $100 each. Henry Mygatt, John H. Kester, E. Huguenin, W. W. Stillwagon, and C. E. Comstock, original Trustees and locators.
(105)

NAPA COLLEGIATE INSTITUTE.

CHAPTER VIII.

CHAPTER VIII.

NAPA VALLEY RAILROAD COMPANY

Certificate filed March 26, 1864. Incorporation formed under the "Act providing, for the incorporation of Railroad Companies, and the management of the affairs thereof, and other matters relating thereto approved May, 1861, and the several Acts supplementary to and amendatory thereof." Capital stock, $750,000, in 7,500 shares of $100 each. Original Board of Directors: Anthony Y. Easterby, John Lawley, James H. Goodman, Chancellor Hartson, Charles Mayne, Samuel Brannan, and Alfred A. Cohen. Original subscribers to the capital stock: Charles Mayne, 30 shares; A. A. Cohen, 30 do.; C. Hartson, 10 do.; S. Brannan, 30 do.; W. R. Garrison, 30 do.; R. B.
(106)
Woodward, 30 do.; H. Barroilet, 30 do.; Edw. Stanley, 5 do.; Jas. Graves, 20 do.; C. F. Lott, 30 do.; S. Alstrom, 30 do.; J. H. Goodman, 10 do.; Thos. Knight, 20 do.; Geo. C. Yount, 20 do.; A. Y. Easterby, 10 do.; J. F. Lamdin, 5 do.; John Lawley, 10 do.; Smith Brown, 10 do.

––––––––

THE BANK OF NAPA.

Certificate filed Sept. 14, 1871, Objects: to invest and loan its capital, surplus and trust funds; to receive money on deposit for such time and at such rates of interest as may be agreed upon; to receive valuable property, packages and papers for safe keeping, and to charge for the care of the same; to act as an agent in the purchase and sales of real and personal estate, in the collection and payment of debts, and in other monetary affairs; to act as trustee in holding and managing real and personal property for the benefit or security of other parties; to act as a receiver of assets belonging to estates, of funds waiting disposition in cases of litigation, and to transact every business that may properly be done by a financial agent, or by a safe deposit, loan, trust, or banking company. Capital, $250,000, in 2,500 shares of $100 each. Original Board of Trustees: John F. Zollner, W. C. Wallace, C. Hartson, Edward Stanley, W. H. Nash, R. H. Sterling, E. L. Sullivan, A. B. Walker, W. W. Thompson, W. A. Fisher, R. B. Woodward, Henry L. Davis, Thos. H. Thompson, I. N. Larrimer, John Lawley, D. McDonald, D. L. Haas.

The present officers are-President, C. Hartson; Cashier, W. C. Watson. Finance Committee-R. H. Sterling, W. W. Thompson, T. H. Thompson.

The Bank was first opened October 2d, 1871, in the building on Main street, occupied by Wells, Fargo & Co.'s Express.

Their elegant and substantial structure on the corner of Main and Second Sts. was completed in the Spring of 1872.

NAPA CITY GAS LIGHT COMPANY.

Certificate filed May 25, 1867. Object, to manufacture illuminating gas, and to distribute and sell the same. Capital, $80,000, in 800 shares of $100 each. Original Trustees and Corporators: James H. Goodman, W. W. Beggs and Jas. Freeborn.
(107)

NAPA VALLEY SAVINGS AND LOAN SOCIETY.

Certificate of incorporation filed Sept. 25, 1871, under the Act of 1862 for the formation of corporations for the accumulation and investment of funds and savings, and all amendatory thereof and supplementary thereto. Capital stock, $100,000, in 1,000 shares of $100 each. Object: to aggregate the funds and savings of the members thereof and others, and to preserve and safely invest the same for their common benefit. Directors: Smith Brown, Henry C. Boggs, Nathan Coombs, James H. Goodman, John M. McPike, George E. Goodman, H. C. Parker and Philip L. Weaver. This institution is doing a safe and prosperous business, and is proving of great public benefit. Its place of business is in the magnificent bank building of Messrs. J. H. Goodman & Co.

The private banking house of James H. Goodman & Co. was first opened September 1st, 1858. It has ever since been doing a prosperous business, and has been a great convenience to the people. Until the organization of the Bank of Napa, this was the only banking house in the town.

PIONEER ENGINE COMPANY NO. 1.

Was organized in April, 1859, by the election of Robert Crouch, President; E. S. Chesebro, Foreman; J. H. Moran, Assistant; J. W. Hemenway, 2d Assistant; Harvey Wilder, Secretary, and B. F. Townsend, Treasurer. The first trial of the engine was on the 6th of June, 1860.

MASONIC CEMETERY ASSOCIATION.

Certificate filed Feb. 29th, 1872. This association was formed at a meeting held at St. Helena Feb. 24th, 1872, at which J. H. Allison was Chairman and A. C. Kean was Secretary. J. H. Allison, D. B. Carver, C. E. Davis, Thomas Greer, Sam. G. Clark, G. S. Chrisman, David Galewsky, L. Lazarus, A. C. Kean, J. R. Wright and Joseph Kaiser were the original associates. Purpose, to procure and hold land to be used exclusively for a cemetery. Original Trustees: C. E. Davis, G. S. Chrisman, D. B. Carver, E. K. Cooley, J. R.
(108)
Wright and J. H. Allison. The Trustees were divided into three classes, viz: C. E. Davis and E. K. Cooley in the first class, to hold their offices for one year; G. S. Chrisman and J. R. Wright in the second, to hold their offices for two years; and D. B. Carver and J. H. Allison in the third class, to hold office for three years.

TOWN HALL ASSOCIATION.

Certificate filed March 3, 1871. Object, the purchase of land and the erection of a Town Hall thereon, and to manage and improve said property and to conduct the leasing and use of said Hall. Capital stock, $10,000, in 100 equal shares. Original Trustees: A. B. Walker, Lyman Chapman, E. Biggs, A. Sampson and G. W. Manuel. Corporators: E. Biggs, A. B. Walker, J. A. Jackson, L. M. Corwin, Ralph Ellis, Lyman Chapman, A. G. Boggs, C. N. Everts, G. W. Manuel, G. N. Cornwell, C. B. Seeley, A. Sampson.

The association erected a building on Second street, 50 by 180 ft., which is used for a skating rink, concerts and other public gatherings. It will accommodate four times as large an audience as any building in the place, and proves a great public convenience.

ODD FELLOWS' HALL ASSOCIATION OF NAPA.

Certificate filed January 2, 1868. Object, to purchase a lot in Napa City and erect a building thereon for the purposes of use and rent. Capital stock, $25,000, in 2,500 shares of $10 each. Original Trustees and Corporators: W. R. Brown, J. D. Blanchar, E. N. Boynton, E. Biggs, A. B. Walker and H. H. Custer. The building proposed by this company has not yet been erected.

NAPA LIBRARY ASSOCIATION.

Certificate filed Sept. 1st, 1870. Purpose, to erect, procure and use a public library in Napa City. Pursuant to articles of association subscribed by citizens, a meeting was called August 27th, 1870, of which G. W. Ford was President, and at an election then held the following gentlemen were elected as Trustees and Officers of the Association: E. N. Boynton, President; H. H. Knapp, Vice-Presi-
(109)
dent; T. P. Stoney, Recording Secretary; J. H. Goodman, Corresponding Secretary; T. N. Mount, Treasurer; R. S. Thompson and F. A. Sawyer. The association occupies the second story of Firemen's Hall on Brown street, and has secured by gift and purchase 1,000 volumes of valuable works, which are kept in constant circulation among the members. It gives promise of great usefulness, and stands high in popular favor.

CALISTOGA HOTEL COMPANY.

Certificate filed April 1st, 1872. Object, to lease, carry on and conduct and manage the Calistoga Springs Hotel, and all business appertaining thereto. Capital stock, $20,000; 200 shares of $100 each. Trustees and Corporators: Alex. Badlam, Jr., Ezra R. Badlam and George Burgess.

WHITE SULPHUR SPRINGS HOTEL COMPANY.

Certificate filed Sept. 7, 1859. Purpose, to purchase the grounds and buildings comprising the White Sulphur and other Springs, and to erect a hotel, and transact such commercial business in relation thereto as may be necessary and proper. Capital stock, $100,000, in 1,000 shares of $100. Trustees: Dexter Tafft, R. E. Brewster and R. J. Van Dewater. Corporators: R. E. Brewster, H. P. Janes, R. J. Van Dewater, S. P. Dewey, Wm. Norris and John Weeks. A magnificent hotel 250 feet long was built by this company, and extensive improvements made to the grounds and drives adjacent at an outlay of $100,000. The hotel was destroyed by fire, with all its contents, a short time after its completion.

WATER COMPANIES.

SPENCER CREEK WATER COMPANY.

Certificate filed October 7th, 1871. Object to supply Napa City and other places in the County with pure, fresh water. Capital Stock $100,000 in shares of $100 each. Original Trustees and corporators, Dwight Spencer, Frank E. Corcoran, Donald McDonald, S. C. Hastings and William Doolan.
(110)

NAPA CITY WATER COMPANY.

Certificate filed September 1st, 1870. Capital Stock $250,000, with 2,500 shares of $100 each. Original corporators and Trustees, A. Chabot, D. P. Barstow and C. H. Potter.

CAYMUS CAÑON WATER COMPANY.

Certificate filed October, 1871. Capital Stock, $500,000. Object "to take and appropriate the waters of the creek in Rector Cañon of Yount Township, and other streams and creeks of Napa County, to supply the towns of Napa, Oakland, Vallejo, Mare Island and San Francisco with pure, fresh water." Original corporators and Trustees, S. C. Hastings, C. Hartson, Wm. Doolan.

NAPA AND VALLEJO WATER COMPANY.

Certificate filed November 24th, 1869. Objects, to supply Napa City and township, and the city of Vallejo with pure, fresh water. Capital Stock $200,000 in 2,000 shares of $100 each. Trustees,

C. Hartson, J. S. Miller, M. M. Estee, E. J. Wilson and R. Burnell. Original Trustees and corporators, C. Hartson, T. J. Dewoody, R. Burnell, D. McClure, and M. M. Estee.

UNOYOME WATER COMPANY.

Certificate filed October 24th, 1871. Object to take the waters of Unoyome Creek, known as the South branch of Tulocay Creek, and also the waters of the North branch of said creek, for irrigating and manufacturing purposes and for supplying pure water for the use of families and residents along the line of the proposed works, and also Napa City. Capital Stock $50,000 in 500 shares of $100 each. Original Trustees and corporators, Nathan Coombs, Thos H. Thompson and J. H. Howland.

HUICHICA WATER COMPANY.

Certificate filed October 28th, 1871. Object to supply farmers and gardeners in Napa and Sonoma counties with water for irrigating purposes. Capital Stock $50,000 in shares of $100 each. Trustees and corporators, Wm. H. Winters, J. C. Hastings, W. K. Salmon, John F. Zollner and A. F. Roney.
(111)

SOSCOL WATER COMPANY.

Certificate filed October 26th, 1871. Objects to irrigate and supply water for domestic and agricultural uses, and for irrigating farm lands in Soscol valley, also for mechanical, manufacturing and dockage purposes in and adjacent to Soscol, using and diverting for such purposes the waters of Soscol Creek, tributary springs and water courses adjacent thereto. Capital Stock $100,000 in 1,000 shares of $100 each. Original Trustees and corporators, Robert Sheehy, Simpson Thompson, Wm. Gouverneur Morris.

CALISTOGA WATER COMPANY.

Certificate filed February 23d, 1872. Object to take the waters of Mill Creek in Hot Springs Township, and other streams and creeks in Napa and Sonoma counties, to supply the counties of Napa, Solano, and Sonoma with pure water for domestic, manufacturing, and irrigating purposes. Capital Stock $50,000. Trustees and corporators, Samuel Brannan, A. C. Palmer, and A. Badlam.

None of the water companies named have erected works or laid down any mains, but some of them will undoubtedly do so at no distant period. There is abundance of water, and the growth of the town will before long compel a supply beyond what wells can furnish. These companies which propose to furnish water for irrigating purposes can easily do so whenever it becomes desirable.
(112)

regulations of the church.

————

BAPTIST CHURCH.

The earliest record of the Baptist Church in Napa is dated February 13th, 1864, showing the appointment of John Norton, A. J. Dotey and Ezra Carpenter as Trustees.

Bank of J. H. Goodman & Co.

(113)

————

CHRIST CHURCH, (EPISCOPAL.)

(113)
————

CHRIST CHURCH, (EPISCOPAL.)

Christ Church Parish was organized August 29th, 1858, at a meeting held for the purpose, Rev. Mr. Ewer presiding. R. D. Hopkins and Richard Dudding were appointed Wardens, and James Lefferts, James McNeil, R. T. Montgomery, Wells Kilburn, and Thomas P. Stoney, Vestrymen.

The original associates for the organization of the Church were R. D. Hopkins, James McNeil, Eugene B. Gibbs, R. T. Montgomery, J. Brome Smith, A. Coles, Richard Dudding, James Lefferts, C. M. Nichols, Thomas P. Stoney, C. W. Langdon, A. J. Donzel, J. L. Egleston, E. B. Eaton, George Fairfield and Wells Kilburn. The canonical consent of Bishop Wm. Ingraham Kip was given on the 18th day of September, 1853. September 16th, 1858, Rev. E. W. Hagar was unanimously elected Rector of the Church. The appointment was accepted by Mr. Hagar October 16th, 1858. July 9th, 1859, James' Hall was rented for the services of the Parish. Rev. Mr. Hagar gave notice of his intention to leave the Diocese on the 15th of October. November 30th, 1859, Rev. Mr. Goodwin was invited to accept the Rectorship. February 28th, 1860, a lot 80 feet square. on Randolph street, was purchased of Richard Dudding for $400 for a church edifice. March 10th, 1860, a plan for a church was prepared by Mrs. Julian Matthieu and was adopted by the Vestry, and proposals published for erecting the edifice. April 16th, 1860, a contract was awarded to John B. Horrell, in pursuance of his bid.

————

THE CUMBERLAND PRESBYTERIAN CHURCH, IN ST. HELENA,

Was organized August 17, 1863, by the election of a Board of Trustees consisting of Thos. B. Townsend, L. Murray, and A. J. Hudson. Corner stone of church edifice laid with Masonic ceremonies July 14th, 1860. The pastor, Rev. Y. A. Anderson, came from Missouri in 1855, and died May 19, 1862.

————

METHODIST EPISCOPAL CHURCH, NAPA.

A lot for church purposes was donated by Hon. Nathan Coombs,
(114)
May 9th, 1853, to Erwin F. Kellogg, Charles Hopper and Nathaniel Squibb, Trustees. The lot was the south half of lot No. 2, block 28, of Napa City. He also subsequently conveyed the present site of the church, 120 feet square on Randolph street, for a nominal consideration. The original church edifice was removed in May, 1867, to Washington street for the uses of the colored Methodist Church, before the erection of the present elegant edifice.

————

CATHOLIC CHURCH.

On the 28th of September, 1856, the lot on which the church edifice now stands was donated to Bishop Allemany by George N. Cornwell, Esq., and the deed was confirmed by a deed dated

Dec. 1866, by Hon. Chancellor Hartson, who also sold to the church lot 7 in block 4 adjoining the original lot. The church was built in 1858, and dedicated by Arch-Bishop Allemany Nov. 6, 1859. The same denomination has erected a neat building at St. Helena, and have a large congregation.

CHRISTIAN CHURCH OF NAPA CITY.

Certificate filed May 25, 1872, under the Act of April 22, 1850, and amendments thereto. Original Trustees: G. W. Deweese, W. W. Smith and J. C. Willson. A fine church edifice was erected in 1871 at a cost of $6,000.

UNITARIAN SOCIETY.

Among the places of worship in Napa City is to be considered the house of meeting, of the Unitarian Society. This society was formed in 1871. It has quite a large membership, and the officiating minister, Rev. Mr. Hudson, has always had fair audiences. So far, the meetings have been held in the Court House Hall.

PRESBYTERIAN CHURCH, CALISTOGA.

The members of the Presbyterian Church at Calistoga, though numerous, had no suitable place of worship till the Fall of 1871. At this time they completed a large and beautiful church edifice at a cost of near $2,500. Trustees: A. Safely, John Wass, Dr. R. Garnett, R. Wright, and John McCausland.
(115)

METHODIST CHURCH, CALISTOGA.

The Methodist congregation at Calistoga in 1869, erected a comfortable church building at an expense of about $2,500. The first Trustees were Wm. McDonnell, Peter Teal, and Alonzo Hopkins. The building was used for a time as a public school house, but since the erection of the fine and commodious school house, is used only for church purposes.

METHODIST CHURCH, ST. HELENA.

The congregation of Methodists at St. Helena worshipped in the Presbyterian church building till in 1867 they erected a building of their own. The Trustees, under whose management the edifice and improvements were made, Wm. McDonnell, Peter Teal, J. B. Risley and John Howell.

BAPTIST CHURCH, ST. HELENA.

The Baptist Church at St. Helena is the oldest church building in that place. In 1857 Hyram Louderback donated a lot for the purpose of a church site to the Baptist Home Missionary Society. John Cyrus, Henry Owsley, and David Fulton were the first Trustees. A suitable building was erected on the lot donated. In the Fall of 1872 the building was moved to the rear portion of the lot and thoroughly repaired and re-arranged.

There are church organizations and large congregations in every neighborhood in the county, but these mentioned above are all that have church edifices especially erected to their use.

NAPA CEMETERY ASSOCIATION.

The Cemetery grounds of 48 4-5 acres was a free gift to the association from Don Cayetano Juarez. There was not in 1858 an enclosed cemetery in Napa County. The Tulocay Cemetery Association was organized by the subscribers thereto January 10th, 1859, at a meeting held at the Court House for the purpose, at which time the deed was delivered by Don Cayetano Juarez to the Trustees. Twelve acres were set apart for the use of the Catholic
(116)
church, and a considerable tract for the burial of paupers. Soon after a substantial stone fence was erected, walks and drives laid out, and a large quantity of trees and shrubs planted. The cemetery grounds are situated on the hill side East of the river and overlooking the town. The situation is one of great natural beauty, and many beautiful monuments already mark the resting place of the dead. The cemetery is a favorite resort of many of our citizens during the Spring and early Summer.

NAPA CHAPTER OF R. A. MASONS NO. 30, NAPA CITY.

Organized May 9th, 1862. Charter members, O. P. Southwell, Geo. C. Yount, H. H. Knapp, M. L. Haas, W. W. Stillwagon, N. A. Greene, Wm. H. Holliday, J. Mecklenberg, D. B. Parks. Present officers, R. Ellis, H. P.; Beeby Robinson, R.; W. C. S. Smith, S.; P. Van Bever, Treasurer; L. M. Corwin, Secretary. Past High Priests, R. Crouch, H. H. Knapp. Number of members, 40.

YOUNT LODGE NO. 12 OF F. AND A. MASONS, NAPA CITY.

Organized May 6th, 1851. Charter members, Wm. D. Deering, James M. Small, M. T. McLellen, W. W. Stillwagon, Geo. C. Yount, Joseph Mount, B. Vines, Thos. Chopson, J. W. Moody, M. H. Kendig. Present officers, H. H. Knapp, W. M.; R. Ellis, S. W.; R. Crouch, J. W.; P. Van Bever, Treasurer; B. H. Gorton, Secretary. Past masters, H. H. Knapp, R. Crouch, Wm. H. Holliday, T. J. Tucker, F. M. Hackett. Number of members, 80.

INDEPENDENT ORDER OF ODD FELLOWS.

Napa Lodge, No. 18, received its Charter from the Grand Lodge, November 26th, 1853. Charter members, J. D. Stetenius, David Monnett, Robert Hopkins, Edward A. Hazen, John H. Waterson, D. C. Tripp. List of members in 1859: All those marked * are deceased. Past Grands, E. B. Eaton, J. H. Waterson, *J. C. Penwell, G. N. Cornwell, *James M. Wilson, *J. M. Dudley, Thos. Earl, *Jonathan Bell, R. D. Hopkins, James Lefferts, C. N. Souther, T. B. McClure, *J. N. Cosgrave.

Brothers of the Fifth Degree: John B. Horrell, M. L. Haas,
(117)
D. B. Parks, J. Magee, Robert Hastie, R. T. Montgomery, J. S. Stark, *L. G. Lillie, J. H. Darnes, *Johnson Horrel, Rt. S. Hardin, *P. Hunsinger, Jacob Blumer, *J. A. Butler, R. B. Adams, Joshua Carter, Samuel B. Snow, L. L. Dennery, D. V. Norton, W. J. Gose, C. W. Langdon, *J. A. McGimsey, Geo. W. Hampton, C. R. McGimsey, Wm. C. Phagan, H. A. Pellett, M. Haller, E. Chatelain, Wm. D. Hensley, Jos. Enright, D. S. Cheney, Charles Marx, J. Chord, *Rees Smith, J. L. Foote, C. B reedlove, *Newton Morse, James Parsley, G. B. Crane, B. M. Townsend, Wm. Morrow, Thos. Horrell, Wm. N. Bell, *Charles Van Pelt, Julius Solomonson, D. Thompson, F. Levinson, Jno. P. Hensley, A. Brannan, J. H. Baldwin, J. B. Walden, Jos. Eggleston, T. H. Ink, T. W. Alexander, Jno. G. West, J. Barnes, E. True, Wm. H. Clarke. Brothers of the Third Degree: N. Coombs, Jerome J. Snow, J. F. Houx, *G. W. Custer, J. C. McWilliams.

Initiates: G. W. Towle, P. Veeder, J. Heath, E. Bounds, W. H. Winters, N. P. Ingalls, A. S. Rooney, H. K. VanBuskirk, Simon Peake, J. M. Snow, George Grigsby, Julius H. Frank.

The above is given merely as a matter of history, to show of whom this benevolent order was at that time composed.

List of members for 1872. Past Grands: H. L. Amstutz, J. N. Reynolds, W. R. Brown, A. B. Walker, G. B. Clifford, E. N. Boynton, W. W. Pendegast, L. M. Corwin, R. N. Steere, J. C. Pierson, W. R. Aldersley, A. Sampson, A. G. Boggs, L. Davis, F. W. Colman, J. Israelsky.

Brothers of the Fifth Degree, 47; of the Third Degree, 5; of the Second Degree, 2; of the First Degree, 2; Initiates, 21.

Officers for 1872: H. T. Barker, N. G.; H. J. Baddeley, V. G.; E. N. Boynton, Treasurer; J. C. Pierson, R. S.; H. L. Amstutz, F. S.

The Lodge is in a very prosperous condition, and has upon its books the names of ninety-five members in good standing.

ST. HELENA LODGE, I. O. O. F., NO. 167.

Charter granted January 31st, 1870. Charter members: C. E. Davis, J. C. Penwell, P. G., J. S. Adams, A. Korns, P. G., H. A. Pellet, H. A. Wyman, J. I. Logan, P. G.
(118)
Number of members November 14th, 1872, fifty-eight; 5th degree members, fifty; 3rd degree members, two; 2d degree members, two; initiates, four.

List of officers at this date: Past Grand, G. W. Montgomery Noble Grand, Robt. Hastie Vice Grand, John Mavity; Recording Secretary, W. R. Wilson Permanent Secretary, E. A. Straus; Treasurer, J. K. Hall; Warden, Wm. McCormick; Conductor, N. Howe; Inside Guardian, P. R. Johnson; Right Supporter to Noble Grand, W. A. C. Smith; L. S. to N. G., Thos Grear; R. S. to V. G., J. Straus; L. S. to V. G., John Keaster; R. S. S., James Lowe; L. S. S., C J Field; Chaplain, J I Logan

---

EMERY LODGE NO 367, ORDER OF GOOD TEMPLARS, NAPA CITY

Charter granted February 11th, 1870. Charter members: F. M. Caldwell, Mrs. A. J. Caldwell, S. N. Mount, J. L. Trefren, Rev. G. W. Ford, R. J. Bishop, Mrs. N. Bishop, Mrs. J. L. Trefren, Mrs. L. A. Ford, F. A. Trefren, W. A. Johnson, F. Adair, A. J. Ford, H. A. Chapman, J. S. Mallony, L. W. Boggs, J. L. Robinson, J. Ritchie, G. W. Manuel, Mrs. A. Lamdin, Mrs. G. Bowman, Mrs. M. Snow, Mrs. Sheppard, Mrs. L. C. Manuel, Mrs. J. Jenkins, H. A. Clark, L. C. Clark, L. Chapman, C. Robinson, E. E. Snyder, M. E. May, G. W. Riley, H. W. Leek.

Officers, November, 1872: J. Eggleston, W. C. T.; E. Clark, W. V. T.; A. J. Clark, W. S.; T. Mount, W. F. S.; Miss L. Grover, W. T.; H. Baterman, W. M. Number of members in good standing, seventy-five.

YOUNTVILLE LODGE NO. 369.

Charter granted February 17th. 1870. Charter members: J. L. Cook, A. E. Cook, A. G. Clark, G. W. Oman, H. Bateman, L. Gilbert, A. J. Clark, S. Clark, C. Clark, S. Kinsey, J. C. Oliver, C. A. Menefee. Number of members, November, 1872, twenty. This Lodge surrendered its Charter a short time since.

MONROE LODGE OF GOOD TEMPLARS, CALISTOGA.

The Monroe Lodge of Good Templars at Calistoga was organized by Miss Emery, State Deputy, about the 1st of February, 1870, with
(119)
twenty-four charter members. This has, since its organization, been a flourishing Lodge. Its present membership is fifty in good standing.

ST. HELENA LODGE, NO. 93, F. AND A. M.

May 6th, 1856, Caymus Lodge of Masons was organized at Yountville with the following Charter members: Simon Rosenbaum, J. W. Deering, G. C. Yount, P. R. Hazelton, J. J. May, Wm. Baldridge, B. Vines, Joseph Evey, Edward Evey, and Wm. Hargrave. The first officers were J. J. May, W. M.; Edward Evey, S. W.; G. C. Yount, J. W.; J. M. Wright, Treasurer; W. Baldridge,

Treasurer; A. C. Kean, Secretary; W. L. Simmons, S. D.; S. G. Clark, J. D.; W. W. Bradbury, Tyler.

_____

OTHER LODGES.

In 1854 there was a division of the Sons of Temperance formed at St. Helena. The meetings were held in a little school house near the present site of the fine residence of Hon. Seneca Ewer. Among the organizers of the Division we mention D. Hudson, Wm. Hudson, J. H. McCord, and W. E. Taylor. At this time the town of St. Helena consisted of only a store and a few other buildings. On account of the fine view obtained of St. Helena mountain, the Division was named St. Helena, and the Division gave the name to the town. The Division soon surrendered its charter.

In 1858 Grand Lecturer Roney organized another Division at the same place with a long list of Charter members. In the following year a Lodge of the Temple of Honor was organized by Rev. B. E. S. Ely, D. G. W. C. T., with the following Charter members:
B. E. S. Ely, Y. A. Anderson, M. Vann, T. H. Anderson, J. T. Edwards , I. F. Kingsberry, J. L. Edwards, D. V. Norton, W. A. Elgin, D. H. Haskin, and Joseph Haskin. A great portion of the (120)
regalia and jewels of the Temple of Honor still remains in the possession of J. L. Edwards awaiting the resurrection of that Order in this State.

April 12th, 1861, Franklin Lodge No. 29, Order of Good Templars, was instituted in Napa City. It continued till the Fall of 1868, when it surrendered its Charter.

In 1864 a Lodge of the same Order was instituted at Yountville, but did not exist long. The records are all lost or destroyed. Also in the same year Grand Lecturer Johnson organized another Lodge of the same order in St. Helena, but it, together with these other temperance organizations, has long since been disbanded.

(121)

CHAPTER X.

(121)

CHAPTER X.

NAPA COLLEGIATE INSTITUTE.

Certificate filed Nov. 22, 1870. A committee appointed for the purpose by the California Annual Conference of the Methodist Episcopal Church of California, Sept. 22d, 1870, appointed the following, persons Trustees to receive, hold and take charge and care of the property in Napa City known as the Napa Collegiate Institute property, and direct and control an institution of learning thereat for said Conference: George Clifford, Nathan Coombs, Geo. Fellows, Henry Fowler, George E. Goodman, Wm. Hamilton, C. Hartson, J. A. Hutton, George Linn, E. S. Lippitt, A. W. Norton, E. Thomas, J. L. Trefren, A. D. Wood and R. B. Woodward-to hold their office

(122)

for one year from the first day of October, 1870, and for such further time as the Conference may determine.

The Institute was originally erected by a subscription of $100 each by the citizens of Napa county. It was first opened August 8, 1860, and conducted by A. N. Hamm as a private enterprise. The country was too new and sparsely populated for such an enterprise, and it was inadequately supported. It was afterwards conducted by Rev. W. S. Turner for two or three years, but, in 1870, fell into the hands of the Methodist Conference of California. The corner stone of the edifice was laid with Masonic ceremonies by, Grand Master W. H. Howard of San Francisco, June 24th (St. John's Day), 1859. The oration was delivered by Rev. Mr. Hagar, the pastor of the Episcopal Church in Napa. The grounds are five acres in area and the main edifice of four stories 46 by 70 feet. It was entirely remodeled at an expense of over $6,000 in 1870, and is now one of the finest school edifices in the State.

Faculty:-T. C. George, A. M., Principal, Mental and Moral Science; W. C. Damon, A. M., Latin and Greek Languages; Mrs. R. R. Thomas, A. M., Preceptress, Natural Science and Modern Languages; Miss M. W. Wells, A. M., English Literature; Mrs. E. L. Smith, Music, Drawing and Painting; Miss Maggie McDowell, Assistant in Music; Rev. George Clifford, Agent.

NAPA LADIES' SEMINARY.

This Institution was established by Miss Harris in 1860, and conducted by her until 1864. After her resignation, and a short interim of a few months, the school was resumed by Miss Maria S. McDonald, through whose untiring energy and indefatigable labors it yearly increased in numbers and influence, by accessions both from home and abroad.

Miss McDonald assumed the position of Principal in 1864, and conducted the Institution for five years, at the expiration of which time Death cut short her usefulness, and overwhelmed the school with sorrow and loss. It is but due to her memory here to speak of the executive talent which she so eminently possessed, also her powers of persuasion, her rare art of discipline, her tact and originality, and

(123)

more than all, her scholarship and Christian culture-all of which adapted her pre-eminently for the profession she had chosen and in which she achieved such signal success.

The event of her death left the school in the care of Miss Sarah F. McDonald, (sister of the deceased), who has since held the position of Principal, with what success the present record and condition of the school testify.

The entire history of this institution has been one of progress, and cherished in the hearts of its patrons, it now stands well defined in its proportions and triumphant in its results.

This Seminary is duly authorized by the Legislature to confer diplomas upon such of its students as may have passed through the prescribed course of study. Since the erection of the new Seminary building, an elegant structure 40 by 55 feet and 3 stories high, the accommodations for pupils are equal to those afforded in any other educational establishment in the State. The Seminary is well supported and merits the high standing which it has attained in the public esteem.

Instructors-Miss Sarah F. McDonald, Principal, and Instructor of Higher English Branches; Miss S. M. Holland, Mathematics, Natural Sciences and Latin; Miss E. A. Follansbee, French and Italian Languages and Instrumental Music; Miss Mary Mulholland, Drawing and Painting; Miss Flora A. Rasche, Vocal and Instrumental Music and German; Miss Ella Lamb, Teacher of Preparatory Department and Gymnastics.

These are all the educational institutions that by their past successes have become permanent. But it must not be supposed that the educational facilities of our county are confined to these. Many private schools in various parts of the county, under the management of able educators, have at various times been opened, but all ceased. The cause was not that the teachers were not in every respect capable, nor that the people were not disposed to patronize the schools, but simply that the public schools have been so good, the teachers, especially in the towns, such superior educators, that the people found that their children progressed better here than in the private schools. Prof. Blake, as elsewhere in this volume noted, recently

(124)

opened a high school for boys in Napa. The number of scholars is limited, and the course of instruction thorough. The Professor is one of the ablest educators in the county, and so far his school promises to become one of our permanent institutions and be of great benefit to the community. Mr. W. A. C. Smith, of St. Helena, for several years that he has been Principal of the school in that place, has had private classes in the higher English branches and in the Classics. He has done an excellent work in educating the community to the importance of thorough schools. Similar remarks might be made about other teachers and other schools in our county, but this must suffice.

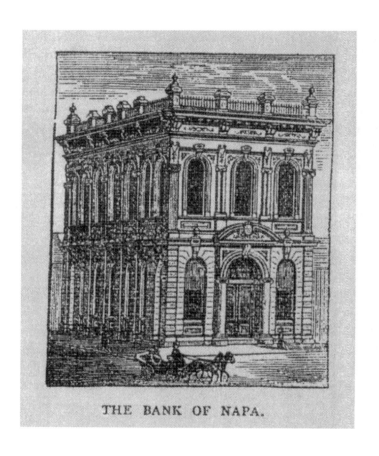

THE BANK OF NAPA.

(125)

ST. HELENA MOUNTAIN, FROM CALISTOGA.

CHAPTER XI.

GEORGE C. YOUNT.

The great beauty, salubrity and fertility of this part of California caused its early settlement by Americans. Several years before the conquest of the country, a number of American emigrants had chosen homes for themselves in Napa Valley and others adjacent to it. As early as February, 1831, George C. Yount reached Napa Valley and settled here having come out with a party of trappers from Missouri which arrived at Fort Yuma in 1827. He was a representative of the pioneers of the Mississippi Valley in the last century. At the age of 18 he had served under two sons of Daniel Boone, against the Indians, in the war of 1815, and had conversed with the venerable Daniel Boone himself. Inspired with the love of adventure, as a trapper he took up the trail on the border of the Missouri, and proceeded westward through the valleys of the Platte, the Arkansas,
(126)
Green River, the Colorado, the Sacramento, and finally the Valley of Napa. So far as is now known he was the earliest pioneer of American civilization from the Sonoma Mission in California to the distant hunting grounds of the Hudson Bay Company, unless we may count as such occasional deserters from whale ships along the coast of the north Pacific, and the Russians who established a colony near Bodega in 1812. Further south a few settlers preceded Mr. Yount. The country at the time of his arrival was filled with hostile tribes of savages. As many as 10,000 or 12,000 occupied the country now forming Napa and Lake counties, of which 3,000, and possibly 6,000, according to Mr. Yount, were dwellers in this valley. Grizzly bears were found in great numbers, and indeed

6,000, according to Mr. Yount, were dwellers in this valley. Grizzly bears were found in great numbers, and indeed are not unfrequently met with among the mountains even at this day. To use the words of Mr. Yount, "they were everywhere-upon the plains, in the valleys and on the mountains, venturing even within the camping grounds, so that I have often killed as many as five or six in one day, and it was not unusual to see fifty or sixty within the twenty-four hours." The streams abounded with fish and the hills with deer and small game, while in the low and marshy tule grounds along the rivers were the favorite haunts of the gigantic elk. Mr. Yount continued his occupations of hunting, trapping and catching the sea otter until 1834, and then spent two years in various occupations in different places, sometimes taking charge of the Sonoma Mission while the Padre was at San Rafael, where another Mission required his attention. In 1836 he finally settled upon "Caymus Ranch," a tract of two leagues of land in the heart of Napa Valley, which was granted to him by the Mexican Government. In the Fall of 1836 he here erected the first log house and raised the first chimney ever built in California by an American. His house was not only a dwelling, but a fortification-having a room 18 feet square below, and another 20 or 22 feet square above it fitted with port holes, and through these Mr. Yount, was often called upon to defend himself by firing upon the savages who from time to time came down from the mountains to attack him. He also erected the first flour and saw-mill in California. At this time his only companion was an old Frenchman who had fought under Napoleon, and his only neighbors five or six fami-
(127)
lies of friendly Indians, who had taken up their abode near by. He had no other neighbors nearer than the Sonoma Mission on one side and the Hudson Bay Company on the other. This brave old pioneer had numerous fights with the hostile savages, but with the aid of a few friendly Indians always succeeded in defending himself.

Mr. Yount obtained another extensive grant of land from the Mexican Government, called "La Jota," situated chiefly in the mountains and broken country on the east side of the valley opposite the town of St. Helena. Both his grants, after long delay and annoyance with squatters and law suits, were confirmed by the United States. Their value was of course enormously increased by the American occupation and the subsequent discovery of gold. He lived long enough to enjoy for a season his large estate, and the universal respect of all who knew him. He was a great hearted, true man, of unbounded generosity, and his house was ever open to dispense hospitality. Even during the later years of his life, notwithstanding his many trials and sufferings, he retained almost the energy and elasticity of youth, and his memory seemed as vivid as ever. He was in manners simple and unassuming, and would relate incidents of his life of the most thrilling nature, without the least display of vanity or egotism. When in the mood, sitting at his own fireside, with a circle of neighbors or visitors, he would allow himself to be "drawn out," and relate his many adventures on the Plains and among the savages with a simplicity and evident truthfulness that charmed all who listened. The writer of this article remembers with pleasure more than one such occasion. Many of the incidents of this sketch were collected and published by the gifted Mrs. F. H. Day, in the *Hesperian* for March, 1859.

Mr. Yount was born in North Carolina in 1794, and died at his residence on Caymus Ranch, Oct. 5th, 1865. He was buried with Masonic honors in the cemetery at Yountville (a town situated upon the same ranch and named after him), and a suitable monument erected to his memory. On the four sides are sculptured representatives of his life as a trapper, hunter and agriculturist.

The white settlers in Napa Valley next after Mr. Yount, were Salvador Mundo Vallejo, Cayetano Juarez and Jose Higuera-the first a

(128)

native Californian and the two others natives of Mexico-who came about 1838. Each obtained a grant of land; the Vallejo grant being north of the site of Napa City, the Juarez grant east, and the Higuera grant southwest. About a year later, Dr. E. T. Bale, an Englishman, married to a native California lady, obtained and settled upon a grant - the "Carne Humana" - north of Yount's grant. These with the Soscol, made six ranches, all of which have been confirmed. Pope Valley was granted at an early day to Antonio Pope and Berryessa Valley was also a Mexican grant. Both the grantees are long since dead. Salvador M. Vallejo and Cayetano Juarez are still living; also the widow of Dr. Bale. The Yount grant, as well as a subsequent one called "La Jota," have been disposed of under the provisions of his will. The widow of Dr. Bale still resides upon the ranch granted to her husband, but a considerable portion of the land has been sold. Cayetano Juarez has sold a portion of his ranch, and still resides upon the remainder. All the other ranches named have passed entirely into the hands of Americans.

It was the custom of the Indians to establish their rancherias upon the grants of the settlers in order to make a livelihood by their labor. In 1843 there were from fifty to one hundred upon the Bale ranch, about 1000 upon the Yount ranch, a large number upon the Juarez and the Higuera grants, and a still larger number at Soscol. A few may be still left upon some of these ranches.

Charles Hopper and Joseph B. Chiles first came out in 1840 overland in the same party with John Bidwell, of Butte county, and others. Both are still hale and vigorous men, and large landholders.

The valley was visited in 1841 by Wosnessensky, a Russian naturalist, who recorded his visit upon a plate of copper at the summit of St. Helena. The plate was removed for preservation by the officers of the geological survey.

William Baldridge, a pioneer of 1843, resides upon his farm near Yountville. Ralph Kilburn, who resides near Calistoga, arrived in 1842.

William Fowler, Sr., and his sons William and Henry, and William Hargrave, are among the earliest settlers. William Fowler, Jr., came across the plains to Oregon in 1841, and returned East.

(129)

All the parties named came to Napa Valley in 1843. Messrs. Fowler and Hargrave are among our most respected citizens.

Harrison Pierce settled in Napa in 1843, having landed in Oregon from a whaleship in 1842. He died in 1870.

The emigration of 1846 was quite numerous. Among the number were Gov. Lilburn W. Boggs and family, who came overland and settled first in Sonoma, and in 1852 upon a beautiful farm in Napa Valley, seven miles above the county seat.

The same year John Cyrus, F. E. Kellogg, R. P. Tucker, David Hudson, L. Keseberg, Col. M. G. Ritchie, Arch. Jesse, Wm. H. Nash, and James Harbin became settlers in the valley. Mr. Nash is well known as the proprietor of one of the earliest orchards and nurseries in the State, and as the present owner of the beautiful Magnolia Ranch, five miles from Napa City.

A list of the early emigrants now residing in this county, and taken from the records of the Pioneer Association of Sonoma, Napa, and Marin, will be found more fully set forth at the close of this volume. To William Boggs, the President of the Association, grateful thanks are due for many points of information contained in this work. Also, to Henry Fowler, Esq., of Napa City.

CAPT. JOHN GRIGSBY.

This gentleman came into the county about the same time as Mr. Coombs, having been for two or three years elsewhere in the State. He carried on a large farm near Yountville until 1861, when he returned Eastward, and is now said to be in Texas.

NATHAN COOMBS.

Hon. Nathan Coombs, who laid out the county seat, came to this coast in 1843, and settled in Napa in 1845. He has served in the State Legislature, and always been a prominent citizen. He has been a liberal contributor to public improvements, and is known all over the State as a raiser of blooded stock and a patron of the turf. His farm, the "Willows," two miles from Napa City, is one of the finest in the valley.
(130)

GUY FREEMAN FLING.

Among the early pioneers of Napa County may be classed Guy Freeman Fling, who, at the age of eighteen, came out upon the whaleship *Courier* from Boston in 1825, and settled at Monterey in 1827. He piloted Mr. Yount from Monterey to Napa in 1831, returned to Monterey and finally settled in Sonoma, whence he came to Napa in 1850. He was at one time an armorer on the United States ship of war *Portsmouth,* Capt. Montgomery, and when on shore followed the trade of a gunsmith. The kind-hearted and eccentric old man was as well known in this part of the State as any other that could be named. He died in Napa City in 1872.

SIMPSON THOMPSON.

This gentleman is well known all over the Pacific Coast as the proprietor of the celebrated Soscol Orchards, and is entitled to the honor of having first introduced the system of fruit culture in California without irrigation. His theory was that thorough cultivation was sufficient without any artificial supply of water, and his experiments demonstrated its truth. At first his experiments were derided, and few could be made to see the correctness of his views. In a short time, however, Mr. Wolfskill and Mr. Wm. H. Nash perceived the advantages of his system, and abandoned their costlier system of irritation. Their example has been generally followed, except in some of the Southern counties, and the practice of irrigation has almost disappeared.
Mr. Thompson was born in Buckingham, Berks county, Pa., in 1803. His great grandfather, John Thompson, bought the old homestead farm in Berks county, directly from William Penn, and it

may be remarked as something very rare in American family history, that the property is still owned by his great grandson, the subject of this sketch. John Willson, his great, great grandfather on the mother's side, emigrated with his family to America and settled in the same township. He was the eldest son of James Willson, who had violated the law of the realm by marrying Isabel, the daughter and heiress of the Earl of Carsik, in Scotland, and had

(131)

been compelled to flee with his bride to the county of Antrim, Ireland. Of the same family, two generations removed, was Margaret Willson, who was in 1685, at the age of 18, sentenced to be drowned in the waters of the Bladnoch, near Wigton, Scotland. An aged lady of 63 years, named Margaret McLachland, was condemned at the same time. Their only crime was refusing to take the oath of recantation, and to abandon the principles of the Scottish reformation. A beautiful cenotaph of white marble was erected to the memory of these martyrs in the city of Stirling, and still commemorates their "faithfulness unto death." The following is an extract from the minutes of the Kirk Session of Penningham Parish, February 19th, 1711: "Upon the eleventh day of May, 1685, these two women, Margaret McLadland and Margaret Wilson, were brought forth to execution. They did put the old woman first into the water, and when the water was overflowing her, they asked Margaret Wilson what they thought of her in that case? She answered, "What do I see but Christ wrestling there. Think ye that we are the sufferers? No, it is Christ in us, for He sends none on a warfare on their own charge." Margaret Wilson sang Psalm XXV from the 7th verse, and the eighth chapter of the Epistle to the Romans, and did pray, and then the water covered her. But before her breath was quite gone, they pulled her up, and held her till she could speak, and then asked her if she would pray for the King. She answered that she wished the salvation of all men, but the damnation of none. Some of her relations being at the place, cried out, she is willing to conform being desirous to save life at any rate. Upon which Major Winram offered the oath of abjuration to her, either to swear it, or to return to the waters. She refused it, saying, "I will not, I am one of Christ's children, let me go." And they returned her into the water, where she finished her warfare, being a virgin martyr of eighteen years of age, suffering death for her refusing to swear the oath of abjuration and hear the curates."

In May, 1852, Mr. Thompson came out to California *via* the Chagres river and Isthmus route, making part of the journey from Gorgona to Panama upon a mule, and sleeping in the open air with

(132)

a box of medicine for a pillow. He came up the coast upon the steamer *Golden Gate* with 1500 passengers, among whom were some 40 or 50 store-aways, who came on board at Acapulco, and who had been wrecked upon another steamer. These were treated rather roughly and made to work at whatever they were able to accomplish. At last, Samuel Brannan, who was aboard, made a speech in their favor and headed a subscription list with $500 for their relief.

William Neely Thompson, brother of Simpson Thompson, with Thomas H., the son of the latter, had come out to California *via* the Horn in 1849, on the ship *Gray Eagle,* 120 days from Philadelphia. William Neeley entered in a co-partnership with Mr. Blackburn in the lumber business in San Francisco, and furnished most of the material for the State House at Vallejo, and in 1851, 320 acres of the Soscol ranch was taken in payment at $12 per acre. Subsequently about 300 acres more were purchased. A town a mile square had been laid out on the property, by Gen. Vallejo. Some of the stakes on the lines are still remaining. When Mr. Simpson Thompson arrived in 1852, his brother had sent men up and planted a small lot with potatoes at a cost for plowing alone of $12.50 per acre. Nothing else was done on the farm, and the man in charge abandoned his place, being completely discouraged. Mr. Thompson had come out for the purpose of taking part in the enterprise of lighting San Francisco with gas, and was provided with some of the necessary fixtures, but when he found that coal cost $50 per ton, abandoned the project, and for want of anything else to do, came up to Soscol and took charge of the place. Here he spent the first six weeks under a big oak tree, making his own bread and doing his own washing. This tree is near the present mansion house, and is surrounded by a circular arbor and cherished with the greatest care. Mr. Thompson found the place in a state of nature. Soscol creek, which is now confined within artificial bounds and empties into the river, in 1852 spread over a wide area, converting it into a morass. This is now reclaimed and constitutes the richest portion of the Soscol orchards. The first trees were obtained from Rochester, N. Y., and from New Jersey. Seeds of trees of many kinds were brought out, but thousands of dollars were sunk by losses in

(133)

transportation. Trees packed in charcoal dried up and died; those packed in wet moss mostly rotted on the way, but those packed in dry moss arrived in good condition. The first peach pits were planted in April 1853, and most of them grew vigorously. Ripe peaches were raised from these pits in sixteen months from the time of planting. The mexican residents when they saw them put out, and preparations making for a nursery, laughed at the idea of such a thing. They said that without water it was impossible, that barley would not grow over two feet and wheat not over six inches, without irrigation, while trees would not grow at all. It may be well supposed that they were somewhat astonished when sixteen months afterwards Mr. Thompson showed them finer peaches than had ever been seen in the State! Apples were also produced from the seed in two years and a half. Garden vegetables of all kinds were produced in abundance, and of great size, without irrigation. The fact stood demonstrated, that nothing more was needed to render the lands productive than deep plowing and thorough cultivation. The Mexicans admitted that Mr. Thompson had produced better results in one year than they had after twenty years of experience. All the fruit cultivated by them was from seedlings, and of course of inferior quality. But a new era was at hand. Mr. Wolfskill and other cultivators at once purchased trees and buds from Mr. Thompson's select varieties, and soon produced the best varieties of fruit in other parts of the State.

The first basket of peaches sold from Soscol orchards, brought $23.75, or about eighty cents per pound. They were retailed at $1.25 each. The first basket of plum peaches brought $34, or $1.12 1/2 per pound. A small area, only about one-fourth of an acre, was planted with gooseberries, and the product was three tons. This fact, when reported at the East by visitors, was rejected as absurd and beyond belief. It may be of interest to some readers to note the prices of fruit at tn early day, and the books of the establishment give the following figures. Wholesale prices of fruit in 1856: Apricots, per pound, 70 cents; early apples, 50 cents; peaches, $9 to $14 per bushel of 28 pounds; peaches, best quality, $18.75 per bushel, or 55 cents per pound; yellow rareripe peaches, 60 cents

(134)

per pound. In 1855, $3 per pound were offered for the cherry crop before they were picked and ready for market.

The prices of nursery trees were in proportion. In 1856, trees in the dormant bud by the 1000 sold for 60 cents each; peaches one year old brought $2.50 each in 1855, and $1.50 in 1856; apple trees sold for 75 cents to $1.50 each; a single fine tree brought $5.

It is stated by Mr. Thompson that in 1856 the trees in the original orchard would have sold for a larger sum than he could now command for the land, orchard, and all included. The farm and orchard that year yielded $40,000, a sum greater than it has ever yielded since, although the area under cultivation is greatly extended, and the product increased ten-fold. Prices of most kinds of fruit are now so low as to leave but a small margin for profit. Mr. Thompson does not speak very favorably of one of his experiments in shipping fruit to the East. Three years ago he shipped sixty boxes of the very choicest Fleming Beauties and Bartletts, each pear wrapped repeatedly in paper, to Chicago and New York. The fruit was of the highest excellence and brought 10 cents per pound in Chicago, and 7 to 8 cents in New York. But after paying freight, commissions, &c., there was left only 42 cents per box for the fruit, just 10 cents more than the boxes cost! Mr. Thompson for many years carried on the establishment in connection with his two sons, Thomas H. and James M. Thompson, and more recently with the assistance of the latter alone. Indeed, James M. Thompson is really the active manager of this magnificent property. The old gentleman, surrounded by everything that could render life enjoyable, and held in universal respect by all, beyond the necessity or desire of active labor, willingly entrusts his affairs to younger hands. The family mansion in which he and his youngest son reside, is a model of convenience, widely known for its generous hospitality. The grounds are laid out with great beauty and dotted over with rare shrubs and trees from every part of the Union. It is a place of great resort for visitors who come here to admire the beauty of the place. Notwithstanding the attractions of Soscol orchard, it is a place of serious business throughout the year. Hard work and plenty of it is always in progress, and a large force of men are em-
(135)
ployed. The reclamation of a large body of tule land is now going forward, which is destined to add greatly to the value of the property.

————

GOVERNOR EDWARD STANLEY

.   Governor Edward Stanley, who died suddenly of paralysis at the Grand Hotel in San Francisco July 10th, 1872, was a pioneer and citizen of Napa County. He purchased a beautiful site between St. Helena and White Sulphur Springs in 1868, and had for many years been a large landholder in the county, although his place of business was in San Francisco. He arrived there early in 1872 from Newbern, North Carolina, the place of his nativity. He was born in 1811. Commenced the practice of law in 1832. In 1837 he was elected to Congress, and was twice re-elected. In 1844 he was elected a member of the lower branch of the Legislature, and became Speaker of that body. In 1847 he was elected Attorney General of his native State. Two years afterwards he was again sent to Congress, where he strongly advocated the admission of California as a State. In 1851, in spite of much dissatisfaction among many of his constituents on account of his voting for the admission of California, he was re-elected. In 1857 he was the Republican candidate for the Governorship of California, but was defeated by the Democratic candidate, John B. Weller. In 1862 he was appointed by President Lincoln Governor of North Carolina, and after having held the position with honor and credit for eighteen months, at a most critical period, returned to California. Governor Stanley was a sincere and upright man, a fearless and able advocate, and a zealous Christian. He held a large landed estate in this county, of which he was one of the most eminent citizens.

————

JOHNSON HORRELL.

Johnson Horrell was born July 3d, 1798, in Tuscarora Valley Juniata county, Pennsylvania, and moved to South Bend, Indiana, in 1834. After having practiced the legal profession and holding the office of magistrate and State Attorney at that place for several
(136)
years, he removed to California in 1849. He erected the first dam ever constructed across the Yuba river, and afterwards aided in laying off the city of Marysville. In 1851 he became a resident of Napa, and took a prominent position in public affairs. He was appointed justice of the Peace in place of Sellers, who was murdered by Macauley, and afterwards held the office of County Judge for three years. He was the owner of the first silver mine opened in Washoe, and disposed of it for a large sum, but which was a mere trifle in comparison to its value as afterwards ascertained. Judge Horrell during the last years of his life was deeply engaged in mining enterprises, and passed through all the changes of good and evil fortune. He was widely known throughout the State as a hard-working and skillful lawyer. His death occurred February 28th, 1867.

————

CAPTAIN ROBERT WEST.

This venerable gentleman was born in Monmouth county, New Jersey, April 14th, 1797, and was engaged in the European and coasting trade for many years. His last European voyage was made in 1847. On the 10th of June, 1849, he came out to California as Captain of the *Pilgrim,* with an assorted cargo belonging to G. W. Aspinwall, of New York. The *Pilgrim* was a canal boat of eighty tons, and had been employed on the route between New York and Wilmington, N. C., *via* the Dismal Swamp canal. She was of the usual scow pattern, and looked like anything, rather than a sea going vessel. She was rigged as a fore-and-aft schooner, and before starting was fitted out with temporary railings instead of bulwarks, and proved entirely seaworthy. On the 2d of January, 1850, she arrived in San Francisco, without the slightest accident or injury to vessel or cargo. In about latitude 10 N. when on the Atlantic, a large English ship passed the little *Pilgrim,* under a press of canvass, and shortly after carried away her foretopsail. Capt. West came up under the lee of the ship and spoke her, inquiring if he could render any assistance. The Englishman appeared quite indignant at the offer, and inquired in reply," What, in ----, assistance can *you* give? and when told by Capt. West that he was bound to
(137)
San Francisco, the Englishman replied incredulously, "San Fran h--l!" The *Pilgrim* made no landing from New York, to San Francisco, and arrived ahead of several vessels which sailed at the same time. Capt. West engaged in the coasting and river trade for two years after his arrival on this coast, employing three vessels, the *Aspinwall,* the *Filt* and the *Pilgrim.* The latter was sold to the California Steam Navigation Company, and converted into a barge, and finally laid up in 1855 at the foot of Third street, Napa City, where she remained several years. She was finally sold

and broken up by Capt. Orloff Reed, and her material used in building the schooner *Zina Reed,* which was lost after a few voyages to the lumber ports on the Northern coast. Captain West became a resident of Napa on the 4th of July, 1852, and has resided here ever since. (The greater portion of his life has been spent on "the rolling deep," and he is never perfectly at home upon land.) He possesses a large store of information, and is universally respected as an honest man and good citizen.

_____

WILLIAM H. NASH.

This gentleman is well known all over the State as a pioneer orchardist and farmer, and his success furnishes a marked example of what may be accomplished by untiring industry and careful experiment. Mr. Nash was born in Claiborne county, Tennessee, on the Clinch river, thirteen miles from Cumberland Gap, on the 11th of October, 1821. He removed to Jackson county, Missouri, in 1838. In 1846 he emigrated to California with a company having sixty three wagons. A portion of this company was destined for Oregon, and a portion for California. They separated at Fort Bridger, twenty-five wagons proceeding by Hastings & Hudspeth's cut-off South of Salt Lake, and others by way of Fort Hall to California. Of the original party the following persons remained together all the way to Napa Valley. Wm. H. Nash, his wife and two children, Enoch Cyrus, Henry Owsley, Zimri Hollingsworth,-- Matthews, father and son, W. Ashley, Wm. Piles and his son, John Lard, -- Whiteman, and some others. Other companies from Westport and In-
(138)
dependence were on the road at the same time, the largest of which was headed by Governor L. W. Boggs.

At the head of the Sweetwater, near the South Pass, the party with which Mr. Nash travelled, met Mr. James Hudspeth and L. W. Hastings, who persuaded them to take the cut-off, which afforded more plentiful grass and water, and would save 500 miles of travel and bring the party to California three weeks sooner than the old route. Fremont had previously discovered the South Pass, but the route had been first passed over with wagons by Messrs. Hudspeth and Hastings, after whom it was named. Mr. Hastings was a gentleman of great abilities, and had in 1842 travelled extensively in California, and on his return to Cincinnati published a pamphlet setting forth in glowing terms the beauties and attractions of this almost unknown region. It was the reading of his work that induced Mr. Nash, in spite of all remonstrances, to venture on the tedious and perilous trip to California. One strong inducement was the offer of grants of land by the Mexican Government. Mr. Nash, found, as he says, that Mr. Hastings' pamphlet was literally true in every particular, although he was prevented by the conquest of the country from obtaining, a grant.

Messrs. Hudspeth and Hastings informed the party that a revolution was going on in California, and hostilities initiated between the Mexican and American population, and therefore urged them to hasten their speed in order to aid their countrymen.

Fremont, who had an exploring party of 130 men at Sutter's fort, excited the jealousy and fear of the Mexicans, although he committed no acts of hostility, and did not even know that war existed with Mexico. The first news he received to this effect was from Lieutenant Gillespie, who had been sent out by the Government *via* Mexico, as a secret agent to confer with him. Gillespie went first to Sutter's fort in quest of Fremont, when he heard that the latter had gone with his party to Oregon. He overtook Fremont at Rogue River, and informed him of the existence of war with

Mexico. The party then returned immediately to Sutter's fort. During the absence of Fremont's party, the Mexicans had manifested a hostile disposition, and murdered two young men, about three miles from

(139)

Santa Rosa, while on their way to Fort Ross. This was the immediate occasion of the formation of the "Bear Flag" party. The Americans were enraged, and hastily collected at Sonoma, declared their independency and resolved to conquer or die. They were but a handful of men, surrounded by enemies, and dispatched Harrison Pierce, one of their number, to ask assistance from Fremont. Pierce rode fifty-five hours on this expedition without stopping, except once at Wolfskill's to change horses. He delivered his dispatch and received Fremont's promise to come on immediately, when with a fresh horse he returned to Sonoma. During his absence the Americans had had their first fight with the Mexicans near San Rafael, killed eight of them, and taken a large number of prisoners, whom they confined in Gen. Vallejo's house at Sonoma. Jacob P. Leese, an American by birth, but long a resident of the country, was taken prisoner also, much to his great surprise and indignation. Fremont's party formed a hollow square about the building and sent in an interpreter to say that the Americans had been civil and harmed nobody, but had been abused and imposed upon; that their only chance left was to leave the country or fight, and that they had chosen the latter alternative. The prisoners assured them that they would all take sides with the Americans against the Mexican Government, and did so. Fremont then moved Southward, arrested the Governor, Pio Pico, in his bed, and sentenced him to be shot, but spared him at the intercession of his family. Pico then, solemnly promised to cooperate with the Americans, and did so, going from Mission to Mission to warn the people of the folly of resistance, and exhorting them to submit to the new order of things.

Having inserted this episode as being of interest in itself and as illustrating the condition of the country at the time of Mr. Nash's arrival, we now return to his personal memories. Mr. Nash purchased 338 acres of land on the Bale Ranch from R. L. Kilburn in 1847 at $2 per acre, naming the place "Walnut Grove." In 1872, 288 acres of this land was sold for $25,000. The discovery of gold, and a mining expedition of a few months to Mormon Island and the North fork of the American River, kept Mr. Nash from settling upon his land until November 26th, 1848, when he camped

(140)

upon it with his family, and erected a shanty of slabs from Kilburn & Bale's mill. For three weeks all the cooking was done under a tree. The place was as wild and uncultivated as nature made it, and he had few neighbors within a distance of several miles.

Mr. Nash commenced his first orchard in January, 1849, by setting out thirty-six 2 year-old seedlings, which had been brought out by Mr. Barnett from Kentucky. They cost $1 each, and there was no way of obtaining any others. In the Fall of 1849, in connection with R. L. Kilburn, a lot of small trees were ordered from a nursery in Pennsylvania, around the Horn. They were packed in moss and boxed, arriving the Spring following. The cost was $1 each. In the Fall of 1850 a further supply was obtained from Quincy, Massachusetts, *via* the Isthmus, and from Portland, Oregon, at the same price.

The only plow in use when Mr. Nash commenced his experiments in agriculture was a forked stick shod with iron, such as is still used by the peons of Mexico, and which is in no respect better than that used by the inhabitants of Judea 2,000 years ago. He was among the first to inaugurate a new and better system of agriculture in California.

He then supposed, as did everybody else, that nothing would grow without irrigation, and accordingly expended some $2,000 in bringing water out of the mountains for his garden and nursery. He continued the irrigation process for eight years, and then abandoned it. We saw his place in 1854, when his conductors and reservoir were still in use. He had no reason to complain of want of success either, having in 1850 sold the peaches upon two three-year-old trees for $300. They were purchased by Mr. Giorgiani, of San Francisco, who retailed them at one dollar each. In 1852 he was led by the example of Simpson Thompson, Esq., of Soscol, to substitute deep and repeated plowing, for irrigation, and did so with the best results. He plowed his ground three times-the last time as late as the 20th of June. He put out thirty acres more of vines and trees, and found that under the new treatment they made twice the growth that had been attained by those which had been irrigated, and indeed, to this day, the unirrigated portions of his old or-
(141)
chard and vineyard have kept up their superiority. The irrigated trees received a sudden check when the water was stopped, from which they have never recovered. The reason is that irrigation causes the trees to throw out lateral roots near the surface, where the ground is naturally dry, whereas in well pulverized ground, without irrigation, the roots tend downward in search of the natural moisture of the soil.

In 1868 Mr. Nash sold his land and purchased the magnificent Magnolia Farm, upon which he now resides, about five miles and a half from Napa City. When he took possession it was a mere wheat field, but it is now the model farm of Napa County. It is beautifully located, and under as thorough cultivation as a garden. No irrigation is used upon the place, nor is it needed where the soil is kept thoroughly pulverized. Mr. Nash has devoted his best energies for the past twenty-six years to the business of fruit raising and general farming, and has experimented extensively, in order to secure the varieties of fruits best adapted to our soil and climate, as well as to ascertain the best plans of cultivation. His success has been great, and he has now a high reputation among the orchardists and farmers of California.

———

MAJOR WILLIAM GOUVERNEUR MORRIS.

The subject of the following sketch is a much respected resident of Napa County. Major Morris is the son of Brevet Major General William W. Morris, U. S. Army, who graduated at West Point in 1820, and faithfully served his country for nearly half a century, he having been engaged in the Yellowstone Expedition, the Black Hawk, Creel, Cherokee, Seminole, and other Indian wars, in the Mexican war and in the defense of the Union during the Rebellion. In the latter war he commanded the Middle Department and Eighth Army Corps. During his long and varied services General Morris received three brevets for gallantry in the field the first being that of Major during the war in Florida.

Major Morris is a scion of an illustrious stock. His great-grandfather was Lewis Morris, one of the signers of the Declaration of Independence, whose half-brother, Gouverneur Morris, occupies a
(142)

prominent place in the early history of our country, he having been a distinguished military officer during the Revolution, and when our national independence was won, he held several important civil offices in New York, his native State, and under the Federal Government. He was elected United States Senator, and was appointed Minister to France by President Jefferson.

Morrisiana, in Westchester county, New York, the ancestral home of the Morris family, is one of the most ancient homesteads in the country, having been granted to Richard Morris by the King of England in 1670, more than two centuries ago. The family is of Welsh origin. Several members of it were distinguished as valiant leaders under the famous Oliver Cromwell, during the Commonwealth in England. Its members have ever been staunch Protestants. Lewis Morris, already referred to, while Colonial Governor of New Jersey, named a county in that State Monmouth, in commemoration of the family estate in Monmouthshire, Wales.

For nearly two centuries the family has had its representatives in the service of the State of New York, in the army and navy of the United States, and among the ministers of the Episcopal Church. Its members are allied by marriage to most of the distinguished old families of New York, including the Knickerbockers, the Van Rensselaers, Schuylers, Jays, Livingstons, Van Cortlandts, Hoffmans, Vanderhorsts, Lorillards, Stuyvesants, Rutherfords, and others. Major Morris is on his mother's side nephew of the late Captain A. A. Ritchie, one of the early settlers in Napa county, who was the owner of Calistoga, Guenoc, and Loconoma grants. His maternal grandfather was a distinguished surgeon in the army during the Revolution. The subject of our sketch is also related to Dr. Hugh Williamson, who was Governor of North Carolina during the Revolution, and to Dr. Archibald Alexander, the distinguished Divine, so long President of Princeton College. Major Morris was born at Brooklyn, New York, in 1832, and has received a liberal collegiate education. After leaving college he studied law at Key West, Florida, with Hon. William Marvin, Judge of the United States District Court, one of the ablest Admiralty lawyers in the nation. During his residence at Key West, Major Morris was elected Clerk

(143)

of the Council, and was appointed Inspector of Customs. In 1855 he obtained the degree of L.L.B. at the Dane Law School, Howard University, and soon after came to California and entered the law office of the celebrated Joseph G. Baldwin, subsequently one of the Supreme Court Justices. In 1856 he was appointed Reporter of the Supreme Court of California, and while filling that position published the "Fifth Volume of California Reports." In 1857 he settled at Visalia, Tulare county, and engaged in the practice of his profession. While here he was appointed Notary Public and State Locating Agent of School Lands. In 1861, during the disturbances among the settlers on the Chabollo grant, in Santa Clara county, when a large body of these settlers were in open, armed resistence to the authorities of the county, Governor Downey selected Major Morris to prevent a rupture of the peace, a mission which he carried to a successful issue. Major Morris has never received the credit he fairly deserved for his management of this delicate business. Had open hostilities broken out between the settlers and the authorities, civil war, which then just commenced at the South, would have been inaugurated in this State. The Major had several conferences with General Sumner, who then commanded the United States forces on the Pacific Coast, and by his tact and skill, the threatened hostilities were averted, and the whole matter was referred to the Legislature, which body subsequently disposed of it to the satisfaction of the parties directly interested.

In September, 1861, Mr. Morris was appointed 1st Lieutenant and Adjutant of the Second Regiment of California Cavalry, commanded by Col. A. J. Smith, of distinguished fame as a cavalry officer, now Postmaster at St. Louis, Mo. In the following March he was promoted to the rank of Captain and appointed by President Lincoln Assistant Quartermaster of Volunteers, a position he held with credit to himself and advantage to the country till mustered out of service at the close of the war in the Spring of 1866. While serving as Lieutenant in the Second Regiment California Cavalry, Mr. Morris performed the arduous and responsible duties of Superintendent of Videttes, and transported the dispatches between the California Column sent to Texas and the head-quarters of the De-

(144)

partment of the Pacific, duties which required himself and his command to be almost constantly in the saddle, and exposed them to the perils of the desert, the Indian, and the rebels on the frontiers of civilization. His duties as Supervisor of Videttes kept him nearly three years travelling between Southern California, Arizona, and New Mexico, the most unpleasant field of duty on the Pacific Coast. On his promotion to Captain and Assistant Quarter-master, his duties became more responsible, and were performed with the same zeal that distinguished him in the field. He constructed Drum Barracks, and the Immense military depot at Wilmington, Los Angeles county, and the military quarters on Catalina Island. For these and other important services, at the close of the war, he was promoted to the rank of Major by brevet for "faithful services." While stationed at Benicia, as Commander of the depot at that place, Major Morris, attracted by the beauty and fertility of the climate and soil of Napa county, determined to settle in this county. With this object in view he purchased a portion of the splendid estate on which he now resides, and which in a few years, when his contemplated improvements shall be completed, will form one of the most pleasant of the private homes in the State.

In August, 1869, Major Morris was appointed United States Marshal for the District of California, a position which he at present fills to the entire satisfaction of the Federal authorities and all who have business with that important office. An examination of the books of the United States Marshal's office, arranged by Major Morris himself, will show at a glance, that as an accountant and statistician, the Major is quite as zealous and efficient as he has proved himself to have been on the field or in the quarter-master's department of the military service.

He is one of the authors of the prize essay on the "Manufacturing Interests of California," a work replete with valuable information relating to a most important subject. The Mechanic's Institute of San Francisco awarded a premium of $400 for this useful essay. In 1870 he had charge of the United States census, in taking which he made such arrangements to secure accuracy, and performed the duty so effectually, as to have won the special commen-

Yours Truly, Wm Gouverneur Morris, U.S. Marshal

(145)

dation of the Superintendent of the Census. Major Morris is a member of many civic and military societies, in all of which he is an active and zealous worker. He is a prominent officer of the military, order of the Loyal Legion; he is a member of the Society of the Cincinnati, the most distinguished society in the United States, which was founded by Lafayette, and is hereditary. Major Morris inherited the position from his grandfather, who was an officer of artillery during the Revolution.

The Major, although taking a deep and active interest in the political and local affairs of Napa county, and enjoying the respect and confidence of its citizens, has never sought any public position at their hands.

The Major's beautiful farm, which he has called "Morrisiana of the Pacific," in commemoration of the family seat in Westchester county, New York, is a portion of the celebrated Soscol Rancho. It contains about nine hundred acres of as fine land as there is in the State, thoroughly cultivated and well stocked, and is supervised by the Major himself, who manages to find time to attend to the onerous and responsible duties of United States Marshal, to take an active interest in the political and local affairs of the county, and to superintend his extensive farm, which includes one of the largest and most valuable fruit orchards in the State, which contains many hundreds of choice apple, pear, peach, apricot, cherry, and other fruit trees.

Major Morris is a bachelor; he is a gentleman of pleasing address, of splendid physique, a most reliable friend and a relentless enemy; liberal and benevolent to a degree bordering on extravagance, he is most rigid in exacting his rights in all matters of business. In politics he is an ultra-Republican, occupies a leading position in that party, is always a member of its most important committees and conventions, and is a good representative member of that party.

Napa county has reason to be proud of such citizens as the subject of our brief sketch, and such men are invaluable in emergencies. Their experience, skill and energies are always available for the public service when required. The greatest defect in the Major's character is his persistent celibacy, a defect we hope to see removed some of these days.
(146)

JOHN LAWLEY.

Mr. John Lawley came to this country from Alabama, his native State, in 1853, *via* New Orleans. He engaged in the warehousing business in Napa City, and did a successful business for several years. In 1867 he purchased an interest of three-fourths in the Phoenix Mine, a considerable portion of which he still holds. After his purchase the mine remained undeveloped for two or three years, when he disposed of a portion of his stock and active operations were commenced. In the Spring of 1866, he in connection with Wm. H. Hamilton and James W. Bostwick, purchased Berryessa Valley for the sum of $100,000, which has been since sold out in farms, and now is the greatest wheat raising region in the county. He has held several public positions with credit, and is well and favorably known in this part of the State.

COL. JAMES CLYMAN.

Col. James Clyman is another of the early pioneers of this county. He was born in Fauquier county, Virginia, A. D. 1793. His father moved to State county, Ohio, in 1812, about the time of the battle of Tippecanoe. Having learned the profession of a surveyor, young Clyman was engaged for a while in surveying Government lands in Indiana, under Major Morris, who had a contract for the work, In 1823, when this was completed, he enlisted in Lt. Governor Wm. H. Ashley's expedition against the Indians up the Missouri, during which he experienced terrible hardships, and was engaged in fierce battles with the Rickarees and other Indian tribes, the marks of which he bears to this day. He returned to the States and remained in Missouri and Wisconsin for seventeen years. He returned just in season to bear a part in the Black Hawk wars, and was out in the whole of it, serving in the same company with Abraham Lincoln.

Bad health induced Col. Clyman in the Winter of 1842-3, to try a trip across the plains. He joined a party at Independence, Missouri, and traveled overland to Oregon, thence by the land route he arrived in Napa in 1845, and returned East the following Summer. Three years after he made a final settlement upon the
(147)

beautiful farm upon which he now resides, two miles Northwest of Napa City. Col. Clyman kept an itineracy of all his journeyings, which he wrote up at night by the light of his camp-fire. It evinces good intelligence, sound judgment and shrewd observation. He describes the soil, scenery, timber, climate, and other peculiarities of California with a minuteness of detail not elsewhere to be met with, giving the most vivid and graphic pictures of the country just as it was in 1845. This venerable gentleman, now 79 years of age, is still in full possession of all his faculties. His life has been strange and eventful, but its evening is full of peace. He is respected by all as a brave, reliable and truthful man.

————

ELISHA G. YOUNG.

Elisha G. Young came to this county in 1850, and has persued the occupation of a farmer ever since. He has been quite successful in his favorite employment, and ranks high as a trustworthy and useful citizen. He merits a notice in a local history, as one of the pioneers of agriculture.

————

RALPH ELLIS.

This gentleman is a native of Pennsylvania, came to California in 1853, and was for two or three years treasury expressman in the mountains for the banking, and express company of Everts, Wilson & Co., whose principal house was at Marysville, with branches at La Porte, St. Louis, Gibsonville, Pine Grove, and Poker Flat. Stages ran only to La Porte. Beyond that point all the coin was sent to the mining camps on the backs of mules, and Gold dust returned by the same conveyance. As much as 300 pounds avoirdupois of dust was frequently carried at a time, and the perils of the business were such as to require the services of men of strong nerve and unflinching courage. Mr. Ellis was elected Clerk of Sierra county in 1857, and removed to Napa City in 1860. He served as Sheriff of Napa county for one term, and then entered upon an extensive warehouse business, and the purchase and sale of grain. As an intelligent and upright business man he has no superior.

(148)
————

PETER D. BAILEY.

Peter D. Bailey, Esq., is a native of Ireland, and one of the pioneers of this county. He came by the overland route to Napa in 1849, and has ever since been a resident. He was among the first who commenced the cultivation of grain on an extensive scale, and demonstrated the value of our valley lands for agricultural purposes. A thorough education and excellent judgment have enabled him to attain success in his favorite pursuits and to win the respect of all classes. He was here when the county was organized, and took part in public affairs in the day of "small beginnings." We are indebted to him for many details of early history which are embodied in this volume.

CHARLES HOPPER.

Mr. Charles Hopper was born in North Carolina A. D. 1800, and although now 73 years of age, has a full head of hair-fuller indeed than most men have at 40. His memory is perfect, even to the smallest details, and the old fire is in him yet. No better example can be cited of the venturesome, courageous, yet wary and shrewd frontiersman. One thing we specially mark and leave to the judgment of the reader. Uncle Charley has a firm and abiding faith in some supernatural power that watches over men. We do not speak of the idea of a general Providence that rules over all things, and which is common to all men. His thought is rather, if we understand him, that, especially, when a good man is alone and in danger, whether from within him or from without, there will come teachings and warnings of supernatural origin and distinctness, entitled to implicit confidence. He gives the following instance, which occurred while crossing the great desert Southeast of Tulare Lake. "Here we were two days without water, and camped at night in the worst of spirits, not knowing whether to go back or keep on, and there was a good deal of murmuring in camp. I do not know how to account for it, unless there was some supernatural in-terference--and I think from this circumstance, as well as others in my experience, that there was-but towards morning, whether in a dream or not, I cannot say, I *saw* a green spot where there was

(149)

plenty of water, and could perfectly see the course that led to it. It was so perfectly plain, and I was so sure of it, that I got up, mounted my horse, and told the party when they got up to follow my trail. I struck out Northwardly, away from the trail we had come over, and everything I came to was *just as I had before seen it,* so that I wasn't *one bit surprised* when I saw a few miles ahead a green, grassy spot, where, when I came up to it, there was the blessed water we so much needed. Can it be that we, who are immersed in the learning of the books, and "tutored in the rudiments of many desperate studies," are less wise than the lonely trapper who rolls himself in his blankets under the silent watch of the stars?

Is it true that there are

> " Airy tongues that syllable men's names on sands and shores and desert wildernesses?"

There are similar experiences in the life of Geo. C. Yount, of which we have memoranda, which we omit as foreign to our present purpose.

He set out in May, 1841, with a party of thirty men, one woman and one child, from Jackson county, Missouri. John Bartleson was Captain of the company, which was increased to seventy-five before starting, by another party commanded by Captain Fitzpatrick, bound to Oregon, and which seperated from Captain Bartelson's company at Soda Springs, near Fort Hall. Mr. Hopper remembers the names of the following persons who belonged to his party:

Col. John Bartelson, Col. J. B. Chiles, (now of Chiles' valley), John Bidwell, (Hon. John Bidwell, of Butte county), Andrew Kelsey, (afterwards killed by the Clear Lake Indians), Nathan Toms, Michael Nye, Captain Rickman, McMahan, Benjamin Kelsey, C. M. Weber, (now a prominent citizen of Stockton), - Chandler, John McDowell, Green McMahan, - Springer, Grove Cook, Mrs. Benjamin Kelsey and child.

He describes San Francisco, then called Yerba Buena, in 1841, as follows:

"It was a miserable place-nothing but a lot of sand-hills, a little trading port of the Hudson Bay Company. There was one hut, said to be a sort of tavern, and Col. Chiles and I went in and called for something to eat. The landlord said, "Gentlemen, I have nothing, in God's world to give you, but will look around and try to get

(150)

you some beef."' Well, he did get some after a while, and broiled it for us. That was the kind of accommodations you got in San Francisco in those days. It's a little different now!"

Mr. Hopper returned to Missouri in 1842 by way of New Mexico, and in 1847 returned to California with his family. He then purchased a large farm on the Caymus Grant from Mr. Yount, upon which he still resides. His early life was spent as a trapper and hunter in the great wilderness between the Mississippi land the Pacific, and many are the hair breadth escapes which he has experienced, from the savages and the fury of the elements. He corroborates Mr. Yount as to the great number of grizzly bears in this region, having killed no less than nine within a mile of his house in the Summer of 1848, and seen great numbers of them. Bear hunting seems to be his favorite sport, and he still sometimes takes the field against them, when tired of the monotony of in-door life. He is apparently as hale and vigorous as a man of twenty, and his eye-sight is as keen as ever. No one stands higher as a conscientious, true-hearted and generous man, whose word is inviolable. He is universally respected, and is affectionately called " Uncle Charley" by all who know this brave old pioneer.

_____

GOV. L. W. BOGGS.

The first great rush of immigrants to California was in 1846, during the pendency of hostilities between the United States and Mexico. Among the arrivals that year was Governor L. W. Boggs and family. Much of the early history of Sonoma and Napa is identified with that of Governor Boggs, and a history of these counties with his name left out would be as the play of Hamlet with the ghost omitted. At the time of his arrival here, Mr. Boggs found the town of Sonoma, then the seat of justice for the Northern District of California, almost deserted. The few native Californians had taken the oath of allegiance to the United States and lived in social friendship with the Americans, were prompt and faithful in the discharge of their duties as citizens, and honorable in all their dealings. At the close of the Mexican war, Gen. Riley appointed Governor Boggs as Alcalde for Sonoma, on account of his former experience as an executive officer.

(151)

Governor Boggs was born in Lexington, Kentucky, 1798. He was at the battle of the Thames under Shelby's command of Kentucky troops. In 1818 he emigrated to Missouri and settled at St. Louis. Here he was married to a daughter of Col. John Bent, and by her had two sons. Soon after the birth of the second son he became a widower. He afterwards married a daughter of Col. Jesse Boone, son of old Daniel Boone of Kentucky fame. His last wife, who still lives at her fine home in Napa Valley, is the mother of nine children. She was married to L. W. Boggs at the age of eighteen. Mr. Boggs was closely related to the Andersons, of Sumpter notoriety, the Olivers and Frazers of Kentucky. Much of his early life was full of adventure and hardships. For a considerable time he was extensively engaged in trading, with various tribes of Indians in the territories, and at another time engaged in the overland trade to Santa Fe. At that early day--from 1826 to 1840--

this Santa Fe journey was considered a very hazardous trip. After successfully following this business for a considerable length of time, Mr. Boggs with his family settled down on his old home and farm adjoining the town of Independence, Jackson county, Missouri. Here he filled various offices of trust from that of post master to the Governor of the State, and took an active part in the framing of many of the laws of that State. During his term of office as Governor, he was often petitioned by the people of Western Missouri to remove the Mormons, who had become a great trouble, both to the people and to the authorities. He finally ordered out the militia and compelled the Mormons to cease their depredations and leave the State. For the firm action of Governor Boggs in freeing the State of this great Mormon evil, he received the thanks of the people and the congratulations of the Governors of other States. But the Mormon leaders selected him for assassination. Joe Smith the Mormon prophet, selected a young man, Orrin P. Brockwell, to proceed to Independence and murder Mr. Boggs. The attempt at assassination was made and came near proving successful. This emissary from Nauvoo had made himself acquainted with the residence and habits of Mr. Boggs, and one evening as the latter took his accustomed seat in his sitting room, fired a charge of some ten or fifteen buck-shots from a large holster pistol. Only four of the (152)

balls took effect. Two penetrated the skull and lodged in the lobe of the brain over the left eye, one passed through the neck and came out at the roof of the mouth, and the other lodged in the neck. Much doubt was long entertained of his surviving, and he never wholly recovered from the effects of the wounds.

Mr. Boggs was one of the first persons who advocated settling the Pacific coast, and he was the author of the first essay in regard to the feasibility of constructing a transcontinental railroad. He formed the idea that a road near the 35th parallel could be constructed and would prove the greatest enterprise of the age. Time has proved the correctness of his estimates. On his leaving with his family for California he was escorted far out on the plains by numbers of his old friends, who bade him adieu, wishing success in his new enterprise. At the time of his departure from Missouri, Governor Boggs was uninformed of the declaration of war with Mexico, and upon being informed by a messenger from Col. Boone of West Port, would have returned, only for the opposition of his son, Wm. M. Boggs, who proposed making the journey, war or no war. The Governor's former experience as a trapper and trader on the frontiers was of great use to him on this journey.

On his arrival in Sonoma, Governor Boggs engaged in mercantile pursuits. He was selected by General Riley as Alcalde for Sonoma and filled that position to the satisfaction of the people. He was at one time an extensive land-holder in Sonoma valley. But disposing of his property in Sonoma, he, in 1852, moved to Napa valley and settled upon a beautiful farm seven miles North of Napa City. He died March 14th, 1860. His older sons are well known as citizens of enterprise and intelligence. Angus Boggs, after a long residence here, removed some years since to San Jose. Henry C. Boggs, although still a property holder in Napa, resides in Lake county, and George W. Boggs in San Joaquin valley. Albert G. Boggs has served the county as Treasurer for many years; and Wm. M. Boggs, a resident of Napa City, and President of the Pioneer Association of Napa, Sonoma, Lake and Marin, is well known and highly esteemed as a citizen of worth. (153)

JOSEPH MECKLENBURG.

This gentleman came overland to California from Ohio in 1853, and has since been engaged in farming and carrying on the business of a miller above St. Helena. His attention, however, has not been confined to his private affairs. He has taken an active part in the political affairs of the county, and for three successive terms filled the office of Supervisor with credit to himself and advantage to the public interests. On all public questions his course has been upright and honorable. Mr. Mecklenburg is a man of large and enlightened views, and when he has once formed a deliberate opinion of a proposed measure, is always ready to stand by it in spite of op- position. Many of our principal public improvements have been either originated or made successful through his influence. He is still a member of the Board of Supervisors.

JOHN STECKTER.

Mr. John Steckter came to this county overland in 1849, and has since resided upon his beautiful and extensive farm near Oakville. There were far more Indians than whites on his arrival. He is one of our most respected and substantial citizens. His description of Napa City as it was in 1849, is brief and graphic, consisting simply in the statement that "there wasn't any such place. The name had got there somehow, but the city hadn't." There were neither streets nor sidewalks, and little to indicate where either were intended to be. The ways trodden by men and horses had a convenient free-and-easy way, of going pretty much where they had a mind to, without much regard to line and compass. Vallejo & Frisbee had a store on the point where the river and creek meet, when Mr. Steckter arrived in the county, and a few scattered shanties on Main street. His farm adjoins the quicksilver region on the West side of the valley.

HORATIO NELSON AMESBURY.

This gentleman is one of the pioneer farmers of Napa county, well and favorably known as one of the most thorough and skillful in his profession. He was born in Stonington, Connecticut, in 1814,
(154)
and came to this State *via* Cape Horn in 1850, in the Fall of which year he settled in this county. He was employed for a while upon the American Hotel, then in course of erection, and shortly afterwards engaged in his favorite pursuit of agriculture. In 1853 he purchased Roscobel Farm in Brown's Valley, the magnificent place upon which he still resides, about two miles from Napa City. When he arrived here there were only eleven buildings in Napa City. Mr. Amsbury remembers the men and events of those days with great distinctness. On one occasion he and Hon. Nathan Coombs had business in Benicia, but Mr. Amesbury declined to go by the usual conveyance, the little steamer *Dolphin*, not considering her safe, and therefore made the journey on horseback. Mr. Coombs took the steamer, and came very near being wrecked by a storm in

the Straits! On his arrival he found Mr. Amesbury had arrived before him, and told him that during the gale when he expected to be lost, he had taken a pack of cards and thrown them overboard, for fear, that if he got drowned they might be found in his pocket. Mr. Amesbury was among the earliest orchardists in the valley, having commenced in 1854, and brought out a large assortment of choice varieties of trees from the East in 1855. He has also experimented somewhat in the cultivation of cotton, tobacco, and Japan rice.

————

LYMAN CHAPMAN.

Mr. Chapman, who now resides upon his beautiful farm about a mile from Napa City, was born at Groton, New London county, Connecticut, in 1821. He with Nathan Coombs and Samuel Starr, built the American Hotel, which is still standing. The raising of this building excited a good deal of attention, as it was the first regularly framed edifice erected in this region. People came even from the Russian River region to see it, and a great crowd was gathered to see the raising. It cost Mr. Coombs about $400 for "egg-nog" to treat them-and he came off cheaply at that, as eggs at that time cost $12 per dozen. Mr. Chapman kept the hotel for three years, and then entered upon agricultural pursuits, which he has followed successfully ever since.
(155)

————

JOTHAM H. HOWLAND.

J.H. Howland, Esq., was one of the early settlers of this State and county. He sailed from Boston, Massachusetts, on the bark *Carib,* and after a passage of 180 days arrived in San Francisco in 1848. The *Carib* was the first vessel from the Atlantic coast that arrived here after the discovery of gold. In 1851 Mr. Howland engaged in mercantile business in Napa City, where he has resided ever since. He has held the offices of Public Administrator and that of County Recorder for several terms with credit, and ranks high for honor and intelligence. Although in the prime of life, he ranks as a pioneer of civilization on the Pacific coast, and is in every sense a true Californian.

————

JOHN B. HORRELL.

J.B. Horrell is one of the pioneer mechanics of Napa, and has been largely engaged in the business of a carpenter and builder since his arrival from Pennsylvania in December, 1849. His first work was upon a building erected for T. G. Baxter for a restaurant, upon the site of Earl's Block, Main street. He was also employed upon the Napa Hotel in 1850. He has lived to see Napa City expand from a little hamlet to its present proportions, and is still in the full strength of manhood. He owned and constructed the first bridge ever built across Napa River, known as the "toll bridge." It was situated a few rods East of Vernon Mills, and was in use down to 1858.

————

SAMUEL HEALD.

Mr. Heald, a millwright by trade, is a native of Ohio, and came out from Missouri in 1849. After remaining a few weeks at Mr. Kellogg's in Napa Valley, he went to Fitch's ranch (upon which Healdsburg now stands) and returned East *via* New Orleans in January, 1851. He then returned across the plains to Napa and was employed the Winter following upon Yount's mill. In the Fall of 1852 he removed to Santa Clara. In the Spring of 1854 he visited the East and in the Fall returned to Santa Clara. In the Fall of 1856, he settled finally in Napa City, where he still resides. He

(156)

was for some time proprietor of the Vernon Flour Mills, first alone, and then as a partner in the firm of Heald, Cooper & Kester. Mr. Heald was one of the first organizers of the Republican party in this county, when the opposite party were so strong as to make immediate success out of the question. He is a man of strong convictions, following out and practising what he thinks to be right, without fear or favor. He is widely known as an advocate not only of total abstinence from intoxicating liquors, but from animal food, tobacco and every other narcotic. What he preaches he practices, and his evident intelligence and sincerity command the respect of even those who hold opposite opinions.

————

WM. H. WINTER.

This excellent citizen and old pioneer is descended from English stock who traced their ancestors back to the Saxons. He was born in 1819 in Vigo county, Indiana. His father had settled in that county when it formed a part of what was known as the Northwest Territory, and died a short time before the birth of our subject. When about five years old, Mr. Winter's mother moved up near Crawfordville, in the same State, and here his boyhood was spent. The only feat of note was his sailing, or floating down the Wabash, Ohio and Mississippi once on a flatboat to New Orleans. This, in those days, was considered a great feat. Soon after his return, he started for this coast. He came out as far as Missouri in 1841, and remained there, in Johnson county, till the Spring of 1843, when he joined a party and started for California. On the Platte River he fell in with the Chiles party. They all traveled together to Fort Hall, when they separated. The wagons came down the Humboldt, guided by the famous mountaineer, Col. Joe Walker. His company again separated at Fort Boise, on the Snake River. He, in company with five others, passed down to Oregon. At Walla Walla the company sold their horses to the Hudson Bay Fur Company, and bought a kind of flat-bottomed boat, propelled by oars, and in this they passed down the Columbia River to Portland. The Winter of 1843-4 was spent at the Willamette Falls. In the Spring of 1844 he joined the Kelsey party, of which William Hargrave and Henry Fowler were members, and came to California. Many hardships,

(157)

adventures and hair-breadth escapes were met with on the way, but no serious accident. They came down the Sacramento Valley to Cache Creek. After leaving the Mission on the Willamette, the party had seen no signs of white people till they arrived at Cache Creek. Soon after, they went to Sutter's Fort. Here he met with a Mr. Williams, with whom he had become acquainted on the Plains, and these two made a journey down through the San Joaquin Valley over to San Jose and Gilroy. At this time no inhabitants lived in the San Joaquin Valley; only wild bands of mustang horses were to be seen. On their return, however, they found that Col. Weber, who had obtained a large grant of land in the San Joaquin Valley, had sent out one Lindsay with a large herd of cattle, and that this person had stationed himself near the present site of Stockton. The Indians were so bad, that the following Winter they killed Mr. Lindsay and drove off the cattle. Thus ended the first attempt at settling the San Joaquin.

After returning to Sutter's Fort Mr. Winter came over into Napa Valley, and visited Mr. Yount's ranch, and then passed over to Sonoma. In the latter place he fell in with Messrs. Fowler and Hargrave, and spent the Winter with them in that valley. In the following Spring, 1845, he and other parties from various portions of the State made Sutter's Fort a rendezvous, to form a party to go back across the Plains. The party, when completed, consisted of thirteen members. This party was the first that ever attempted to cross the Sierra Nevada Mountains going East. A few parties had found their way over the mountains into the State, but none had attempted to recross. They crossed over in safety; passed up the Humboldt and Bear River; camped for a time with a party out recruiting; crossed to the South Pass, and traveled on to Fort Laramie. Here the party separated. The Indians were very bad, and some of the party wanted to halt and go from there through to the Missouri River with the provision wagons; seven, of whom Mr. Winter was one, concluded to attempt to go straight through. They succeeded without any great accident. On reaching the Missouri the company disbanded, the parties going to their several homes. He and his companion, Mr. Johnson, traveled on together to Indiana, retaining all the way their pack animals with which they left this country.

(158)

Mr. Winter remained in Indiana till the Spring of 1849, when he got up a company and came out to California. On the head waters of the Blue River, before starting across to the Platte, the party found they were the head train of the season. The company crossed with nothing more than the usual number of accidents and losses allotted to such perilous journeys. After reaching California, Mr. Winter settled near Mokelumne, and engaged in mining. He opened a provision and grocery store, and obtained a postoffice for the place-afterwards known as Winter's Bar-and did considerable business. In 1850, however, he sold out and went back home by way of the Panama and Chagres River route. Soon after his return to Indiana he was married and engaged in farming. In 1851, becoming dissatisfied, he traveled through Texas in search of a better country, and not being satisfied with that State, returned in 1853 with his family to California. The Winter of 1853-4 he spent in Colusa county, and in the following moved to Lake county. In Lake county he found one of the best places he had ever seen for gratifying one of his greatest passions-bear hunting. The bears were plentiful all over the county. In 1855 he came over to Napa and bought a tract of 664 acres on the Huichica; some time afterwards he purchased 600 acres more. This place he has ever since made his home. Mr. Winter's life has been an eventful one; and the many incidents, travels, hardships and hair-breadth escapes that have been allotted to him would, if collected, make a volume more entertaining than the finest romance. From youth till his settling in Napa, his life was one of continual adventure. As a trapper, mountaineer and explorer, he had few equals. Since his settling down on his farm in this county, he has surrounded himself with all

the comforts and conveniences of life. He has made very extensive and beautiful improvements, and his farm now is regarded as among the best in the county. He has, also, been an extensive stock raiser, and in taking care of his herds has spent much time in various parts of this State and in Nevada. Mr. Winter has always taken an active part in whatever was of interest to the county and the State. He has, though never a politician, always taken a deep interest in the political changes and transactions in the county. He has always been an advocate of the principles (not the practices) of
(159)
the Democratic party. As a stock raiser, a farmer, vine grower, he stands second to few in the county; and as an upright, honorable and trustworthy citizen, has no superiors.

THOMAS EARL.

This gentleman is a native of Canada. He emigrated in 1835 to Richmond, Ray county, Missouri, where, with the exception of one year spent in Lexington, Kentucky, he remained until 1850. On the 20th of May of that year, with three others he started overland from Independence with a team of mules. The party were three months making the journey to Sacramento. In a short time he visited Napa, tried the mines awhile, and finally established the pioneer saddlery and harness business in Napa City. In this pursuit he was very successful, and satisfied with the prospects of this part of the State he determined to become a permanent resident. He accordingly purchased 85 acres of land from James M. Harbin, and erected a house thereon near the homestead lot of R. T. Montgomery, in 1853. The tract was used by tenants for farming purposes until 1858, when it was sold to John Lawley, Esq. In 1853 Mr. Earl bought a lot 60 feet square on Main street adjoining the lot on the corner of Main and First street, owned by Wm. H. James. In 1856, after much urging, the latter joined with Mr. Earl in erecting a substantial brick block on the two lots, being the first brick building erected in Napa City. The brick were procured by Mr. Earl in Sacramento. The first floor was used for stores, and the second story of Mr. Earl's part of the building was occupied for several years as a Masonic Hall. In 1857 Mr. Earl erected another brick store of 36 feet front adjoining the first. The upper story was finished in one room 36 by 55 feet, for a public hall for lectures, theatrical performances, etc. It was known as Earl's Hall, but is now occupied as a Lodge room by the Independent Order of Odd Fellows. This building had the first iron front ever erected on the north side of the Bay. In 1859 Mr. Earl erected a second iron front building adjoining the former. He has the honor also of having erected the first concrete building, in Napa county. It is 34 by 34 feet, 2 stories high, and a very substantial structure. It will be seen that Mr. Earl has done his part toward improving the appearance of the town.
(160)
He also contributed liberally in time and money, in 1857, to prevent the recession to Solano county of a strip of territory annexed to Napa by the Legislature in 1855, and also toward purchasing the toll bridge across Napa River and making it free for the use of the public. Hon. Nathan Coombs contributed $200 for the same object. The territory in dispute is one of the richest portions of this county, and pays an important share of the public taxes. Old residents will remember the very active exertions of Mr. Earl to save this important portion of our territory, as well as his efforts at a more recent period to secure the establishment here of the State Normal School and Odd Fellows'

College. He believes in the manifest destiny of Napa, and has always done his utmost to promote its growth and prosperity. His record is that of a useful, unostentatious man, who seeks rather to promote quietly, the welfare of the place than to have the honor of doing so.

A. B. WALKER.

This gentleman emigrated to this county from Sandusky City, Erin county, Ohio, in 1852, and was engaged in mercantile pursuits in company with J. C. Penwell, on the corner of Main and Second streets. He has since been prominently known in connection with the political and public affairs of the county, having served one term as Assessor and three terms as Sheriff. Notwithstanding the decided stand he has always taken in politics in exciting times, he has always retained the respect even of his opponents, and after several years of service in responsible positions, his record is irreproachable as an upright and faithful public officer.

WM. BALDRIDGE.

This old pioneer was born in East Tennessee, 1811. In 1819 he left his native State and emigrated to Missouri, where he learned the trade of millwright.

In 1830 Mr. Baldridge, while in a hotel, heard a man named Mills, partner of Mr. W. L. Sublett, the celebrated Rocky Mountain trapper, describing the soil, productions, and climate of California. Mr. Mills had passed the previous Winter here, and gave a

GEORGE C. YOUNT.

(161)

glowing description of the country.   Mr. Baldridge was struck with this description, and knowing, that a warm climate agreed with his constitution, determined to come out here. In 1840, his friend, Col. J. B. Chiles, now of Chiles Valley, had returned from Florida, and while on a visit to Mr. Baldridge, spoke of the benefit his health had derived from traveling. These two agreed to make a journey to California the following Spring, but on account of having considerable work to finish, Mr. Baldridge was unable to come as agreed. So Col. Chiles came out with the party that Spring and returned. He followed his trade in Missouri till 1843, when, in connection with Col. J. B. Chiles, he formed a company and came out to the Pacific Coast. The company left the Shawnee settlement on the 29th of May of that year, and traveled together to Fort Hall. Here it separated, one portion with Col. Chiles at the head, taking the Pitt River route, the other, in which was Mr. Baldridge, together with the wagons coming down the Humboldt River and crossing the Sierra Nevadas at Walker's Pass. They did not arrive at Sutter's Fort till January, 1844. Their Christmas dinner, consisting of horse flesh boiled in an iron kettle, was eaten on the bleak mountains East of Tulare Valley. He came then direct to Napa Valley. In 1844 he built the grist mill in Chiles Valley. In 1846 he joined the Bear Flag party, and was with the army during its operations in California under General Fremont. In 1851 he settled on his farm near Oakville, where he has ever since resided and where he has gained the esteem of all who know him. He is brave and generous to a fault, a man of extensive reading and sound judgment.

E. BIGGS.

Mr. E. Biggs is one of the pioneers of the State, having crossed the plains to this coast in 1849. He has made Napa City his home since 1859, and has always enjoyed the confidence and esteem of the people. At the first municipal election held in Napa City, in the spring of 1872, he was elected City Marshal, which office he filled with credit to himself and profit to the town.

GEO. N. CORNWELL.

Mr. Cornwell was born in Waterford, New York, in 1825. He
(162)
spent his early life in his native State, working at the trade of cabinet maker. He enlisted and came out to California in Colonel Stevenson's Regiment, Company H, Captain J. B. Frisbie. He arrived in San Francisco in March, 1847. He was stationed at San Francisco and the Presidio until the Summer of 1848, when Company H was removed to Sonoma, and in the Fall was disbanded. After the disbanding of his Company, Mr. Cornwell spent a short time mining near Hangtown, now Placerville, afterwards at Big Bar on the North fork of the American River. But he soon tired of mining and returned to Sonoma, where he engaged in the merchandising business with Vallejo & Frisbie. He established for this firm a store at a point South of First street, between Napa Creek and river. He continued in the mercantile business in Sonoma and Napa until 1853. In addition to the business at these two places, he also had an establishment opened at Benicia. In 1849 and 1850 he was Secretary to the Prefect for the Sonoma District. In 1853 he was elected to the Legislature from Napa county, and served one term. He was Post Master in Napa City for eight years, and served three years as Supervisor. He served six years as under Sheriff, and as such gave good satisfaction and proved himself one of the most efficient officers Napa has ever had. He was one of the original locators of the Redington Mine, and is the only one of these locators who now hold an interest in the mine. He is one of the present Board of Directors.

Mr. Cornwell has always been known in politics as a Democrat. He has made his life a season of hard study, and is well posted on all questions of general interest. He is a man of strong convictions, and is frank in the avowal and advocacy of his sentiments, ever ready to give a reason for the "faith that is in him."

ROBERT CROUCH.

Among the well tried, faithful and efficient servants of the county, few can claim to be peers with the subject of this sketch-none superiors. Mr. Crouch is a native of Ohio, where he was born in 1823, and where he lived till 1844. He then moved to Farmington, Illinois, where he studied medicine, and for many years practiced as a physician. In April, 1852, he started overland for Cali-
(163)

fornia. He reached Salt Lake City in August of that year, and spent the Winter in Mill Creek Cañon near that city. During the time he remained there he worked on a saw mill, and at other severe labor. In May of the following year he left Salt Lake for California, arriving at Sacramento in June. Thence he went to Marysville and worked at the carpenter business. Later in the same year he came to Napa Valley, continuing to work as a carpenter. In 1854, in connection with James H. Page, he built the old White Sulphur Springs Hotel for Lillie & Evey, The Winter Of 1854-5 he spent in Campo Seco, but returned to Napa early in 1855. In April of that year he received the appointment of under Sheriff, and soon after, on the resignation of the Sheriff, was appointed by the Board of Supervisors to fill the unexpired term of that officer; but the Coroner claiming to be Sheriff by virtue of his office, Mr. Crouch would not qualify, and returned to his trade. In the Fall of the same year he received the appointment of Deputy Clerk under A. J. Watson. At the election of 1857 he was elected County Clerk, which office he held until 1863, when he was elected County Judge. He served as Judge till 1871, when he was succeeded by Hon. T. P. Stoney, who still presides. He his since his term of office expired, been engaged in the practice of law with Mr. D. McClure as partner.

Mr. Crouch is a Republican, of strong convictions. Yet he did his duty so well as an officer, and was so courteous to opponents that he always carried a large vote among the Democrats. He served the county longer, made more friends and fewer enemies than probably any other man who was ever here.

––––––

JOHN M. PATCHETT.

Among the most respected of our pioneers is the subject of this sketch, Mr. John M. Patchett. He was born in Lincolnshire, England, in 1797. In 1817 he removed to the United States and settled in Pennsylvania, where he lived till 1835. In the Fall of that year he removed to Illinois. in 1837 he moved to Iowa and laid off the town of Philadelphia on the Big Bend of the Des Moines River. In 1840 he moved up the Des Moines about seventy miles, where he resided till 1850. In Pennsylvania he followed the busi-
(164)
ness of a brewer, and after leaving that State engaged in farming which occupation he has mainly followed since. In the Spring of 1850, attracted by the favorable reports of the richness and the pleasant climate of California, he started in company with many others for this State. After a tedious journey of five months-a journey which must be gone through with to be fully realized and appreciated-he arrived at Placerville. Later in the Fall he removed to White Oak Springs, Eldorado county, and remained here till 1853. In 1852 he had made a visit to Napa Valley, and being favorably impressed with the valley, purchased a tract of about 100 acres adjoining his present homestead. In 1853 he came down to his property here, and just before moving, purchased his present home in the Western part of town. On his settling in Napa he engaged in agriculture, and has ever been esteemed as one of the foremost cultivators of the soil in the county. Though repeatedly solicited to, he has never consented to accept any office, prefering the quiet and more agreeable labors of farm life. He was the first person who planted a vineyard worthy of any note in the county. His vineyard was of Mission grapes and planted in 1850. The same year he also planted out an orchard of about eight acres. In 1859 having become convinced that the business

of raising grapes and making wine could be made remunerative, he erected a stone wine cellar 33x50 feet. He had made about 600 gallons of wine the year previous, selling it at $2 per gallon. The stone for his cellar was quarried out of the hills back of the residence of Cayetano Juarez. The cellar is still standing and is as good as ever.

————

DR. W. W. STILLWAGON.

Dr. W. W. Stillwagon was born at Connellsville, Fayette county, Pennsylvania, in 1827. He studied and practiced medicine there till 1848, when he removed to Illinois. In March, 1850, he started across the plains, and arrived in Sacramento in August of the same year. He spent a short time at mining near Oroville, but in the Fall of the year came to Napa and commenced the practice of his profession. He has ever since been a resident. He served one term as Coroner. He had been elected to the office but refused to give bonds and qualify, yet was, by popular sentiment, compelled

(165)

to serve, and his acts afterwards legalized. He has at different times filled the position of County Physician for the space of five years, and always gave satisfaction. In 1871 he was elected to the Assembly, from Napa and Lake, and while in the Legislature did much towards so presenting the desirability of Napa, that the Branch Insane Asylum was located here. He was acting in getting several bills of a local nature passed.

As an officer he always acquitted himself with credit, and as a physician he has few superiors.

The Doctor was a Whig when he came to the county, and affiliated with that party till the formation of the Republican, of which he has ever since been a prominent member. But party lines have never been strictly drawn in local affairs in Napa county, and as a result she has always had good and efficient officers: Dr. Stillwagon was one of the Charter members of Yount Lodge No. 12, of Masons, and labored earnestly in the establishing of that Order in the county. He was also one of the Charter members, and the first Noble Grand of the Odd Fellows in Napa City. He has of late years been devoting much of his attention to quicksilver mining in Pope Valley.

————

A. Y. EASTERBY.

This gentleman was born in the county of Surrey, England, January 1818, and is of the family of the Easterbys of Northumberland. At the age of fourteen he went to sea in the merchant service of Great Britain, and during the year 1836, accompanied the expedition to the river Euphrates for the purpose of opening an overland route from the Mediteranean to the Persian Gulf. At the age of twenty-three he became Commodore of the first Mediterranean line of screw steamers laid on from Liverpool to the Levant. This line was owned by A. Mongradine of Liverpool. Cunliffes & Co. of London, and A. Y. Easterby, who was Captain of one of these steamships, the *Levantine*. In 1848, Mr. Easterby came out to Chili, and in October met Commodore Schenck, then Lieutenant, in Piata, and from there accompanied him to Panama. In consequence of this gentleman's representation he returned to Callao, and here induced parties to lay on a ship to San Francisco, and con-

(166)

signed his portion of her cargo to DeWitt & Harrison. On the 1st day of January, 1849, Mr. Easterby arrived in San Francisco, and there in company with his brother-in-law, Frank Gray, purchased a number of vessels and converted them into store-ships. Among these ships were the *Lindsay, Edwin, York, Mentor, and Henry Ewbank,* all deserted by their crews on the breaking out of the gold fever. The *Edwin* was the first bonded warehouse in San Francisco, and she laid on the mud flats at the corner of Pacific and Front streets, from whence she was cut out in 1855. He remained in business in San Francisco till the above year, and then came to Napa City and bought out the firm of Schultz & Miller, on the corner of Main and Second streets, where now stands Wm. Quentin's Bank Exchange. In February 1864, Mr. Easterby purchased the store and fixtures of Lamdin & Coghill, directly opposite his old stand, and during the month before his removal to his new quarters, his old store and nearly all its contents was consumed by fire. He remained in business on the East side of Main street up to 1872. He then went into the real estate, mining, canal, and farming business in which he is present engaged.

Mr. Easterby has never run for any office in this county, but has been Chairman of the Republican County Committee. He was the first President of the Napa Valley Railroad, of which he was also one of the original incorporators. He is a Royal Arch Mason, and with the late Governor Geary opened the first Chapter of Royal Arch Masons in San Francisco in 1850.

———

DAVID HUDSON.

Mr. David Hudson was born in Missouri in 1821. His early life was spent in the frontiers and was full of trials and adventures. He emigrated to California in 1846, and lived in various parts of the State, but being attracted to Napa by the salubrity of the climate, and the advantages of pasture, as well as the fertility of the soil, he made this county his home. He purchased an extensive tract of land Northwest of St. Helena from Mr. Bale, and improved it for a homestead. He was a large stock-raiser, and devoted much of his time and attention to this pursuit, yet he found time to engage very largely in agriculture. He was always regarded as one of the lead-
(167)
ing men in his neighborhood, and none stood higher than he for probity and honor. In 1872 he disposed of his fine farm near St. Helena, and is now a resident of Lake county, engaged in his favorite pursuit, stock raising. He has always taken a deep interest in public affairs, though never agreeing to receive anything at the hands of the people.

———

JOHN YORK.

Mr. York came to California overland among the emigrants anterior to the gold discovery. He is from Tennessee, where he was born in 1820. Mr. York settled near St. Helena as early as 1849, where he has ever since resided, and is one of the prosperous farmers of that part of Napa county.

WILLIAM RUSSELL.

Mr. Russell is a native of the State of Maine and arrived in San Francisco Bay in 1846, on board a whale ship, of which he was carpenter. He was a member of Fremont's Battalion, and was with it and shared in its hardships on the famous march southward in the Winter of 1846-7. Mr. Russell is still a resident of Napa county, and enjoys the esteem of all who know him.

A. G. CLARK.

The subject of this sketch was born in Butler county, Ohio, in 1818. When about six years old his parents moved to Montgomery county, Indiana, where he resided till 1835, occupied on a farm and as a clerk in a dry goods store. He was also employed for a time as clerk in Michigan City. In the Fall of 1837 he moved to the lead district of Galena and Dubuque, and soon after went to farming in Jackson county, Iowa, and was also engaged in merchandising. He continued here till in 1849, when he removed to Council Bluffs on the Missouri River. In the Winter of 1849-50, he went on a trading expedition with the Indians up to the Big Sioux River, and in the Spring of 1850 started overland for California with his wife and three children. After traveling for some distance, owing

(168)

to the scarcity of feed, the train, which consisted of thirty-two wagons and accompanying stock, was separated. Mr. Clark and two others agreed to travel together into California. Soon after the separation the men connected with these two wagons and their families were all taken sick, and for a period of six weeks it devolved upon Mr. Clark and two young men with him to care for the sick, take charge of the wagons, and stand guard at night. This was indeed a gloomy time. At Fort Hall they were advised by the Commandant, Major Grant, to take the road to Oregon. They did so, and came through to the Dalles on the Columbia River with nothing more than the usual incidents of such journeys. At the Dalles they sold their wagons and sailed down to the Cascades on a kind of yawl boat. Thence they passed down to Astoria on the first steamer that ever sailed on the Columbia River. The vessel was an old whale boat fitted with a small engine, and the deck stood but a few feet out of the water. On the way down it devolved upon Mr. Clark as his business to keep the boat in trim and keep both wheels in the water by rolling a barrel of flour from one side to the other, as the boat changed position. We imagine he was anxious for passengers to remain quiet. From Astoria he took the steamer *Panama,* the first steamer that ever went up the coast, then on her second trip, to Sail Francisco, where he arrived on the 29th of September. After a short time spent in the mines he went over near the foot of Mt. Tamalpais in Marin county, and worked as a carpenter in the erection of two saw-mills. He remained there about fifteen months, receiving wages of $1 per hour.

At the close of this time he purchased property in Port Orford, Southern Oregon but in going up to it was on the 26th of January, 1852, wrecked in Humboldt Bay. Escaping with his family from the wreck he built the first residence in Eureka. He remained in Eureka most of the time till 1856, engaged in lumbering, mining and land speculating. He made an expedition to the mines up near Klamath River, found fine prospects, laid off a city called Soda City and left for home, intending to return in a short time. Soon after he left the Indians destroyed the camp and killed twenty-two of the men. He never went back. While a resident at Humboldt Bay

W. H. WINTER.

(169)

he became intimately acquainted with General Grant, while the latter was stationed at that point.

In 1856 Mr. Clark left for San Francisco, and was in the latter place during the reign of the Vigilant Committee. In this year he purchased a large tract of land near Yountville and moved on to it with his family. Here he remained engaged successfully in farming till in the Fall of 1871. Since December, 1871, he has been engaged in the hardware business in Napa City.

Mr. Clark has been a close observer of the progress of California, and always taken a deep interest in public affairs. Up to 1855 he affiliated with the Democratic party, but that party, in his estimation becoming so corrupt and abandoning its principles, he left it and united with the Know Nothing party. He supported Gen. Fremont for President in 1856, and has since affiliated with the Republicans. He was a zealous supporter of Lincoln's Administration and is now of that of President Grant.

Mr. Clark is a man of positive character, is either a warm friend or a relentless foe. He has for years been an earnest advocate of temperance principles. He was one of the Charter members of Yountville Lodge of Good Templars, and is now an active worker in the Lodge of that Order in Napa City.

JAMES H. GOODMAN.

Mr. J. H. Goodman a native of New York, came to California and settled in Napa at an early date. In 1858, in connection with his brother, Geo. E. Goodman who served one term as Treasurer for Napa county, he opened the first bank in Napa City. Since then he has confined himself principally to the business of banking. He and his brother have been earnest laborers for the building up and prosperity of Napa. Their banking house has been a great accommodation and benefit to the people of the county, and by their fair dealing, they have won many warm friends. They took great interest in getting the bill passed through the Legislature of 1871-2 incorporating Napa City, and in securing the location of the Branch Insane Asylum, and various other important measures looking to the interest and welfare of both city and county.
(170)

PETER STORM.

The history of this old Swede is so familiar to most Californians as the man who rudely sketched the famous Bear Flag, that little may be said beyond the fact that he still lives near Calistoga, and though over seventy years of age, is in good health, with a prospect of living out another decade.

WILLIAM POPE.

William Pope, the pioneer from whom Pope Valley derived its name, was born in Kentucky. From there he went, when a young man to New Mexico, and for twenty years lived as a hunter and trapper, traveling over the regions now comprising the Territories of New Mexico, Colorado, Utah and Arizona. He spent much time in trapping beaver on the sloughs extending from the head of the Gulf of California. In 1830 He came into the Mexican town of San Diego for the purpose of procuring supplies, and was there arrested because he had violated the Mexican laws in entering, their dominions without a passport. He was kept in confinement at San Diego for about a year, when the captain of an American merchantman which had entered the port, having heard of Mr. Pope's situation, took the matter in hand, and prevailed upon the Mexican officials to release him-they affecting not to have understood his case. Thankful for his unexpected deliverance from imprisonment, the daring pioneer hastened to his family in New Mexico, and in 1836 he emigrated to Los Angeles. Having obtained a grant of land in Pope Valley from the Mexican Government, in 1841 he brought his family to Geo. C. Yount's ranch, in Napa Valley, which he made his headquarters until he had erected buildings upon his grant. His grant was six miles in length and three in width. During the last of May, 1841, he moved upon his ranch, of which he was justly proud, but his happiness was destined to be of short duration. In the Fall of the same year, while hewing out some logs for building purposes, be accidentally cut his leg very badly, severing an artery. In those days doctors were unknown and his wound after having been bound up by his friends many times, finally broke out bleeding, and all attempts to stop it proving fruitless, he expired in November, 1841, just twelve days from the date of his wound.

(171)

Mr. Pope's wife was a Mexican lady by whom he had five children. They continued to live in the valley until the greater portion of the grant was sold. Several of the children are yet living among whom is the wife of Mr. Juan Burton, a resident of Pope Valley.

————

ELIAS BARNETT.

Mr. E. Barnett, now a resident of Pope Valley, is one among the oldest pioneers in the State. He was born in Prestonburg, Floyd county, Kentucky, in 1805. After traveling in Virginia, Ohio, Illinois, Indiana and Tennessee, during his early manhood, he settled in Jackson county, Missouri, in 1831. He joined the emigrant train of which Chiles and Hopper were members, elsewhere noticed, and crossed the Plains to California. The portion of the company with which he traveled on into California after the separation near Fort Hall, came into the Stanislaus, but the company suffered greatly for want of food after leaving the Humboldt till they reached this State. At one time the company was compelled to subsist on horse flesh, mules and coyotes. In Barnett's language, "I was so near starved that the coyote did taste good, but hang me if I could make the horse or mule taste well; it was too bitter." The company reached Dr. Marsh's place, near Mount Diablo, on the 20th of November, having been over six months on the road. After a few days' rest the most of the company went to Sutter's Fort. Mr. Barnett remained during the Winter and then went to Geo. C. Yount's in the Spring of 1842. During the time that Mr. Barnett was at Sutter's he aided in putting in a crop of two hundred acres of wheat. As an example of productiveness of the soil at that time, he says that Sutter sowed 300 Pounds of a variety of wheat which he had received from the Russians, upon ten acres of choice land, and received 510 bushels. He stopped with Yount for a few weeks, and then went to Alexander's place, near where Healdsburg now stands, where he worked in building an adobe house. At this time Mark West, Mrs. Carrillo and Alexander were the only settlers in Santa Rosa Valley. Deer, bear, and other game were found everywhere in the valley and on the hills. In the Fall of 1842 the Americans at Alexander's place received news, by a rumor, that Capt. Graham, of Santa Cruz, with a com-

(172)

pany of foreigners had reached Sutter's Fort and was waiting for white settlers to join him for the purpose of wresting the country from Mexico. Barnett hastened to Sutter, and after the plan had been given up, he returned to Billy Gordon's place on Cache Creek, where he remained during the Winter.

After spending some time working for Yount and hunting, Mr. Barnett came to Pope Valley in 1843. In the Spring of 1844 he was married to widow Pope, and has, almost ever since, made this valley his home.

Mr. Barnett joined Sutter when he espoused the cause of Mitchell Toreno, the Mexican Governor, against the native Californians, under Generals Castro and Pio Pico. In this campaign the foreigners on either side did not engage, but withdrew by mutual consent to witness the bloodless battle of San Fernando Plains, in Los Angeles, which secured the authority of Pico as Governor.

Mr. Barnett was one of the famed Bear Flag Party, and in 1846 enlisted under Gen. Fremont for his march to Los Angeles. The army started in September, 1846, and reached its destination in March, 1847, after undergoing untold suffering from drenching rains and fatigues of the march.

————

R. D. HOPKINS.

Mr. R. D. Hopkins, formerly editor of the Napa *Register,* is a pioneer of this State, having come out in the great rush overland in 1849. He is a native of Maryland. He studied law and was admitted to the Bar the year previous to his coming out to California. He settled in the mines, and served as District Attorney of Placer county two years from 1851 to 1853. In 1857 he became a resident of Napa. From 1859 to 1861 he was District Attorney for the county. During 1868-9 he was a resident of Vallejo, and editor of the *Recorder,* a paper then published in that city. From 1869 to 1872 he was editor of the *Register* of Napa. In the Fall of 1872 he sold out to Mr. Henning, and has since been editing the Yolo *Mail.* As a Christian and a man of strict integrity Mr. Hopkins stands high wherever known.

————

R. T. MONTGOMERY.

Mr. Montgomery, who is well known as the editor of several news-
(173)
papers in Napa during the past seventeen years, and who is compiler of a portion of this book, was born in Richmond, Virginia, in 1821. It would be difficult, and superfluous if it were not, to follow the erratic wanderings of an old printer. From early manhood he has been connected with the printing business in various capacities. Coming to this State in 1853, he employed himself as school teacher until December, 1856, when he took hold and assisted Mr. Cox in the Napa *Reporter* while in its infancy. He has been a resident of Napa ever since, and almost constantly, engaged in the newspaper business. As a talented and vigorous writer he is too well known to need extended notice.

————

A. J. COX.

There are few names more familiar in this and adjoining counties than that which heads this paragraph. Cox is a native of Charleston, South Carolina, where he served an apprenticeship at the printing business. In 1846, while in New York, he joined Stevenson's Regiment, and in one of the transport ships arrived in San Francisco Bay in March, 1847-so that, like Mr. Cornwell, he is a soldier pioneer. He has had his share of the vicissitudes of life in California in early days. It was not until 1852 that he resumed the business of printing, when he established the Sonoma *Bulletin,* the first newspaper north of San Francisco. Mr. Cox has, at different periods, started five newspapers in this State, which argues that in his younger days he was not idle-that he contributed much in labor to public enterprise, though of little profit to himself.

———————

COL. J. B. CHILES.

Col. J. B. Chiles is a descendant of an old Virginia family. He was born in Clark county, Kentucky, in 1810. His parents were among the pioneer settlers in the present State of Kentucky. Mr. Chiles lived in his native State till the Fall of 1831, when he emigrated to Missouri. In 1838 he went with Col. Gentry's Regiment to Florida, and was engaged there in hostilities with the Indians. For his conduct in this war, Mr. Chiles was brevetted Lieutenant. He was in the battle of Ocachoba, where Col. Gentry was killed. After he left Florida he returned to Missouri, and in 1841 started

(174)

for California with the Bartleson company. Col. Chiles, C. Hopper and Benj. Kelsey guided the party through, and they arrived at the foot of Mount Diablo in October, 1841. Here the company separated. Mr. Chiles and Mr. Hopper traveled together during the whole of the ensuing Winter. After passing up Napa Valley, they crossed over into the San Joaquin and prepared for a return trip to Missouri. The return was made by way of New Mexico, and was made under great hardships and many strange adventures. In 1843 Mr. Chiles came out a second time across the Plains. This year Mr. Chiles brought out from Missouri the family of Geo. C. Yount. The following year he settled in the valley to which he gave his name, and where he has since resided. In 1844 he obtained a grant of two leagues of land, where he now resides. He accompanied Commodore Stockton's forces back across the Plains, and in 1848 returned, bringing his three daughters and one son. In 1852 he returned to Missouri by way of the Isthmus, was married to his second wife, and in 1854 again crossed the Plains. Since this time he has resided most all the time at his farm in Chiles' Valley. He has been engaged extensively in stockraising and agriculture. Like other old pioneers, Col. Chiles has passed through many adventures, and has seen more of the hardships of life than most men. His history is so closely related to that of other pioneers in our valley that we refrain from entering into further details.

———————

WH. H. BAXTER.

The subject of this short sketch is a native of New York, where he was born in 1825. His youth was spent in his native State, working on a farm. At the age of fifteen he was apprenticed to learn a mechanical trade, and after serving out his time as apprentice, spent several years in the Southern States. He married early in life. In 1850 he came by way of the Isthmus to California. On his arrival in San Francisco he was employed as agent of the Atlantic and Pacific Express Company, a short lived institution of early days in California, and as such won great credit by the promptness and energy displayed in carrying on the business of the company. This was at the time when California applied for admission into the Union, and the news had to be brought by way of the Isthmus; so that a

(175)

great rivalry existed between the various express companies of that day to get the news first on the arrival of the steamers and distribute to the city and country. Mr. Baxter won the reputation of excelling all others in getting and distributing news.

After remaining in San Francisco a few years he went to Nevada City and engaged in mining. He was quite successful and accumulated a large amount of wealth; but he was induced to invest in a smelting furnace, one of the first on this coast, and in this operation sunk all, or nearly all, he had previously accumulated. After this severe reverse of fortune he returned to San Francisco and engaged in merchandising. Getting interested in mining stock in the city he again sunk a fortune. In the Spring of 1869 he came into Napa Valley. His objects were to engage in sericulture. He purchased a farm a few miles from Napa City, named by him the Spring Dale Farm, and he has made it one of the prettiest places in this section. Mr. Baxter is a man of great activity and energy, and has won the esteem of a large number of friends for his enterprise, industry, and sterling integrity. Since coming into the county he has identified himself with all the movements promising a better system of industry, and freeing of the people from the extortions of carriers and middlemen. In March, 1873, he instituted the first Lodge, or Grange, of the Order of Patrons of Husbandry, in Napa City. His silk experiment will be duly noticed in our review of the agricultural resources of the county.

E. N. BOYNTON.

Dr. E. N. Boynton is a pioneer and one of the substantial citizens of Napa. He was born in Bainbridge, Chenango county, N.Y., in 1834. He studied medicine and graduated in 1843 from the Medical College at Geneva, in his native State. He practiced his profession there successfully till 1850, when he emigrated to California. He crossed by way of Santa Fe and Arizona, and arrived in San Diego about the first of September of that year. He engaged in mining, near Auburn and on the Feather River till 1853. In the latter year he came to Napa, and was for two years engaged in merchandising and practicing his profession in this and Lake counties.
(176)
In 1855 he moved to Vallejo, and there engaged in practice and as a druggist for a period of three years. In 1859 he moved back to Napa, formed a copartnership with Dr. W. W. Stillwagon in the practice of his profession. Soon after, they purchased the stock of drugs, medicines, etc., of L. J. Walker, who kept in the store now occupied by Messrs. Colman & Co., and conducted the business of druggists and apothecaries with that of their profession. In 1864 he moved into his present place of business.

Although he ranks as a pioneer, he is still in the prime of life. He has served the county three years as Supervisor, and is widely known as a most worthy and public spirited citizen, awake to everything tending to the enhancement of the interests of his county and State. He also stands high in the ranks of Odd Fellows, and has done much to make that benevolent Order prosper in the county. He was among the most zealous laborers to get the Odd Fellows College and Home located here, and was among the last to acknowledge that the Order would not erect the College as proposed. Dr. Boynton is also a member of the Pioneer Association of Napa, Lake, Sonoma and Marin counties.

Beeby Robinson is a native of England, where he was born in 1814. He lived in the northern part of England till he was about seventeen years old, when he moved to the United States and settled in the city of New York. He was here married to Miss Emeline Parker daughter of Hon. Joseph Parker of that city. In 1837 he removed to Missouri and settled in Jefferson City, where he was engaged in building the State Capitol. He afterwards settled in Jackson county, in the same State, where he remained till 1849, when he emigrated to California. In 1850 he established himself in Benicia, where he built the first magazine for the War Department. This was at the time Capt. Jones, since General, was in command there. In 1856 he removed to Napa City, and has ever since made this his home. Mr. Robinson was educated to the business of carpenter, builder and architect, and has followed this through life. He has, while working at his trade, been employed in various parts of the country and in Canada, so that he has traveled very extensively. Since his locating

THOMAS EARL.

(177)

in Napa he has been engaged in building in the county. Many of the public buildings, bridges, school houses, etc., have been erected by him. In 1872 he completed the elegant and substantial building for the Young Ladies' Seminary, one of the most imposing buildings in the town. Mr.

(177)
in Napa he has been engaged in building in the county. Many of the public buildings, bridges, school houses, etc., have been erected by him. In 1872 he completed the elegant and substantial building for the Young Ladies' Seminary, one of the most imposing buildings in the town. Mr. Robinson has raised a large family, most of whom have married and settled in this county. His son, Joseph L., has for several years been engaged with him in his trade. Mr. Robinson has always been one of the most respected citizens of the community.

C. P. BRIGGS.

Charles P. Briggs an early resident of Napa, but now living in Charlestown, Massachusetts, first arrived in California in 1845, and was also attached to Fremont's Battalion, in which he served very creditably. On the breaking out of the late civil war, Mr. Briggs left Napa to join the Union forces, and has not since returned.

R. C. GILLASPY.

Among the prominent residents of Berryessa Valley is R. C. Gillaspy, who is also one of the early settlers in Napa county. He was born in Madison county, Kentucky, in 1829. In 1849 he came to Monroe county, Missouri, where he remained till April, 1852, when he started to seek his fortunes in California. The company of which he formed a part consisted of sixty-two men, women and children, with fourteen wagons and about four hundred head of cattle. The company suffered a great deal from sickness during the trip, resulting in the death of Wesley Hill, Nancy Jane Hill, all connected with the Hills now of Soscol, a Mr. Quigley, and a negro boy. One pleasant and happy circumstance connected with the journey was the arrangement for the future marriage of Mr. Gillaspy to Miss Angeline M. Hill, daughter of Wesley Hill who died on the plains. The proposed marriage took place on the 22d of May, 1853, at Soscol.

The journey's end was reached on the 14th of October, 1852, at the present ranch of Mrs. James Hill, of Soscol, where the cattle were turned out in wild oats as high as a horse's back. When he reached Soscol there were but two or three families nearer than Napa and Vallejo; and ladies were so seldom seen in California during
(178)
the early settlements that it became a proverbial saying "That the sight of a woman was good for the sore eyes," and "Uncle Bob," as he is familiarly called, says his eyes were very weak "them days," and hence he made good use of the remedy by his frequent calls on his intended.

At that day there were thousands of wild cattle, horses, and game of all kinds roaming over the valleys and mountains. Mr. Gillaspy, lived in Soscol, Napa county, from his arrival in California till the grant of Berryessa Valley was divided up and opened for settlement, when in 1866, with his family, ten persons in all, he moved into Berryessa, Napa county, where there were few settlements and no schools. He organized the first school district, and was one of the first in aiding in organizing a congregation of Christians in the valley. At the time he moved into the valley a town had been laid out by a company who had bought the grant, but no building had been done. The town has since sprang up into a lively little village called Monticello.

After he moved to the valley he spent four years in managing the large ranch of W. H. Bostwick, of San Francisco and becoming so well pleased with the healthfulness of the climate and fertility of the soil, he bought a portion of Mr. Bostwick's ranch, where he is now pleasantly situated and devoting himself to wheat raising and wool growing.

Mr. Gillaspy has served the people of Berryessa for several years as justice, and has in all his actions acquitted himself with credit, and none stand higher in the esteem of his neighbors for honesty and integrity. Yet, he is a firm believer in the correctness of the adage "laugh and grow fat," and is ever ready to enjoy a good joke.

————

SIM BUFORD.

This gentleman is a native of Missouri, where he spent his early years working on a farm. He worked a considerable time learning the trade of printer. He came out to California in 1849, and on his arrival in this State engaged in mining. He followed the life of a miner principally in the Northern districts, with varying success till in 1854, when he started for home. He took passage in the
(179)
Yankee Blade, and was wrecked off Cape Aguilar, in Santa Barbara county. He returned to San Francisco, and embarked the second time in the Fall of the same year. He remained in Missouri, Wisconsin and Minnesota till in 1856, he returned to California by way of New Orleans and the Isthmus. After returning he went up to the Salmon River Mines, but did not succeed well. In 1858 he came to Napa Valley, and has been here ever since. Till 1868 he was engaged in farming and stock raising in Soscol; and since then he has been a resident in Berryessa Valley. He has a large tract of land near Monticello, and has been doing a successful business in farming. He is one of the most prominent and respected citizens of his section of county.

————

CHANCELLOR HARTSON.

Hon. Chancellor Hartson is one of the pioneers of Napa county, and has acted a very important part in the history of the town and county. He was born in Otsego county, New York, in 1824, graduated at Madison University in the same State in 1845; was admitted to the practice of law in the Supreme Court in 1848, just having closed a course of study at Fowler's Law School, then established at Cherry Valley; came to California in 1850, and settled in Napa Valley in July of the following year. He entered upon the practice of law, and in September of that year was elected District Attorney. In the following September and at the close of his term of office in 1853, was elected County judge and administered this office until 1858.

In 1856 helped to organize the Republican party and elected to the Assembly in 1861, and to the Senate in 1862. In both Houses was Chairman of the Committee on judiciary, and took an active part in legislative proceedings. In the years 1867 and 1868 was the nominee of the Republican party for Congress, but failing of an election by 375 votes at the first contest and 263 at the second. In 1867 George C. Gorham being candidate for Governor, and in 1868 General Grant being candidate for President, neither of whom had a majority in this District.

In 1871 retired from the practice of law and aided in the organization and establishment of the Bank of Napa, and was then elected
(180)
President thereof, which position he still holds. He has taken an active part in almost every work of improvement in the county, and has done more, probably, than any other one man towards the building up of Napa City. He was chiefly instrumental in getting the Branch Insane Asylum located here and has occupied the position of President of its Board of Directors since the location.

SAMUEL BRANNAN.

Mr. Samuel Brannan was born at Saco, Maine, in 1819, and there spent his youth and received his education. In 1833 he removed to Lake county, Ohio, and was apprenticed to learn the printing business, but did not serve out his full term. In 1836-7 he was infected with the great mania for land speculation that so raged in those years throughout the whole Union. But he did not succeed well in this land-jobbing arrangement, and soon returned to the press, and for the next five years traveled from town to town and State to State, experiencing the grim delights (fully known and realized only by his fraternity) of a journeyman printer. During these five years of toil and vicissitudes, he learned much of the world that was afterward used to advantage. In 1842, having become acquainted with the teachings of Joe Smith, the great Mormon prophet, he connected himself with that sect, and for years labored in disseminating its doctrines. He was for a considerable time engaged in publishing the Mormon organ, the "New York *Messenger*." In 1846, having heard so much of the Pacific Coast, he determined to come here and, if possible, establish a colony. He chartered a ship, the *Brooklyn*, fitted it up for passengers, and invited adventurers to embark with him. Two hundred and thirty six passengers, about sixty of whom were females, and forty children, embarked. These passengers were mostly, if not entirely, Mormons. Mr. Brannan at that time, most likely entertained the idea of planting this Mormon colony on the coast, gradually growing powerful, till this coast should be in the possession of that sect, and an independent government here established. Mr. Brannan provided a liberal outfit for his colony for the new country. Among the articles supplied was a printing, press, types, and a stock of paper, machinery for flour mills and various agricultural implements. The *Brooklyn* sailed from New
(181)
York on the 4th of February, 1846; five months after touched at the Sandwich Islands where provisions, arms and ammunition were purchased for the colony, and arrived at Yerba Buena (now San Francisco) on the 31st of July. His colony settled on the sand hills of Yerba Buena, and all their business was carried on in the name of S. Brannan & Co., till 1847, when the concern was dissolved. In 1846 Mr. Brannan had erected two flouring mills in that place, and in January, 1847, he commenced the publication of the pioneer paper of San Francisco, the *California Star*. This paper was the parent of the *Alta*. Mr. Brannan was likewise engaged in farming in the San Joaquin Valley, and in merchandising, at Sutter's Fort. In the first he failed entirely, but in the latter succeeded beyond expectation. The discovery of gold drew crowds to California, and his

store was the only one in the whole Sacramento valley so that fabulous prices could not only be asked but obtained. It is stated on good authority that during 1848 and 1849 the average monthly sales reached the enormous sum of $150,000. At the same time, Mr. Brannan was a large speculator in town property in the infant city of Sacramento, and owing to the unprecedented rise in real estate there, caused by the great mining excitement, he found himself suddenly possessed of vast wealth. In 1849, in addition to his business as land-jobber in San Francisco and Sacramento, he embarked in merchandising with China, and in 1851 purchased extensive property in the Sandwich Islands. In nearly all of his early business transactions in California he was eminently successful. Indeed, it seemed that, Midas like, whatever he touched turned to gold, till he was considered the richest man on the coast.

In 1859 Mr. Brannan came into Napa Valley and purchased of Capt. Ritchie a square mile of land at Calistoga. On this tract are situated the famous Hot Springs. Soon after, he purchased other lands of Messrs. Fowler and Hargrave, till his landed possessions about Calistoga exceeded 2,000 acres. It was his desire to make of this place, called by him the Saratoga of the Pacific, a great watering place. His expenditures for buildings, laying off of grounds and other improvements at this place, has probably not been less than half a million dollars. Mr. Brannan has spared no effort to make his chosen town of Calistoga, and the whole upper part of the county, (182) prosperous. He has, since permanently locating there, added largely to his landed possessions, and has ever been liberal to actual settlers and those desiring to carry on trade and business calculated to enhance the value of property by making the community more prosperous.

Since locating in Napa Valley Mr. Brannan has continued his varied business affairs; but it seems that the talisman is gone, for of late years serious financial reverses have overtaken him. He has, since the first foundation of government here, taken a deep interest and performed an active part in all public measures. But his character and history are too well known to need further notice.

B. W. ARNOLD.

This gentleman is a native of Massachusetts, where he was born in 1823. He lived mostly in Rhode Island till in 1849, when he took passage on a sail vessel and came around Cape Horn to San Francisco. After arriving in San Francisco he went to San Jose and Santa Cruz for the benefit of his health. He then went into the mines. In the Fall of 1850 he went up to Trinidad to engage in merchandising, and, up to the time of his removal to Napa Valley, was engaged at various places in mining, merchandising, and other pursuits. At one time he went out to the Salmon River mines, when freight cost $1.75 per pound. In 1857 he removed to Yountville, Napa county, where he has, until lately, resided, engaged a greater part of the time in merchandising. He held the position of Postmaster for several years. At the election of 1863 he was chosen Assessor for Napa county, which office with the exception of two years, when he was deputy, he has ever since held. Since first arriving in the State he has never left it. His family came out by way of the Isthmus in 1853. His continually being kept in the service of the people is more demonstrative evidence of the high esteem in which he is held than any encomium we could offer.

CAYETANO JUAREZ.

"Don Cayetano," as he is familiarly known by so many, is a native Californian, born in 1810, in Monterey, the former capital of Upper California. In 1827 Mr. Juarez came to Sonoma in the capacity
(183)
of a soldier, serving under Commander M. G. Vallejo, who had just established that, the first Mission or settlement, north of the Bay. After a time he obtained a grant of two square leagues of land in the locality now occupied by him, and in 1840 settled on his ranch. His generous gift to the public of Tulocay Cemetery has already been noticed in the beginning of this work. He has always been-even in the days of the Bear Flag party-a staunch friend to the Americans, and contributed liberally to relieve the necessities of the early emigrants. He is one among the few native Californians who have had the shrewdness to retain a goodly portion of their original estates. Though now 63 years of age, he is as vigorous as a man of 25, and bids fair to survive many more years. Mr. Juarez has reared a family of 11 children, 8 of whom are living.

JOHN S. STARK.

Mr. Stark is one of the ante-gold-discovery pioneers, having arrived here overland in 1846. He is a native of one of the Western States. He served as Sheriff of Napa county, from 1856 to 1860, and did the duties of his office satisfactorily. Mr. Stark has always been esteemed as an honorable and useful citizen.

M. D. RITCHIE.

Col. Ritchie is a native of Pennsylvania, born in 1805, but lived in Illinois for many years before coming to California. He arrived here overland in 1846, and settled in Sonoma; a few years after he moved to Napa Valley, where he still resides. Col. Ritchie was the first man who made an effort to rescue the Donner party who were snow-bound at Donner Lake in the Winter of 1846-7.

C. H. ALLEN.

Col. Allen is a native of Providence, Rhode Island, born in 1817. He sailed from Stonington, Connecticut, in the ship *Calumet,* for California *via* Cape Horn, and arrived at San Francisco in March, 1850. Col. Allen came to Napa in November, 1853, since which time he has been a permanent resident, thoroughly identified with and taking an active interest in the gradual growth of the place. He opened the first tin and hardware establishment in Napa City, which
(184)

old pioneers whom we have been unable to see, and therefore unable to give them a notice. Some have refused to give us any information in regard to their lives, and some were unknown to us till it was too late to get their lives. We therefore close, assuring all that we have not intentionally slighted any nor given any unmerited notice.
(185)

VIEW IN COBB VALLEY.

CHAPTER XII.

TOWNS AND WATERING PLACES OF NAPA.

Among the important elements going to make up the history of a county, is the rise and progress of the towns of the county. They are, in fact, the centers of historical transactions. We shall, therefore, devote a short space to these. Also, the watering places, or general resorts for tourists, are important as they go to make up the desirability of a country for travelers and settlers. Napa City, having been so thoroughly noticed in noting the progress of the county, we omit from the list.

YOUNTVILLE

YOUNTVILLE

The little village of Yountville is situated near the center of the valley on the line of the railroad, about nine miles above Napa City. It took its name from Mr. Yount, the first white settler in the county. His homestead, where his widow still resides, is about
(186)
two miles north of the present town. It is in the center of a rich agricultural section, but, owing to its proximity to Napa City has never done much business. Yet it has, probably, one of the most equable temperatures in the county. It is far enough from the Bay that the winds, so disagreeable to many, are tempered down to pleasant breezes, and it is not far enough in the interior to be cut off from these breezes, and to be subject to intense heat. In the early part of 1870, Mr. J. Groezinger, of San Francisco, purchased a large tract of land having a fine vineyard thereon, of H. C. Boggs, and has erected there one of the largest and most substantial wine cellars in the State. More particular reference will be made to this cellar in our review of the vineyards of the county.

ST. HELENA

This town is one of the most pleasant places in the whole county. It is situated on the line of the railroad, eighteen miles north of Napa City. Its first beginning was in 1853 when a Mr. Henry Still, who owned a large tract of land there, in connection with Mr. Walters built a store and dwelling house. The valley surrounding was sparsely settled; but some even at that early date, had an idea that at no distant day a considerable town would grow up there. In 1855, Mr. Still announced that he would donate lots to any persons who would erect business houses on the same. Among those who accepted the offer were John S. Keister, who erected a shoe shop on the present site of the National Hotel; Mr. J. Howell, a black-smith shop, and Robert Calderwood a wagon shop on a lot adjoining the present St. Charles Hotel. The infant town was christened St. Helena, from the name given to the Division of Sons of Temperance established there about this time.

In 1856 a hotel was erected by A. Tainter on a lot nearly opposite where the Pope Valley road now intersects Main street. This hotel was destroyed by fire in 1860. The next building of note was the Baptist Church edifice, [noted in the chapter on Churches and Benevolent Organizations; also the other churches and Lodges are duly noted in the same chapter.]   At the laying of the corner stone of the Presbyterian Church, there was the grandest time that the town had ever before known. People came from Sonoma, Napa and other
(187)
places to witness the laying of the corner stone and hear the oration delivered on the occasion. The following are some of the articles placed in the corner stone: A copy of the Napa County *Reporter;* the confessions of faith of the Cumberland Presbyterian Church; names of the members of the Church and of the Sunday School; constitution and by-laws of the Sons of Temperance and

of the Temple of Honor, and also of the Masons; a copy of the Cumberland Presbyter, a church paper published at that time in Santa Clara county, and some pieces of coin.

The second hotel was erected in 1862 by John Wolf, on the same site as the first one. This one likewise was destroyed by fire in 1866, and has never been rebuilt. In 1865 Mr. Rampendahl completed the National Hotel. This has since its erection been the resort for large numbers of persons visiting the White Sulphur Springs, and going to enjoy the pleasant climate and beautiful scenery of this section of the valley.

In 1867 Mr. J. Vick purchased a lot of H. H. Dixon, and on it erected the large and commodious brick building, the St. Charles Hotel. He has the greater part of the time, till the Fall of 1872, conducted the hotel, it which time he leased it to Mr. Reeve. St. Helena is the centre of an extensive agricultural region, and is in direct communication with the mining districts of Pope Valley and Knoxville. It is in the great vine growing section of the county, and bids fair soon to become an important point for the Eastern wine trade. The community surrounding St. Helena, in a moral, social and intellectual view, is probably not excelled in the State. There are four church edifices, Presbyterian, Methodist, Baptist and Catholic; two Lodges, Odd Fellows and Masons; and one of the best schools in the county.

MONTICELLO AND BERRYESSA VALLEY.

The town of Monticello is a thriving little village in the rich valley of Berryessa. It has been entirely erected since the purchase and division of the valley. Berryessa Valley is one of the chief wheat growing districts in the county. It has not been settled thickly, still being owned by a comparatively few persons. The Berryessa grant originally contained 36,000 acres. As only a slight general descrip-
(188)
tion of this valley is elsewhere given, we here note the following items: The valley lies between two spurs of the Coast Range Mountains, running about 29 degrees west of north, and lies 24 miles north of Napa City. Putah Creek, a most beautiful mountain stream. runs through the valley, filled with a great variety of fish-while along the foothills and even on the mountain tops are found numerous springs. Putah Creek runs through a cañon bearing the same name, to the southeast into the Sacramento Valley, where its waters sink in the tule. Putah Cañon has been surveyed for the purpose of building a railroad into the valley from Sacramento Valley. The route is a very feasible one, as the cañon forming a natural inlet to the valley, has a fall of but 14 feet to the mile, and has a fair wagon road through it at the present time. It is merely a matter of time as to the building of a railroad into Berryessa; and the time will be very soon after the dividing up of the extensive farms into smaller ones for actual settlers. The valley is capable of producing sufficiently, we think, to warrant the construction. The valley is about 20 miles long and from 1 to 3 wide, and is, together with the surrounding mountains, covered with an abundance of timber, while the scenery is the most picturesque and beautiful in the State; and the healthfulness is not excelled anywhere, separated as it is by three ranges of mountains from the Bay winds; the air becomes dry, extremely bracing and healing to the lungs, and thus it promises a safe retreat for the afflicted. The soil is rich and fertile, producing large crops, and is very promising as a fruit and especially a grape growing region. From the contour of the valley it has evidently been an inland sea at or not far

from the time when the great throes of Nature brought into existence not only the coast range mountains, but opened the "Golden Gate," formed the fertile valleys of the Pacific Coast, and laid out the beautiful county of Napa. The surrounding mountains of Berryessa furnish an abundance of wild game. Mount "Sugar Loaf," being the principal peak, lying southwest of Monticello, is easily recognized by its conical shape.

The first settlers of the valley were Cap. Hardin, John Adams, Wm. Moore, Edward Cage, and Andrew Wester, who were in the valley before the grant was divided. The first houses erected in the valley were the Berryessa adobe, the Wester adobe, and the Cap.
(189)
Hardin adobe. After the division of the land, R. C. Gillaspy erected the first house for J. H. Bostwick, and Ezra Peacock built the first house in Monticello. There are four school districts in Berryessa Valley and two religious organizations, the Cumberland Presbyterians and Christians.

Berryessa Valley, like many other localities in California, is suffering greatly, from land monopolists. Such large ranches prevent settlements from advancing, strangle the surrounding villages, and make sickly schools. A change in this matter must take place soon: we must have smaller farms and manage them better.

CALISTOGA.

The beautiful town of Calistoga, situated in the Northern part of the valley, and at the terminus of the Napa branch of the Pacific Railroad, has become famous on account of its medicinal springs and fine scenery. These Springs, though known to the Indians and Mexicans long before, seems to have attracted little or no attention till about the time Samuel Brannan, in 1859, purchased the extensive tract of land on which they are situated. They were known to the native Californians, Mexicans and Indians as the *aguas calientes,* hot springs, and their curative properties were by these early inhabitants occasionally used. The Springs are situated in the level valley, and are surrounded except on the South side by high and picturesque mountains. After the purchase of the property, Mr. Brannan immediately commenced improvements on an extensive scale. He set about making all the improvements and furnishing all the comforts necessary to render this the most attractive places of resort for invalids as well as tourists in the State. The main grounds belonging to the Springs proper consists of a tract of about one hundred acres near the center of which stands a small hill called Mt. Lincoln. On the summit is an observatory, from which a fine view of the whole of Calistoga and of the surrounding country can be obtained. On this hill is a reservoir which holds ninety thousand gallons. The water is brought from Napa River by means of steam.

At the foot of Mt. Lincoln, on the Western side, is the hotel and the pleasure grounds. There are near twenty-five neat and comfortable cottages for the accommodation of guests. The grounds are
(190)
laid off into walks and ornamented with choice selections of trees shrubbery and flowers. West of the Spring grounds lies the business part of Calistoga, while the county road passes along the Western side of the valley. The town is quite a lively place for business, being the terminus of the railroad and being closely connected by stage lines with Lake county, the Geysers, Healdsburg, and Santa Rosa.

The waters of the springs hold in solution sulphur, iron, magnesia, and various other chemical properties. A few years ago a well was bored directly in front of the hotel. At the depth of seventy feet rock was struck which prevented further progress. The water now stands in this well at the uniform temperature of 185^0. There is a Russian steam bath formed by having the bath room erected immediately over a spring of the temperature of 195^0, with apertures for letting the steam come up into the room. A window is provided for letting the bather get fresh air, and slides are provided for regulating the issue of steam. There are a vast number of different kinds and temperatures, but we refrain from further detail. One spring or well of hot sulphurous water has a most peculiar taste. With a little seasoning of salt and pepper, it has a very decided taste like unto restaurant chicken soup, and is much relished by a great many. The writer calls to mind a ludicrous scene that took place at this "soup bowl" during the political campaign of 1871. Four candidates for official honors were assembled around the "bowl" regaling themselves upon the chicken soup, when one of them stooping down to help himself to a second plateful, fished up a small animal of a suspicious looking nature, and jumped up triumphantly exclaiming: "Here's your chicken, here's your chicken!" There was an immediate complaint of want of appetite.

The compiler of Bancroft's Tourists' Guide thus speaks of Calistoga:

"There is evidently some mysterious agency at work underground at Calistoga, not quite comprehensible to visitors. Chemists and *savans,* indeed, explain the matter in the most learned and scientific manner, by speaking of chemical reaction among mineral substances and the like, and make out a very plausible theory. But the explanation, to many people, needs as much explaining as the

(191)

mystery itself; and when a man finds the ground under his feet to be hot, and the waters issuing from it to be in the neighborhood of the boiling point, he cannot well help harboring a suspicion that the *diabolus ipse* is at work within perilous proximity, especially since the imagination is somewhat helped to the sinister conclusion by a prevailing and most Stygian odor.

"A well was bored at this place, preparatory to the erection of the bath house, to the depth of sixty-five feet, when the boring instruments were blown out with tremendous force, high into the air, as if some unseen power beneath was resenting the intrusion of mortals upon his domain. The workmen ran for their lives, and could not be induced to resume operations on any terms.

"Here is another evidence that the presiding genius of the place does not like to be disturbed. An attempt was made to pump water from this well. After a few strokes a violent stream was blown out of the well, ten or fifteen feet high. If the pumping was stopped the blowing would stop also, but renewed afresh as often as the pumping was resumed. The water at the top being cold, seems to hold in abeyance the steam and intensely hot water below; the action of the pump relieves the superincumbent pressure, when the hot water below rushes out."

One other feature of considerable interest is a grotto erected in the shape of a Druidical Temple solely of petrified wood. It is about fifteen feet high and twenty-five in circumference. The material consists of pieces of logs from two to three feet in length, the apex being occupied by what was once the knot of a tree, in which is a small flag-staff. The wood or rock was brought from the celebrated Petrified Forest.

During four months of 1872, April, May, June and July, the number of visitors to this favorite watering place was 3,020. From the hills surrounding the valley flow fine streams in which trout are abundant, and in the hills are to be found deer and various other kinds of game, with an

occasional bear. A few years ago, Messrs. Brannan & Keseberg erected an extensive distillery and wine house some of the "California Cognac" from this distillery is said to rival the finest brands of French brandy. But Mr. Brannan did not long continue in the concern, and since his retiring, the business has been limited.
(192)

The temperature at times is very warm, at times for a portion of the day the thermometer running up to 110^0 but the average is very pleasant. Entries are made upon the hotel register at 6 A.M., 12 M., and 6 P.M., and the average yearly temperature for these respective hours was in 1871-2, 56^0 71^0, and 65^0. For the months of May, June, July and August, 1871 the averages were 67^0, 80^0 and 75^0. In 1871, Mr. McGeorge commenced the publication of the Calistoga *Tribune,* and excepting a few intervals of cessation, has continued it till the present time.

————

THE WHITE SULPHUR SPRINGS.

One among the many attractions to St. Helena is the celebrated watering place, the White Sulphur Springs. These springs are situated in a deep but romantic cañon, nearly two miles west of St. Helena. Nature has lavished her beauties upon this place, and art has added many attractions. A stream flows down the cañon or gorge in the hills, which adds much to the scene, and affords a find place for anglers. The stream is of the finest water and beautifully shaded, with trees and shrubs. The mountains on either side are high and rugged, mostly covered with a dense growth of a kind of grease-wood-like bush, known as chimisal. A flat on the north side of the mountain has been cleared and planted in vines and trees, but few other attempts have been made to change the natural beauties of the place. The hotel is a large and commodious one, and the cottages of which there are quite a number, all cozy and pleasant. This place early attracted attention, and, as early as 1855 we find that a fine hotel had been erected there by Tafft & Brewster. There has been a fine road constructed from St. Helena to these springs, a telegraph line erected, beautiful flowers and shrubbery planted, and everything done that can add to the pleasures or comforts of guests. The Springs have for many years been under the management of Mr. Alstrom, and a more attentive host can nowhere be found. The scenery from the mouth of the cañon is grandly beautiful. The valley, dotted over with vineyards and farm-houses, and the rugged hills to the east and north, form a contrast that impresses every one who views it, and compares favorably with many
(193)

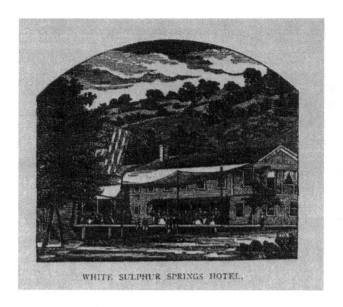

WHITE SULPHUR SPRINGS HOTEL.

The roads leading from the Springs, and about St. Helena, are kept hard and smooth, affording fine drives. During the traveling season the hotel and cottages at the Springs are most always crowded, and many visitors get board with private families, while others board at the hotels in the village.

NAPA SODA SPRINGS.

The Napa Soda Springs, from which is obtained the pleasant cooling beverage, the Napa Soda, are situated on the western side of the mountains east of the valley, about five miles from Napa City. This locality is finely suited for a favorite watering place, but, for the want of hotel and other accommodations it has not as yet become noted, except for the water. The landscape from the Springs is very extensive and very attractive, and we doubt not that ere long suitable buildings and improvements will be completed to render this second to no place in the county as a resort for travelers and invalids. A fine hotel, erected in 1856, was burned only a short time after completion, and no further attempts have been made to provide accom-
(194)
modations for travelers. The property has changed hands several times and been much in litigation. This probably has been one of the greatest reasons why accommodations have not long since been provided. The water of these Springs hold in solution soda, magnesia, lime, iron, alumina, and other properties, and is considered not only a pleasant but a healthful beverage. It is bottled on the grounds, and hauled in wagons to Napa City, where it may be shipped.

PETRIFIED FOREST.

One of the interesting features closely connected with Calistoga is the Petrified Forest, five miles west of south from that place, and near the dividing ridge between Napa and Santa Rosa Valleys. The road from Calistoga to the Forest is picturesque and beautiful. The hills are covered with groves of pines, oaks, madronas, manzanitas and other growths, and as the tourist passes over the road he cannot but be struck by the beauty and grandeur of the scene. The Forest is on the north side of a deep ravine or cañon, and covers an area of two or three hundred acres. The trees are from a hundred to a hundred and fifty feet in length, and from two to seven feet in diameter, and are broken up into logs of various lengths. These trees are only partially unearthed-they evidently having been covered by dirt and rock of volcanic formation, which has only been partially washed away by the agency of water. The logs bear almost the exact appearance of wood, and are in every state of crystalization. In one place is a large tree growing between and upon the fragments of a log of rock, which strikes the beholder as a genuine curiosity of nature, and proves that these logs have existed for countless ages. The trees are nearly all lying with the tops *from* St. Helena Mountain, which would seem to indicate the fact that they were overwhelmed by lava from that direction.

The existence of this forest was first made known by Mr. C. H. Denison, of San Francisco, in 1870. Various theories have been advanced as to the cause of this petrifaction. Not being experts in geological science we refrain from expressing any opinion, and close by giving the views of Prof. O. C. Marsh, who visited the spot in 1870. He says:
(195)

"It is about two thousand feet in height, and is mainly composed of metamorphic rocks of cretaceous age, which are in places, as we ascertained, overlaid uncomformably by later tertiary strata, consisting of light-colored, coarse sandstones and beds of stratified volcanic ashes. This ridge had long been covered with a dense growth of chaparral, but just before our visit a destructive fire had swept over a portion of it, rendering it comparatively easy to examine a large tract of country, which apparently had never been explored. A careful examination of the locality where the first prostrate trunks had been discovered, soon made it evident that those now on the surface had all been weathered out of the volcanic tufa and sandstones, which form the summit of this part of the mountain ridge. Several large silicified trees were, indeed, subsequently found in the vicinity, projecting from the side of a steep bluff, which had partially escaped denudation."

————

MOUNT ST. HELENA.

This mountain; whose summit rises to the height of 4,343 feet, and is a point from which run lines dividing Lake and Napa counties, is the culminating point of the Coast Range in this section of country. From Calistoga it is about five miles to the foot of this mountain, and near ten to the summit. A good trail has been made for the accommodation of tourists which renders the ascent easy. From the summit a grand and magnificent view can be obtained of the surrounding regions of our State. With a good glass, in clear weather, many towns in the Sacramento Valley can be seen, together with the Sierra Nevada range, for over a hundred miles of its course. San Francisco Bay, and a large portion of the city, can be seen when not enveloped in the dense fogs, so common to the Bay region. Towards the North Clear Lake lies mapped out in plain view. Many of the valleys, mountains, towns, rivers and cities of the finest portion of California can be examined in a panorama of Nature from this elevation. On the West, beyond the Coast Range, extends the

VIEW AT THE GEYSERS.

CHAPTER XIII.

AGRICULTURAL RESOURCES.

Napa county has two important sources of wealth-her mines, sufficiently noted elsewhere, and her agriculture and kindred resources. Up to the last few years little attention was paid to developing the resources of the soil, wheat raising being the chief occupation of the farmer. There are some fields in the county, off of which for the last fifteen years, an annual wheat crop has been reaped. There are few localities in the world where wheat will grow better than in Napa Valley, but then such a succession of crops must greatly exhaust the

(197)

soil. Nearly the whole of the land in the valley is well adapted to all kinds of cereals, and with judicious rotation would produce a large crop every year. Some of the land along the foot-hills is too gravelly to produce wheat to much advantage, but then this land is valuable for other productions. Oats and barley grow equally well with wheat, and fields have been planted in Indian corn producing crops that would compare favorably with those of the Wabash bottoms. Yet corn does not grow thus in any but the rich valley lands. Early sugar corn matures well on the higher lands, but it must be planted early.

The land below Napa City down to Soscol is a kind of adobe, but not very heavy. A great portion of it is swamp and overflowed-commonly called tule land, and only waits to be reclaimed to be the richest and most valuable land in the county. It requires comparatively little labor to reclaim these lands, and experiments about Soscol prove that when reclaimed they are unsurpassed for the production of grasses, beets, sorghum, and other vegetation. Messrs. Thompson have reclaimed quite an extensive tract of this land, and find that it surpasses any other they have.

The land below Napa City down to Soscol is a kind of adobe, but not very heavy. A great portion of it is swamp and overflowed-commonly called tule land, and only waits to be reclaimed to be the richest and most valuable land in the county. It requires comparatively little labor to reclaim these lands, and experiments about Soscol prove that when reclaimed they are unsurpassed for the production of grasses, beets, sorghum, and other vegetation. Messrs. Thompson have reclaimed quite an extensive tract of this land, and find that it surpasses any other they have.

Along the foot-hills on either side of the valley the soil is gravelly and not well adapted to grain. Yet, this land is the best that can be found for vineyards. It is also very extensively used for grazing purposes. The quantity of this grape land is very great, and could be made valuable. About St. Helena, the finest vineyards that are to found, are on land that was formerly called waste land, covered with chemisal. The fine vineyard of Mr. G. S. Burrage, Northeast of Yountville, is on the hillsides, which were useless for any other purpose, barely affording a scant amount of feed a short season of the year. Indeed, for land that will produce the finest flavored grape, and one from which wine of the finest bouquet can be made, we must look to these hill lands.

HOP CULTURE.

The soil and climate of Napa seem peculiarly adapted to the raising of hops. The vine grows and bears well, needing but little labor in harvesting. The hops grown in California contain a larger proportion of resinous lupulin than the imported article, and this
(198)
gives it a greater value for brewing purposes. The main production of hops in this county has been about St. Helena. Mr. A. Clock came into that section in 1867, and rented a piece of land from Mr. D. Cole on the rich bottom land near the river. The first year he planted fifteen acres, and till 1871 gathered fair crops, but the market price was low, so that he did not realize much of a profit, and had he not been possessed of great energy would have given up the enterprise. But in 1871, although his crop was light, the quality of the California hops had begun to be appreciated, and he realized a handsome profit. Off of the fifteen acres he gathered over ten tons, selling the same for an average price of about sixty cents per pound. This brought him in a revenue of near $12,000. He purchased a tract of land and set out thirty acres more in hops, and erected a large concrete dry house 54x70 feet, two stories high. Mr. R. F. Montgomery whose farm is situated about one mile North of St. Helena, has also engaged to considerable extent in hop culture, and feels well satisfied with the enterprise. He has erected a dry house 30x40, two stories high. From the ample experiments of these two gentlemen there is no longer a question as to the adaptability of the soil and climate of Napa for hop culture, nor of its affording a remunerative source of employment. There are now hundreds of acres along Napa River well adapted to the culture of hops, which now lie idle, covered with briars and willows, affording little or no revenue to the owners.

THE TEA PLANT.

Mr. S. Brannan a few years ago started a small tea garden near Calistoga. Everything started off with promise of complete success, but the garden was soon neglected, so that the experiment proves only that the plant grows finely. It is probable that if planted in the foot hills, and cultivated with care, that a good quality of tea would be produced. Owing to the very large and increasing consumption of the plant it is to be hoped efforts will be made to test thoroughly the adaptability of our soil for its culture.

FRUITS AND NUTS.

It would be superfluous to enumerate the different kinds of fruits
(199)
of Napa County. They are too well known to need any notice. Suffice it to say that nearly every variety has been produced, and of the finest quality. Besides the common fruits, experiments have been made at raising oranges, lemons and other semi-tropical fruits. Oranges have matured on the ranch of Geo. C. Yount, near Yountville, and there is little doubt but that in sheltered localities on the hill-land, where frosts are light and rare, that oranges can be grown well. Gen. M. G. Vallejo, of Sonoma, has oranges, lemons and olives growing and bearing in his garden. The oranges mostly grown here have been from the seed, and consequently are not as good as the grafted ones of Los Angeles. Our climate is peculiarly adapted to the drying of fruits and raisins. When proper care is taken in the picking and drying of fruits they command the highest market value, owing to their superiority. Dr. D. K. Rule, of St. Helena, and W. H. Crabb, of Oakville, have cured raisins which, were superior to any of the imported article. The grape mostly used for raisins has been the Muscat of Alexandria. The experiments made in producing raisins prove conclusively that the only reason why this is not now a lucrative business is because proper care and attention has not been devoted to it.

STOCK RAISING.

A great portion of the hill land in the county is unsuited to cultivation for other purposes than grapes, and has thus far been used for pasture. Large herds of cattle and flocks of sheep have been kept upon these hills. Cattle can be raised in California at less cost than in any other country, but a greater range is required, owing to the absence of Summer rains. After the grass is once eaten down the drouth prevents much of a growth thereafter. Formerly the hills and valleys of the county, were covered with wild oats, affording the finest of pasture; but the stock has almost entirely destroyed this. Now, owing to the native grasses on the hills drying up so early in the season and affording so scant a pasture, those who are largely engaged in sheep raising find that the quality of the fleece from their flocks is benefitted by preparing better feed, and much attention

has of late been paid to the growing of grasses for feed. Alfalfa has been raised extensively and found to be very good. Ex-
(200)
periments with timothy and other Eastern grasses have not been favorable. Some parties in this and Sonoma counties have experimented with the Texas Mezquit grass and report quite favorably, but as yet little is known of it. The finding of some grass adapted to our soil and climate is for our stock raisers a great desideratum. It is evident that the pastures are gradually failing and something must be done to supply the deficiency.

————

OTHER PRODUCTIONS.

There are many kinds of productions which the quality of the soil in Napa, and the climate give assurance could be raised at a profit, which never have been attempted. Among these, one is rice. We do not believe that any attempt has yet been made to raise rice in this State, except as an experiment, yet the experiments prove that our tule lands when reclaimed, are excellent for this production. It is more than possible that at no future day rice may be counted among the staple productions of our State and county. Flax is also another production for which large quantities of our land is well suited, and for which a ready market could be found. Flax, hemp, ramie and jute could all be produced in Napa Valley, and thus a very large bill for importations be saved to our producers. These are among some of the possible productions and the evidence for their adaptability is similarity of soil and climate to countries where they grow, and the few experiments made with them. The great demand for sacks in the State to ship the wheat crop makes it appear strange that no efforts as yet have been made to raise these textiles and supply the home market with the manufactured articles. Over fifteen hundred pounds of flax seed have been gathered from an acre in other parts of the State, and the stalk above the average in other countries in regard to strength and the quality of the fibre. And this was on land no better than hundreds of acres in Napa Valley. Another production that offers great inducements to capitalists to engage in it, is that of raising beets and making sugar. The beet grows finely all along up the rich bottom lands of our valley, and in the tule lands wherever reclaimed. There have been two sugaries in active operation for quite a time in the State, and they have proved eminently successful.
(201)

————

SERICULTURE.

Several extensive experiments have been made in this county in sericulture. That the mulberry will grow here, and that the worm will do well, admits of no question. The trees make a wonderful growth, and the silk produced is of a superior quality. We do not claim a superiority for any one county, but over other silk producing countries. Several years ago Mr. Brannan planted out quite a large field in mulberry trees, and these have made a fine growth, and now produce a large quantity of leaves for feeding. In 1872 a house or room was fitted up for a feeding room for the worms, and the business carried on quite successfully. The mulberry orchard and feeding house have since been placed under the charge of an experienced sericulturist, and more extensive improvements made. It is rumored that in a short time a silk manufactory will be erected at that place.

Messrs. Hallin & Amerup also planted large numbers of trees in Brown's Valley, West of Napa City, but so far nothing more than the setting of the trees has been done.

Wm. H. Baxter, of Springdale Farm, commenced the culture of silk on his arrival in this county in 1869, and has pursued it since with varying success. As yet, sericulture is almost a new industry in California, and the processes necessary to its successful development are things of but yesterday. It was found what was good in Spain and France would not always be well here. So that many failures have been sustained, is not surprising. Mr. Baxter shared these early losses fully, but now he has succeeded in making this a hopeful and paying industry. He has abandoned the use of artificial heat in his feeding house, finding that the climate of Napa is all that is needed. Mr. Baxter now has over 50,000 trees of the *Moretti, Alba,* and *Multicaulis.* Last year, (1872), he fed over 300,000 worms, of the French annuals. Thus far he has done little in the silk culture, having used most of the eggs in filling large orders from France. The foreign demand for California eggs, which are found to be the best that can be had, is very great.

One great drawback to silk culture in California is the high price of labor. It is questionable whether the cultivator can afford to pay the wages asked by laborers to gather the leaves and feed the worms.

(202)

Yet, as the whole season requires less than two months' work, we have hopes of seeing this difficulty overcome. The work seems well suited to women and children. But the greatest obstacle to this industry is that the two silk factories in this State have not, so far, supplied machinery necessary for reeling the silk from the cocoons, but have required this work to be done by the producers. Doubtless this want in the silk factories will soon be supplied, and the person who has a few trees, and produces a small quantity of cocoons, find a ready market for them. Then silk culture may be regarded as a success. California presents more advantages for the prosecution of this industry than any other country. It requires less outlay and less care; the worms are free from disease and the growth of the tree is most exhuberant. Everything, except the obstacles above noted, points to this State at no very distant day as the greatest among silk growing countries.

VINICULTURE.

California seems to be the natural home of the vine. Though there are some favored localities where the finest flavored grapes grow, yet hill and valley alike produce an excellent quality. The distribution of the grape is general, not only over Napa, but almost over the State. It was discovered, by the missionary Padres more than 100 years ago that the soil and climate of California were well adapted to the culture of the grape. Wine was made on a small scale for home use long before the conquest of the country by the United States. But the Mexican and early American settlers planted a few vines, which are still in vigorous growth. There are several small vineyards in this county over twenty years old, the trunk of the vines being from four to six inches in diameter, which produce an enormous amount of grapes. Some of these old vines may be seen upon the farm of Col. J. B. Chiles, in Chiles' Valley, at Wm. H. Nash's former vineyard above St. Helena, and at the ranch of Geo. C. Yount, deceased. These vines were all of the Mission variety.

It took several years for our farmers to learn that the planting of vineyards on a large scale could be made profitable, and the manufacture of wine an important and extensive branch of industry. (203)

The first one to plant a vineyard of any consequence-one for any other purpose than for grapes for table use-was J. M. Patchett. As early as 1850 a small vineyard had been planted on the property which he afterwards purchased. The year of his purchase he planted a greater number of vines and also an orchard. In 1859 he was so well convinced that wine-making could be made remunerative that he erected his cellar, now standing.

The first vineyards were planted in valley land suited to the culture of cereals, and grew luxuriantly. It was found, however, that the grapes produced a wine inferior to those planted in a more gravelly soil, or in the foothills upon each side of the valley. Year by year the area planted in vineyards is extending, the amount of grapes increasing with the number of vines and the age of those already planted. There must be in the future a vast extension in viniculture and the manufacture of wines for export. The home market is scarcely sufficient for the wine product of a single county. Viniculture has already become a most important industry in this county. Instead of the old Mission variety most of the vines recently planted are the best obtainable in Europe. Careful experiments have been made to ascertain which varieties are best suited to our soil and climate, and men of great experience and capital have embarked in the wine business. Extensive cellars have been constructed, and all the necessary appliances provided for the production of excellent wines upon a large scale.

A great change has taken place in the wine business. It has become, to a great extent, centralized in a few hands. The proprietors of small vineyards no longer attempt to make their own wine, but sell their grapes to large establishments which have the necessary capital and conveniences for the business. This plan has proven advantageous to all parties, and has yielded to the vineyard owner a larger profit than he could have made by cultivating grain.

Since the time when Mr. Patchett commenced his vineyard the industry has grown till now it stands foremost in the county. The first shipment of wine from Napa county took place in 1857, and consisted of six casks and six hundred bottles; in 1871 the export was over half a million gallons. And still the industry is but in its infancy. Among the first who looked upon the wine business as a
(204)
lucrative industry, were Drs. G. B. Crane and D. K. Rule, of St. Helena. Both these gentlemen had been practicing physicians and apothecaries in Napa City for many years, but in 1859 Dr. Crane, becoming wearied with the profession, and seeking for a country home bought a tract of land on the Bale grant and commenced the planting out of a vineyard. His vineyard, one of the largest in the county, is planted mostly with Mission vines. Much of the land for his vineyard was such as people, at that early day regarded as almost worthless. His first cellar was erected in 1862, a diminutive affair, built of wood. In 1870 he commenced the erection of a concrete cellar 44x75, two stories high. Dr. Crane labored hard to get California wines introduced into the Eastern markets. He established a wine house in St. Louis, and carried it on till the last year or more.

Dr. D. K. Rule, in 1860, also purchased a tract of land on the Bale grant, about one mile southeast from St. Helena, and planted a small vineyard. His vineyard was planted on land cleared of the chemisal brush, and that was considered valueless. But he found that this soil was preeminently adapted to grapes. He has at different times sold off portions of his farm as first purchased, so that now he has but a comparatively small vineyard. A considerable portion of his vines are of the finest foreign varieties. He has no cellar and does not manufacture wine, but sells his grapes.

Mr. Charles Krug, whose vineyard lies about one and a half miles north of St. Helena, is a native of Mainz, on the Rhine. He came to America in 1851, and to California in 1852. In 1858 he entered into the wine business in Sonoma, and the same year was employed by Mr. Patchett, of Napa, to make wine. In 1861 he obtained a tract of land near St. Helena of 800 acres, and set out 15,000 vines. He has continued increasing his vineyard till at present it covers 68 acres and has 60,000 vines, 40,000 of which are fine foreign varieties, among which are Johanisberg Riesling, Franken Riesling, Rhenish Muscatel, Burger, Chasselas, Malaga, Muscat of Alexandria, Zinfindel, Black Malvoisie, Flame Tocay, Rose de Peru, etc. Mr. Krug's first wine cellar, still standing, is 14X20 feet., 2 1/2 feet in the ground and raised 5 1/2 feet above. covered first with straw, then with earth, and finished with a roofing, of redwood shakes.

The rapid growth of the vineyard and large increase of wine
(205)
necessitated building additional cellar room from year to year, until the past season, when the present large and substantial concrete was completed which is capable of holding from 250,000 to 300,000 gallons. It is from outside to outside 90x104 ft., the middle or main building being two stories. The upper room, 44x100 feet clear of posts, will be the press room or general manufacturing room. Immediately under is a room 43x100 feet that will have all the modern apparatus for keeping an even temperature for fermenting wine. The west room, 21x100 feet, contains the distilling and stores for new wine, with office room at one end. The east room, 21 x100 feet, will contain the old wine, except the very old, which will always be found in the old cellar. Mr. Krug takes great pride in brandy making, and employs an aged and very competent French distiller making cognac from clean wine that is only equaled, and not surpassed, by the best French brands of the same age.

Messrs. Pellet & Carver are more widely known as wine makers than as grape-growers, yet their vineyard is among the best in that vicinity. It is situated adjoining those of Drs. Crane and Rule, and contains 36,000 vines, mostly foreign, of very much the same varieties as those of Mr. Krug. Their vines, like those of Dr. Rule, were planted on land cleared of a heavy growth of chemisal. Their cellar, one among the earliest built in that section, is 50x64 feet, partly under ground, two stories high. The wine from this cellar ranks among the best in the valley.

The Giaque Brothers have a cellar two miles south of St. Helena. It is of concrete, 26x100 feet, two stories high. The grapes mostly used are purchased.

Mr. J. Backus, who purchased of Dr. Rule, has a small vineyard, but nearly all of select foreign varieties. In 1872 he completed a concrete cellar 30x80 feet, lined inside and out with wood. The temperature is remarkably uniform.

Gen. R. W. Heath, in 1972, purchased the fine ranch of Gen. E. D. Keyes, near the mouth of Sulphur Spring cañon, one and a half miles southwest of St. Helena, on which is a vineyard of near 40,000 vines, nearly all foreign varieties; also a stone cellar three stories high and most conveniently arranged. The cellar was erected
(206)
by Gen. Keyes, and is so situated at the base of a hill that wagons can be unloaded into any one of the stories.

About three miles north of St. Helena is the farm of Rev. T. B. Lyman, formerly owned by Mr. Kellogg. There are about 800 acres in the farm. There are near 25,000 vines, mostly Mission. A concrete cellar 30x100 feet, two stories high, was erected in 1871.

H. W. Crabb, near Oakville, though not a wine maker, is extensively engaged in raising grapes. His farm, consisting of 240 acres, is a model for neatness and business thrift. He has forty orange trees grafted from the grandiflora, all of which grow well and are beginning to bear. He likewise has a number of Italian chestnuts which are growing well. He also has seventy acres planted in vines, the greater portion bearing.

Mr. Eli Lewelling, adjoining Mr. Crabb on the East, has an extensive vineyard and orchard, but does not manufacture wine. His farm consists of 120 acres, on which is a fine nursery, an almond orchard, and 40,000 vines. He is also experimenting, in the cultivation of oranges.

J. C. Davis, near Oakville has one among the handsome pieces of property in the county, and one that is admirably located for a vineyard. He already has about 28,000 vines, mostly on fine hill land.

Mr. G. Groezinger, of Yountville, only recently became possessed of his fine tract of land. He purchased the large farm and vineyard of H. C. Boggs in 1870, and since the purchase has made extensive and permanent improvements. The vineyard has been enlarged and one of the finest cellars in the whole State erected. At the expense of being prolix, we here annex a description of this cellar and that of Messrs. Burrage & Tucker, prepared by us and formerly published in the Napa *Reporter*. The main cellar structure, built entirely of brick (a quantity of which was made on the spot), is 150 by 80 feet and two stories high. Its wine capacity is 400,000 gallons. At the North end of the building, a wing extends back 84 feet, and is 60 feet wide, the same height of the main building, with a cellar underneath. Joining on to this wing, and running along the back of the main edifice, is the fermenting room, 105 feet in length and 30 in width. A portion of room is used for steaming and

(207)

cleaning casks, etc. The roof of the fermenting room is nearly level, and comes up within six feet of the eaves of the main cellar. This roof is very strongly built, and is on a level with the upper story of the cellar. On this is all the grape crushing done, in the open air, skylights being fitted in directly over large fermenting vats below, into which falls the juice from the crushers. These crushers take a box of grapes, containing from 55 to 60 pounds, every seven seconds, and their capacity for juice is from 6,000 to 6,500 gallons per day. A platform leads from the roof to the ground, and one also from the upper floor of the cellar, and as a load of boxes of grapes is pulled up one platform by a horse below, a load of empty boxes goes down the other one. On this roof is also made all the Port, Muscatel, Sherry and Angelica. Two hydraulic presses that have a power of thirty tons each, are used in this establishment to press the pumice. The different varieties of wine made at this cellar are as follows: Port, Muscat, Muscatel, Angelica, Sherry, White Wine, Claret and Mountain Wine. In the rear of the wine cellar, at the distance therefrom prescribed by law, is the distillery, where some of the best California brandy made in the State is distilled. Here are two stills, whose united capacity is about 150 gallons per day. A steam engine is here employed, which performs almost all the work done on the premises. Everything here, as in every portion of this vast establishment, bespeaks the tidiness of the Superintendent, Mr. F. Schweitzer, who has combined, all over the premises, the three best elements of successful wine making: order, neatness and convenience. Everything that will take a polish shines, even the floors are swept clean enough to delight the heart of a tidy housewife, and all the casks are numbered. The rubber hose and all the various implements in constant use in an edifice of this kind, are to be found in their appropriate place, and can be made available even in the dark.

The cellar is located in an eminently favored location. In the rear the vineyard rises gradually and forms a background almost as picturesque in January as it does later in the season, when the grape vines are covered with green leaves. About 150,000 vines are growing here, though not all in full bearing, and only 25,000 of these are native or Mission grape. As the estate is large, more
(208)
vines will be set out every year till the whole place shall become one vineyard, before which time, however, its proprietor will have purchased what adjacent land his neighbors will let him have, so that there is no telling to what extent this vineyard may reach. The water used on the premises is furnished from springs on the property, of sufficient altitude and force to throw water all over the building. Four reservoirs have been constructed at the springs above mentioned, and now Mr. Groezinger proposes to tap another spring on the property of A. G. Clark, And bring that down also. A switch from the Railroad Company's track is laid within a few feet of the wine cellar door, and cars can either be loaded with full casks or the empty ones loaded on and then pumped full of wine.

The Vine Cliff Vineyard, Messrs. Burrage & Tucker, proprietors, is situated about three miles northeast of Yountville. One of the most romantic spots in Napa valley is this same vine Cliff Vineyard. A semi-circle of inaccessible rocky side-hills, in the cañon in which nestle the buildings, has, by the energy of man, been turned into a useful and picturesque piece of property. Hundreds of tons of rock have been patiently gathered off the hill-sides, which now team with grape vines, and hauled away. Truly does it look to one who saw it a few years ago as though the finger of enchantment had been pointed at its frowning, rocky surface, and changed it into a "thing of beauty and a joy forever." This vineyard, which now contains 65,000 vines, only 10,000 of which are native or Mission, was commenced seven years ago. A bull tongue and cultivator have done nearly all the plowing for this flourishing vineyard, which, in the last two years, has turned off 19,000 gallons of wine. The wine cellar is four stories high, the lower story of masonry, the stories above of lumber. The cellar is so built into the precipitous hillside that every floor is approachable by wagons, save the upper, where a truck is used to haul the boxes of grapes into the building along a platform just the right height on to which to unload a wagon easily. The grapes are thus crushed in the upper story without any hoisting process. Through this floor the juice falls into the fermenting vats on the floor beneath, where it can be either lowered in casks, or by hose, to the floors below, or loaded into wagons at the door. In the second story a furnace stands, used to keep the wire at an even tem-
(209)
perature or to generate steam with which to cleanse the casks. From every floor of this cellar a beautiful view greets the eye, no matter which way one may happen to look. The live oaks around the dwelling house, the clusters of toyone with its ruby berries, and the ornamental trees, planted by the proprietors, all tend to enhance the beauty of this place. In a grove of live oaks, is the spring house, just high enough to force water into every room in the dwelling house, and allow a fountain to throw its fanciful spray before the door. Orange and lemon trees can hardly help flourishing in this favored locality, and as it is the intention of the proprietors to plant some of these trees this

season, we may hope, one of these days, to eat oranges and lemons in Napa, grown on our own hills.

Extending all along the foot-hills of the valley are smaller vineyards of from two and three to fifteen and twenty acres of vines. Among these we mention only a few: Mr. Charles Hopper, near Yountville, has about twenty acres in vines. Mr. Hopper's place is very romantically situated on the West side of the valley, in a grove of live oaks and madronas that border a living stream. This is a portion of the section purchased in 1849 of Mr. G. C. Yount at $1.50 per acre, now worth near $125 per acre. Blackberries and other kinds of fruit grow well here. Adjoining Mr. Hopper's place is a tract formerly sold by him, now owned by Mr. Wm. Locker, of Oakville; also near by that of Mr. Greenup Whitton. Further up the valley we come to the home of Mr. Wm. Baldridge, another one of the old Pioneers, who has established himself for the remainder of his existence in a very cozy nook in the hills that border immediately on Napa valley. Almost every variety of grape vine and fruit tree have been grafted, planted and raised here by its even now indefatigable proprietor. An everlasting stream of water flows to his house from a mountain spring, and every comfort that nature can lavish or industry furnish in the shape of fruit, can here be found. Near the house still stands the old log cabin erected here when first taken possession of by this gentleman, in whose memory lies enthroned the history of many a stirring scene in the annals of California.

Just below Oakville is the large farm of Mr. John Benson. It consists of 400 acres, about 84 of which are set in vines, most white

(210)

Muscat of Alexandria. This vineyard was only planted in 1872, and when the blocks are filled will contain over 60,000 vines. Also, the same year he started a nursery in which were set 60,000 grape cuttings-same variety as the vineyard.

In this same section, about a mile south of Oakville, lies a tract of land, now owned by Mr. G. L. Kenny, of the firm of A. L. Bancroft & Co.; also one by A. L. Bancroft. These gentlemen have superior land, and are having the same highly improved.

Mr. Stoneberger, whose property is nearly opposite Oakville, has only a small vineyard, about ten acres of the Black Malvoisie. He has become better known as a successful grain grower, and more lately of fruit. He has an orchard of 1,200 almond trees, and various other kinds of trees.

Near Rutherford Station, a little place nearly midway between Oakville and St. Helena are the vineyards and property of Judge S. C. Hastings. His family residence is on the Home Farm southwest of Rutherford; here he has twenty-eight acres of vines. Near Rutherford he has two other vineyards, one of thirty-three acres, the other of forty-three. The greater portion of his vines are foreign varieties.

Adjoining the Home Farm, above mentioned, we come to a spot on the edge of our beautiful valley, on which nature has lavished her happiest charm. With a back ground of hills, sufficiently romantic to make an Italian envious, through which bubbles a clear and limpid trout stream, whose silvery sheen can at times be caught sight of from the county road, is the vineyard of W. C. Watson. Here are 50 acres in vines, mostly Black Malvoisie. An extensive orchard has likewise been planted here, and such is the immense advantage of the water privilege that everything that heart could wish, or eye desire, can be raised here. An artificial pond has been formed, fed from the mountain stream, in which trout could be easily raised. This water is of sufficient depth to admit of a spring-board, from which the swimmer can take a dive, and large enough to take a pretty fair swim. The house is situated in a grove of large trees, mostly planted there years ago, which shade without hiding it.

H. N. Amesbury, C. H. Clark, S. L. Marshall, T. A. Mann, the Kneif Brothers, and several others out towards Brown's valley, have small vineyards, many of which are foreign varieties and doing well.

(211)

Mr. J. J. Sigrist, whose farm is but a few miles from Napa, is both a grape-grower and a wine-maker, and both on a large scale. His first cellar, together with all the contents, were destroyed by fire a few years since. His present one is of a capacity of 100,000 gallons. He has about one hundred acres in vines, the oldest of which were planted in 1860. He makes his wine from each variety of grape singly. His crushing machine has a capacity of 2,500 gallons per day, and during the vintage is kept constantly going.

Mr. F. A. Roeder, adjoining Mr. Sigrist, has a vineyard of forty acres, all foreign vines, mostly Black Malvoisie, and all in good bearing.

Further out in Brown's valley is the fine property lately owned by Dr. Lockwood. In this vineyard are 50,000 vines, only one-third of which are Mission, and all bearing. There is a cellar of the an capacity of 15,000 gallons. This property consists of 100 acres, and is located on both sides of Napa Creek.

William Woodward, whose farm lies near four miles northeast of Napa City, has one among the best vineyards in the county. It is situated along the foothills of the mountains, and is excellent vineyard land. He has a large area in bearing vines on the place and a cellar with all the appurtenances common thereto; also a distillery. The brandy made here is of fine quality, and the sherry wine, which seems to be a specialty, unsurpassed. Mr. Woodward's whole farm bespeaks order and business thrift in every part. He has all the convenience of water power that could be desired-a living stream coming down from the hills. In addition to the large business carried on in the wine and brandy manufacture, he has a dairy and a large farm. He has done much for the developing of the natural productions of that part of the valley.

In and about Soscol the land seems not so well adapted to the growing of the grape. Grains and fruit trees do well, and the vine grows finely, but the quality of the grape, and especially the bouquet of the wines, is inferior to that grown upon the hill lands higher up the valley. But the grapes grown in this section are good, and always bear a highprice in the market. This section of the county seems better adapted, if possible, to fruits than any other part of Napa county. The extensive orchards of the Messrs. Thompson,

(212)

Mr. R. E. F. Moore, and various other persons, amply testify to this.

East of Yountville, on the foothills, the quality of the soil and its adaptability to grapes is fully established. Mr. Terrel Grigsby has a large vineyard in good bearing condition, and his grapes are equal to the best. He is not a wine-maker. Along up the eastern side of the valley are quite a number of vineyards, lately set out. Among these, one of the largest and one set with the finest grapes, is that of Mr. Geo. Linn. This gentleman, in addition to his vineyard situated northwest of the property of Mr. Burrage, elsewhere noted, has one of the finest tracts of rich, alluvial bottom land anywhere to be found. This tract is situated just east of the town of Yountville, and is the family homestead.

About five miles northwest of St. Helena, on the eastern slope of the mountains west of the valley, is a small vineyard of choice varieties of foreign grapes, belonging to Mr. Jacob Schram. He also has a small cellar, and makes his own grapes into wine, which, from its excellence, ranks among the best in the whole State.

Above the lands of Mr. Krug is the large vineyard and cellar now owned by Mr. Weinberger, and above his the extensive vineyard of Mr. Sayward. One notable feature about Mr. Sayward's vineyard is that it is set on a rocky hillside that was useless for any other than vineyard purposes.

Mr. David Fulton, deceased, owned a large vineyard near St. Helena, only a portion of which are foreign vines. On the premises was erected a large cellar and distillery. But little has been done in the way of wine or brandy-making for a year or more, owing to the closing up of the estate after Mr. Fulton's death.

Near the base of the mountains west of St. Helena, is the magnificent farm and vineyard of Mr. John York. Mr. York commenced the planting of his vineyard soon after Messrs. Crane, Rule and Krug commenced the enterprise. It is on gravelly land; the vines grow well and the grapes are much liked by wine-makers. The same remarks will apply to the vineyard formerly owned by Mr. David Hudson. Besides the vineyards mentioned near St. Helena, there are a great number of smaller ones. In fact, there is scarcely a single place but has a number of vines planted, some only a few hun-

(213)

dred vines, and some five, ten, fifteen and twenty acres. The aggregate of these small vineyards is very great.

Of the many large vineyards near Calistoga, we will only mention one, that planted by Judge Evy, and now owned by Dr. R. Garnett. This vineyard is situated about three miles north of Calistoga, near the mouth of the cañon through which runs one of the head branches of Napa River. The first portions of the vineyard were of Mission grapes, but those set out later are foreign varieties. Judge Evy, while he had the place, erected a small cellar and made a limited amount of wine; but the present proprietor has not engaged in winemaking. The vineyard is on gravelly but rich soil. In addition to the extensive vineyard there is also a large orchard of choice varieties of fruit. The Doctor likewise has one of the finest stock ranches in the county.

The lands in the upper parts of Carneros and Huichica Creeks are well adapted to grape growing. Mr. Wm. H. Winter, in addition to his fine orchard, has an extensive vineyard, and has found that the grapes grow and mature as well as elsewhere. His vineyard consists mainly of Mission grapes. He has a cellar and a distillery connected with his vineyard.

Besides the cellars noted in the foregoing pages, there are several smaller ones which are omitted. In Napa City there are two wine houses that simply manufacture wine. One is the cellar of Mr. G. Migliavacca, the other of Messrs. Van Bever & Thompson. Mr. Migliavacca is a native of Italy, came to California in 1858, and commenced the wine business in 1866. At first he had only a small house on Main street. In the back part of the house he began the manufacture of wine on a small scale. The quality of his wine was good, and met with ready sale. He kept gradually increasing the capacity of his house, till finally he got his present building. In addition to the storeroom in this house on Main street, he has a portion of the large brick house commonly known as Crowey's store, east of the bridge on First street, and used it for the purposes of a cellar. Mr. Migliavacca, by his industry and his skill, has built up a fine business for himself in Napa. Messrs.

Van Bever & Thompson commenced the manufacture of wine on a large scale in 1871. After moving their store from its previous position on First street,
(214)
near the bridge, to their present commodious place, they used the old storeroom as a cellar. Here they made a large quantity of wine; but in 1872 they obtained the old Banner Warehouse on Main street opposite the Depot. This was fitted up for a cellar, and is now occupied by these parties as a wine house. The wine from this house, "Uncle Sam Vineyard Cellar," as the proprietors call it, bears a good price in the market, and is said by experts to compare favorably with the best.

Notwithstanding the great numbers of vineyards now growing in the county, the work of planting out more is continually going on. Those who have vineyards and vacant land, keep year by year increasing the number of their vines, entertaining no fears of the business being overdone. In 1872 the Assessor returned 2,324,545 bearing vines in the county. This number will be very materially increased the present year by large numbers of vines previously planted coming into bearing. New cellars are being projected and the business of viniculture in Napa is indeed assuming wondrous proportions.
(215)

POINT ARENA LIGHT HOUSE.

CHAPTER XIV.

THE FUTURE FOR NAPA

Of course in speaking on what will be the future condition of a country we can not speak certainly. We can only form estimates from the past and the present. But, judging from these we think we can speak with considerable probability of correctness that the future for Napa is destined to be glorious. Our proximity to the great centers of trade and commerce give us assurances that we shall continue to grow and improve, that the resources of our soil shall be more fully developed and new industries started, till for material wealth and enterprise we shall be second to but few other countries. The pleasant climate in Napa Valley, and the facilities for travel,

(216)

have already attracted many from the city, and we find the valley gradually being divided up into small tracts for homesteads, and elegant improvements being made. The wealth and culture of the city is in great numbers looking to this valley for a country seat, for a pleasant home where the substantial comforts of rural life may be enjoyed, and still the facilities of a rapid transit place them at the doors of the metropolis. The peculiar adaptation of the soil and climate of Napa render it easy in a brief time to improve a home so that shade and ornamental trees, flowers and shrubbery can be had in abundance, and add their charm to the surroundings.

Already there are numbers of elegant villas and suburban residences in the county, and the number is being increased yearly. As an evidence of what kind of palatial residences and pleasure grounds may be expected in the future we will notice one of the many now existing, the Oak Knoll Farm.

The Oak Knoll Farm, of which Mr. R. B. Woodward is the present proprietor, originally formed a part of the grant known as the Rancho de Napa. It came into the possession of Otto H. Frank, and was in 1858 transferred by him to J. W. Osborn, afterwards assassinated by a desperado named Brittan. In 1862 it was sold to the present proprietor for the sum of $61,976.85. The main farm, as given to the Assessor in 1872, consists of 1583 acres. This is rich valley land, and is under the highest state of culture. One of the largest orchards in the State is here set out, and the pleasure grounds about the buildings are richly supplied with the choicest evergreens, flowers and shrubbery. In 1872 the present palatial residence was erected. Mr. Woodward, as the proprietor of Woodward's Gardens, in San Francisco, is too well known to need any notice here. He is justly esteemed one among Napa's best citizens. He has since living in Napa, identified his interests with those of the county and has done much to advance the general prosperity.

The population of Napa county is now estimated by the most accurate calculators who are acquainted in the county at between 11,000 and 12,000 inhabitants. This is a meagre number compared to what it is capable of supporting. There are now hundreds of acres only partially cultivated that might, and ere long will be utilized to support a greatly increased population. When the re-

(217)

sources of the soil are more full developed by not making the cereals such a specialty, but by planting more fields in mulberries; carrying on the culture of flax, ramie, jute, or other textiles; by paying more attention to the supplying of the market, as we are capable of doing, with choice dried and canned fruits and raisins; by devoting more acres to the culture of hops; by increasing the extent and quality of our vineyards; and by starting and maintaining the varied branches of industry for which nature has specially endowed us, we may know that we will be on the highway to a successful career.

The prices for land vary greatly, according to the quality, the nearness to the railroad, and other circumstances. The rich bottom lands, lying along near the line of the railroad, or near the towns, commands a high price, ranging from $50 to $150 per acre without improvements. Vineyards are valued according to the age of the vine and the kind, and to their location, whether on high or low land, for from $300 to $800 per acre. But, the lands lying along the foot-hills, finely adapted to the grape or to sericulture, are much cheaper. In Gordon, Berryessa, Pope, Chiles, Conn, and many parts of Napa, such lands rate at from $5 to $25 per acre, according to quality and position. The tule lands rate low on account of the out lay necessary to their reclamation. The cost of reclamation is not very heavy, and then they become the most valuable.

THE LABOR PROBLEM.

One of the most important questions presented to the agriculturist is that of labor. The farmers frequently find it impossible to get laborers to perform their work. A great portion of the labor employed during the vintage in picking and shipping grapes is Chinese. People are not favorably disposed to these Asiatics, but often find themselves reduced to the necessities of accepting these or none. There is no State in the Union where the laborer has so easy a time as in California, but this very fact has an injurious effect upon the laborer. It is harder here to find good and trustworthy laborers than elsewhere. Few think farther than the best means of shirking responsible labor, of getting the largest sum and making the least return therefor. Many, after the week's work is over, stroll away to

(218)

dens of vice and crime, to come away, by no means benefitted.

And frequently, those who claim to be laborers can not be induced to leave these haunts to accept the best position in the country. They prefer lounging around town, doing little jobs to gain a bare subsistence in the cities, than leaving for the interior. They waste their energy in complaining of hard times and cursing the Chinese, while they use no efforts to do anything for themselves. Especially does it seem that in the matter of house servants it is an utter impossibility to get white persons; and the scarcity of these teaches the Chinese to be more insolent and more exacting. It is next to an impossibility to induce a female servant to leave the city and go into the country, at any wages. Of course there are many exceptions, but this is the rule.

The mere fact that Chinese have obtained positions does not explain the scarcity of good white laborers. We know politicians have harped upon the wrongs of the white laborers on account of the employment of Chinese, but it has been merely to gain a few votes. The cause for the condition of the laborers, and their scarcity cannot be accounted for on the mere fact of the presence of the Chinee.

The system of farm labor pursued in California is, in our estimation, chiefly responsible. Farmers have no occasion to employ laborers but a few months in the year. During the season of seeding and harvest laborers are in great demand, but when the rush is over, they are dismissed. Between these two seasons come long periods when it is impossible to get employment. Some may get jobs of cutting wood, a few may be retained as permanent hands on large farms, but the majority are set adrift, to get work for a subsistence as best they may. Thus from the severest of all farm labor, harvesting, the laborer is thrown into complete idleness. Of these some drift off into other States, some seek other occupations, while others, generally the majority, seek the towns, and by performing little jobs, and by the multifarious ways known to the loafers around a town, eke out a subsistence, and never dream of their importance except about election times.

Such alternate changing from severe toil to utter idleness is demoralizing to the best of men. If it is hard for those who are busy

(219)

to act right, how hard shall it be for these who are idle such a large part of the time? And this enforced idleness is in no wise the result of the presence of the Chinese.

The remedy for this state of affairs, is to be found in a more varied agriculture, and sources of labor. Break up the great wheat growing mania, and diversify the work so that it will not, as now, come in two seasons of the year, but extend the year round. Open manufactures and such as depend in some considerable degree upon agriculture, and a better day will dawn upon us. At present, comparatively few can purchase lands and become producers. It is useless to seek for immigration, for the laboring portion of the people can see, in farm labor in this State, nothing but alternately the most enervating idleness and the most exhausting labor. The "bone and sinew" of other States and countries dread to come among us, not that they fear to compete with Chinamen, but that they fear they cannot find labor, because it is not.

If our State would progress and consummate the glorious achievements the future has in store for her, something must be done to ameliorate the condition of farm labor. We must have more intelligent laborers, and we must have some means of giving them employment more than a moiety of the year. This we cannot do so long as we remain so exclusively a wheat growing people. Unless we introduce new kinds of agricultural production, new sources of employment for labor, we need not expect much immigration from abroad; we need not expect to find better nor greater numbers of laborers; and we must, instead of deprecating the presence of the Chinese, look upon them as the only possible class that can be had to perform a very great part of our work.

One of the greatest drawbacks that Napa now has is the want of manufactures. True, there are a few. Various agricultural implements are manufactured here, not only to supply the home demand but also that of other counties. The vineyard plows patented by M. P. Rose of Carneros, and by J. C. Potter of St. Helena, and the gang plows of the Manuels of Napa City, are widely known and growing in favor. The planing mills, first started by H. T. Barker and the Groat Brothers, now owned by J. A. Jackson & Co., is doing excellent work. But when these and a few others are counted, the

(220)

list of our manufactures is numbered. Napa presents more facilities for successfully carrying on various kinds of manufactories than most other places in the State. Besides the facilities of the railroad for travel, all the conveniences of water privileges are afforded. Rents are low, fuel is cheap and abundant, and nothing but the capital and enterprise are lacking to make Napa an important manufacturing place. There probably is no place in the State where a beet sugarie could be started with more assurances of success. This and many other industries could easily be started here.

But, so far, those in the town and county who view such enterprises as feasible, and who would be willing to engage in them, have not had a sufficiency of capital to guarantee commencing operations. There is an abundance of capital, but those who control it rarely think of the material growth of the town and county. Instead of developing the resources of the county by investing their capital here, giving employment to more mechanics and more laborers, creating a home market for more of the agricultural products that are now shipped away, and supplying the people with many of the necessities of life, now imported, they only seek the best securities and the highest rate of interest for their loans. They are particularly interested in nothing except the perfect security of one and a quarter per cent per month. It is a great convenience to farmers at times to get a loan; but instead of having a number of capitalists who, leech-like, live off the substance of the community and add nothing thereto, how much better it would be to have men who would work to do away with the necessities of borrowing by making the community more prosperous? But the natural advantages of the place so recommend it to the people that we feel confident that at no distant day capitalists from abroad will be found who will build up these industries.

LAKE COUNTY

144

(223)

UNCLE SAM MOUNTAIN LOOKING FROM LAKEPORT.

CHAPTER I.

GENERAL DESCRIPTION.

The territory now known as Lake county, was first included in the Northern District of California, and upon the formation of Napa county, composed the northern portion thereof. It is bounded on the North by Colusa and Mendocino, South by Napa and Sonoma, East by Colusa and Yolo, and West by Mendocino and Sonoma. It is about twenty-five miles wide by seventy-five miles long. This county has the most natural boundaries of any other one in the State. The whole of it lies between two main branches of the Coast Range. The mountains to the West are a continuation of the Mayacamas;

(224)

those on the East are locally known as the Bear Mountains. Both these ranges are formed of narrow ridges of broken mountains, and present some of the most magnificent scenery. From the beauty and grandeur of the scenery, this county has justly been named the Switzerland of America. The culminating point to the South is Mt. St. Helena; to the North, Mt. St. John, near four thousand feet high but near the upper end of Clear Lake rises Mt. Ripley, which, next to Mt. St. Helena, is the highest peak in the range. Bounded on all sides by mountains, the arable land of the county is in the valleys between these ranges. Lying about the center of the county is Clear Lake-one of the most beautiful of mountain lakes. It derives its name from the clearness of its waters. It is about twenty-five miles long, with an average width of seven miles, and divided into the Upper and Lower Lakes by the peak called Uncle Sam, situated on the Southern side of the lake, and about equidistant from the Northern and Southern extremities. Rising, abrubtly to a hight nearly two, thousand six hundred feet above the lake, and extending one of its arms therein, forms "The Narrows"-one and a half miles in width and some two miles long, and connecting the Upper and Lower Lakes, the whole composing Clear Lake. This body of water is much the shape of an old-fashioned silk purse-the well-filled extremities forming, or representing, the Upper and Lower Lakes, the ring in the center "The Narrows." The water is cool, clear as crystal and pleasant to the taste, generally placid, varying in depth from eighteen to one hundred and twenty feet. Pike, blackfish, pearch, trout, suckers, silver-sides and many other varieties of the finny tribe abound in both lakes. The water fowls are only plenty during the winter season.

Clear Lake is estimated to have an elevation of about 1,500 feet above the sea level. It is sixty-five miles from Suisun Bay, and thirty-six from the Pacific Ocean.

Northwest of Uncle Sam Mountain, rising gradually from the lake and tending to the upper end of the main valley, is a fertile tract known as Big Valley. In this valley are situated Kelseyville and Lakeport. It is crossed by several small streams, the largest of which is Kelsey Creek. North of Lakeport, and separated from Big Valley by a low range of hills, is Scott Valley. Extending around to the

(225)

northern part of the lake to the little town of Upper Lake is a small area of arable land lying between the lake and the mountains. On the eastern side of the lake the mountains extend down close to the water, so that there is but little arable land. A great many streams flow down into the lake, and there is to most of these small bottoms of fine rich land.

The Blue Lakes, covering an area of about four square miles, are situated about five miles northwest of Clear Lake, and twelve from Lakeport on the road to Ukiah. During the wet seasons they are connected with Clear Lake. The water is a beautiful sea blue and of a wonderful depth. They are surrounded by high rugged mountains, which are covered with large pine and fir trees, whose silvery tinged tops are rocked "high in the ethereal air" by the gentle motion of the mountain breeze. The eastern shore is sheltered by very high mountains even to the water's edge, while on the western side there are pretty little nooks with cottages presenting a beautiful view from the grade, which is several hundred feet above the level of the lake. These lakes, according to Indian tradition, have in their waters a huge monster resembling a half fish and half horse, to which they are pleased to give the euphoneous appellation of Devil Fish. Different reports as to size of this monster vary the length from ten to twenty feet. Its presence in the lake, according to Indian history, is some hundred years. The monster is held in great dread by the Indians. It is said to make its appearance on the surface of the water only once in ten years. It is asserted that his presence is followed by great calamities befalling the Indians. This monster, or Devil Fish, was seen by the Indians in March, 1872; hence large gatherings of all the tribes, congregating in Big Valley, on the shore of Clear Lake, to indulge in a grand pow-wow and making peace offerings to the Great Spirit, to appease his anger and avert the pending evils hanging over their wigwams. The hotel erected on the margin of these lakes is quite a paying institution in the summer season.

At the southern extremity of Clear Lake is the town of Lower Lake, and the surrounding agricultural country. A short distance east of the narrow arm of Clear Lake, and separated from it by a low ridge, is Borax Lake. This is a beautiful sheet of water, its

(226)

surface smooth and bright as burnished silver, covering from two to four hundred acres, according to the season of the year. The mountains through Lake and Napa counties are of metamorphic cretaceous formation, but around Clear Lake there is unmistakable evidence of volcanic action. The hills around Borax Lake are of volcanic materials heaped loosely together, and consist in great part of scoriae obsidian, and pumice stone. The appearance of the land indicates this lake at one time extended much farther to the southeast. The land for nearly a mile to the southeast is raised but a very little above the level of the lake, and wells sunk in it fill with water similar to that of the lake, and rise and fall similarly. The waters of the lake contain in solution a large per cent. of borax, carbonate of soda, and chloride of sodium. The land lying about the lake was located by the California Borax Company, and was first worked by W. S. Jacks, of Napa City, for this company in 1864. The manufacture of borax in large quantities was carried on till in 1869, a disagreement among the members of the company occurred, and work was stopped.

Dr. J. A. Veatch in 1859 discovered the Lake and detected the presence of borax, but it was not till some time afterwards that the existence of large beds of crystals of this valuable material was discovered. On the bottom of the lake is a jelly-like bed of black mud, some three feet thick. This mud contains large quantities of the crystals of biborate of soda. Underlying this bed of mud is a layer of blue clay, also containing large quantities of these crystals. It has been ascertained by experiments that the mud and clay as far down as tested, about sixty feet, are highly charged with this material. There is another smaller lake, Little Borax Lake, situated a short distance Southwest of Clear Lake, just at the foot of Uncle Sam mountain. There are numerous Springs and small ponds lying in other parts of the county, also highly charged with borax.

The Sulphur Banks is another feature of great interest, as showing not only the geological formation of this county, but its commercial value. It lies about a mile beyond the ridge bordering Borax Lake, and near a small arm of Clear Lake. The Banks cover an area of near 40,000 square yards, and from beneath them

(227)

appear to flow the hot borate springs found near by. It consists of decomposed volcanic rock splintered and fissured in innumerable places. Through these fissures gas and steam are constantly issuing. All over this mass large quantities of sulphur have been deposited, and solfatara is still going on. At a little distance this mass looks like solid sulphur. On being refined it yields about eighty per cent. of pure brilliant sulphur. Near the Sulphur Banks on the edge of the Lake is a hot borate spring which is estimated by Dr. Veatch to yield three hundred gallons per minute, and the waters of which percolate through the sands over an area of 75 by 150 feet. The flow of the water, however, seems to vary according to the season. The waters of this Spring are of such a remarkable character that we here subjoin an analysis of them made by Mr. Moore:

	Grains in one gallon.
Chloride of potassium	trace.
Chloride of sodium	84.62
Iodide of magnesium	.09
Bromide of magnesium	trace.
Bicarbonate of soda	76.96
Bicarbonate of ammonia	107.76
Biborate of soda	103.29
Sulphate of lime	trace.
Alumina	1.26
Carbonic acid (free)	36.37
Silicic acid	8.23

Matters volatile at a red heat 65.77

$$\overline{484.35}$$

Prof. J. D. Whitney, State Geologist, makes the following remarks on this spring:

"In this table the constituents are necessarily calculated as anhydrous salts; the biborate of soda, however, contains about 47 per cent. of water when crystallized, and the 103.29 grains given above correspond to 195.35 of crystallized borax. The most extraordinary feature in the above analysis is the very large amount of ammoniacal salts shown to be present in this water, in this respect exceeding any natural spring water which has ever been analyzed. Mr. Moore thinks that, as in the case of the boracic acid waters of Tuscany, this

(228)

ammoniacal salt may be separated and made available for economical purposes. This locality is worthy of a most careful examination to ascertain how considerable a flow of water can be depended on."

One of the most wonderful features connected with the Sulphur Banks is a large spring, boiling and bubbling up as a mighty cauldron, but which, though in the immediate vicinity of the Banks and the hot borate springs, is almost cold as ice. This spring was opened or discovered in 1871 in the following manner: One of the men was digging sulphur just above it, when suddenly the earth gave way under his feet, and he fell in up to his arm-pits, and having his arms extended was all that saved the poor fellow from going down in this bottomless well or cave beneath. This commotion of the water, this rolling and boiling, is always the same-the bulk of the water never increasing or diminishing. The gas from it is so strong as to almost take the breath. In fact, when it was first opened birds flying over it would drop dead. Hares, rabbits, and many animals were killed here by approaching too near and inhaling this gas.

Petroleum has been found in large quantities in several parts of Lake county, but nothing of a commercial value has been discovered.

Between the Clear lake valley and Napa county lie Coyote and Loconoma Valleys. These are small valleys mostly used for pasture lands. Guenoc is the only town in Coyote, and Middletown the only one in Loconoma. There are various mineral springs throughout the county, which are becoming celebrated for their medicinal virtues. A notice of these will be found elsewhere in this volume.

Cobb Valley, one of the most beautiful valleys in the county, lies on the road between Kelseyville and Calistoga. Cobb Muontain, nearly of equal altitude with Mt. St. Helena, lies west of this valley and Pine Mountain, and the cinnabar region to the east.

(229)

CHAPTER II.

HISTORICAL SKETCH.

The first white settlers in Lake county were Kelsey and Stone, who, in the year 1847, drove a large band of stock into what they christened "Big Valley." Ranching their stock in this valley seems to have been their only intention, as they made no efforts at cultivation of the soil, nor did they erect any buildings. Their intercourse with the Indians-the Mayacamas tribe-seems to have been friendly until December, 1849, at which time they (Kelsey and Stone) were murdered by the natives near the present site of Kelseyville.

In 1851 a party of U. S. troops under command of Capt. Lyon, consisting of infantry and cavalry, and having two pieces of ordnance, arrived at the outlet of Clear Lake-Cache Creek. Finding no Indians in the Lower Lake country, the infantry and ordnance were sent by boats to the Upper Lake, the cavalry, going by land around

(230)

the west margin of Clear Lake. A junction was made on the north shore of the Upper Lake, near which the Indians had assembled in a strong natural position, from which they deemed it impossible they could be dislodged. The cannon was brought into use, loaded with grape and cannister, and at the first discharge produced the utmost dismay among the Indians. Resistance was forgotten, flight seemed their only safety, and they "stood not on the order of their going." The cavalry followed and cut down all alike. About two hundred were slain, without the loss of even one white man. In 1852 Capt. Estell arrived in the Lake country with the "peace and treaty mission," and succeeded in making a treaty that has not to this day been broken. After the expedition of 1851, under Capt. Lyon, many persons visited the country, some on hunting tours, some prospecting and some hunting homes. Among the latter were C. N. Copsey and L. W. Purkerson, in the Summer of 1851. In 1853 these two men returned, and on the 12th day of February commenced building a house near the head of Cache Creek--the only outlet of Clear Lake-which building still stands, being now near the town of Lower Lake, and the first erected in Lake county. During the same year Jeff Warden settled on Scott Creek, in what is now called Scott's Valley.

In April, 1854, a party of emigrants arrived in Big Valley and settled along the lake shore. In this company were Martin Hammack and family, Brice Hammack and wife, Woods Crawford and wife, John T. Shinn, J. B. and W. S. Cook. Of these were the first white women in the county. The following Summer came W. B. Elliott and family, Ben Duell and family, and others, who settled on the northwest of the Upper Lake, near the present town of Danville. Here was erected the first grist mill in the county.

In 1853 Capt. Steele and R. H. Sterling commenced the erection of what is now known as the Rock House in Coyote Valley. In June, 1854, they moved into the house and occupied it till 1856. At the time Mrs. Sterling came on the ranch to live, there were but two or three other ladies living in what are at present the bounds of Lake county, and she would be for several weeks, sometimes, without seeing the face of a white woman, except when she went to Napa Valley.

(231)

The first school in the county, was opened by Mrs. Parmley, in 1855. The first public school was opened two years after by Mr. Walter Revis, near where the present fine, large public school house at Lakeport now stands.

In 1857 the population of the country now known as Lake, but then a portion of Napa, had increased to some two hundred. The nearest officer was the magistrate at St. Helena, distant some sixty miles. This year a new township, that of Clear Lake, was created and Woods Crawford was elected justice of the Peace, and John T. Shinn as Constable. On the 21st of May, 1861, the county of Lake was created by Act of the Legislature. The first election held after the organization of Lake county resulted in the election of W. W. Pendegast, joint Senator; John C. Crigler, Member of Assembly; O. A. Munn, County Judge; W. R. Mathews, County Clerk; W. H. Manlove, Sheriff;

W. A. Marshall, District Attorney. Marshall never qualified for the office, and Woods Crawford filled the position. The records of Lake county were all destroyed on the night of February 16, 1867, when the Court House at Lakeport was burned. For this reason no election returns previous to that date can be given. However, at the first election Lakeport was chosen as county seat, and two years later, in pursuance of an Act of the Legislature, an election was held to re-decide the same question, Lakeport and Lower Lake being the contestants, when, as before, Lakeport was successful. Below is given election returns from 1867 to 1872 inclusive:

THE ELECTION OF 1867.

Sheriff-W. H. Manlove*, 412; Isaac Alter[r], 307. Co. Clerk- S. Bynum*, 520; Z. Cushman[r], 222. District Attorney-S. K. Welch*, 508; L. D. Winchester[r], 234. Treasurer-W. S. Cook*, 519; J. G. Manning[r], 58. Assessor-H. H. Nunnally*, 463; W. H. Goldsmith[r], 266. Co. Surveyor-J. N. Chapman*, 438; L. W. Music[r], 277. (* Democrats, [r] Republicans.) At the Presidential election of 1868, Seymour received 452 and Grant 248 votes.

The election of September, 1869, was as follows: Member of Assembly- J. C. Crigler, D., 408; J. E. Pond, R., 68. Sheriff-T.
(232)
B. Burger, D., 411. Co. Clerk-S. Bynum, D., 432 - Treasurer- W. S. Cook, D., 429. Assessor-H. H. Nunnally, D., 336; W. H. Goldsmith, R., 26; R. Kennedy, R., 91. Sup't. Public Schools-M. Mathews, D., 240; H. W. Turner, R., 135- Co. Surveyor-Geo. Tucker, D. 418. Coroner-W. R. Mathews, D., 240; Geo. Bucknell, R., 123. Public Administrator-Joel Jenkins, D., 394. County Site-Lower Lake, 375; Lakeport, 368.

The result of the general election in September, 1871, was as follows: Sheriff--T. B. Burger, D., 502; A. B. Ritchie, R., 285. Co. Clerk-S. Bynum, D., 788. District Attorney-Woods Crawford, D., 447; W. D. Morton, R., 289. Treasurer-J. W. Everett, D., 403, W. S. Cook, Ind't. D., 372. Assessor-Hiram Allen, D., 771. Sup't. Public Schools-Mack Mathews, D., 758. Co. Surveyor-Geo. Tucker, D., 785. Public Administrator-J. O'Shea, D., 455. Coroner-H. H. Sull, D., 479.

At the Presidential election, 1872, the vote was: Greeley, 355; Grant, 202. For Congress-J. K. Luttrell, D., 456; J. M. Coghlan, R., 142.

It will be recollected that in 1869 the choice of county seat, was in favor of Lower Lake, that place having a majority of seven votes. This election was contested on the ground that fraud was practiced at Lower Lake. While in the Courts, and before a decision was had, by Act of the Legislature an election was held May 2d, 1870, to determine this question. The result was: For Lakeport, 479; Lower Lake, 404 votes. This result once more brought the county seat to Lakeport. In the latter part of May, 1870, the removal was made.

On account of the uncertainty of the "county town," no public buildings had been erected, and the consequence was that the Baptist Church was now used as a Courtroom. New public buildings were at once, however, put in process of erection, and in the Fall of 1871 a neat, roomy substantial brick Court House and Jail were completed. This building contains offices for all the county officials, besides a good Court-room, well furnished. The public square, upon which the Court House and County Jail stand, is now being enclosed and ornamented, and will compare favorably with the improvements of many older and wealthier counties.

(233)

During 1864 the "Bensley Water Company," sometimes called "Clear Lake Water Works," whose ostensible aim was, and is, to convey water from Clear Lake to the city of San Francisco, commenced building a dam across Cache Creek, near the lake. This dam, constructed for the purpose of obtaining motive power for their extensive mills, being on the only outlet to the Lake, caused the waters thereof to rise about thirteen feet above the medium hight. Thousands of acres of naturally dry land, and of great fertility, was thereby overflowed and rendered worthless to the owners. Many suits for damages were instituted against "the Company," but some were compromised, some dropped, and none prosecuted to judgment. On the 14th of October, 1868, some three hundred armed men arrived at the works of the Company, tore out the dam, removed the machinery from the mills, and the buildings were that night destroyed by fire. The "Bensley Water Company" instituted suit against the county of Lake to recover $200,000. after many delays the suit was set for the May (1873) term of the District Court in Yolo county.
(234)

CHAPTER III.

SOURCES OF WEALTH.

Lake has several important sources of wealth. In the Southwest portion are several quicksilver mines that prospect well, and will doubtless prove of great importance. Several mines have at different times been located in the county, and some of them are now being developed. One of the most important of these mines is the American, situated on Pine Mountain about seven miles Southwest of Middletown. It was discovered by John McFarland, of St. Helena, but was not worked till in 1871, when it fell into the hands of Messrs. Lawley, Lamdin, Perchbaker, and others. The St. Louis Mine is situated a short distance Northeast of the American. As early as 1861, considerable interest was manifested in quicksilver mining in this county. Companies were formed and much work done. The "Cincinnati," "Dead Broke," "Pittsburg," "Pioneer," and "Denver" were some of the claims located about this time all lying near Pine Mountain. On the road from Lower Lake to Sui-
(235)
sun, about eighteen miles from the former place, is situated the "Lake Mine," and a few miles further down the "Excelsior Mine." These mines were worked as early as 1863. Although the mines in the county have been known and some of them worked so many years, yet no adequate works have been erected, so as to develop any of them. Judging from the prospects so far as made, it is thought that Lake is destined to be one of the foremost quicksilver producing counties in the State. Silver and gold bearing quartz have been found in several parts of the county, but nothing of value has yet been discovered.

The only minerals that so far have been obtained in sufficient quantities to become remunerative are borax and sulphur. The California Borax Company during the time they had their works in operation shipped large quantities of borax. The demand for the borax is very great, and it is to be hoped that the Company will soon resume operation. They now have probably $200,000 worth of machinery lying idle, rusting away and becoming worthless. And this not because there is any doubt of the remunerative character of the business, but because of a disagreement among the members of the Company. Dr. Ayres is doing a successful business refining and shipping borax from Little Borax Lake. At the Sulphur Banks extensive works are erected refining the crude sulphur, and are producing about fifteen hundred tons of pure sulphur annually.

Although there is a large area of fine arable land in the county, yet the distance from market has prevented much attention from being devoted to agriculture. Grain is grown to supply the demand of the inhabitants and to feed to stock, but for no other purpose.

No accurate agricultural reports are accessible, it is probable they have never been regularly made.

The first farming was commenced in 1854. In 1866 the number of acres of land enclosed was 46,963.

In 1866 the number of acres of land under cultivation was 4,500

" 1867 "   "   "   "   "   "   "   "   "   5,160

" 1868 "   "   "   "   "   "   "   "   "   8,730

" 1870 "   "   "   "   "   "   "   "   "   12,000

" 1872 "   "   "   "   "   "   "   "   "   13,652

" 1872 "   "   "   "   "   "   enclosed   "   90,614

(236)

The small grains predominate, and an average yield of thirty bushels per acre is in general received. Indian corn is cultivated largely in the Northwest portion of the county.

Stock raising is the chief source of natural wealth outside of the mines. The hills are devoted to stock, and so much of the valleys as are not used for the production of grain, etc., to supply domestic demands, is used for the same purpose. Around the lake are some of the finest dairies any where to be found. Butter and cheese are produced and shipped in large quantities. The rich land bordering the lake seems especially adapted to grazing. Clear Lake cheese is recognized in the markets as the finest that can be found.

Viniculture and fruit growing on account of high rates of transportation, has been confined to domestic demands. The soil and climate are proven, however, especially adapted to these branches of farming, and now that railroad connection is drawing the county nearer the great marts of the State, vineyards and fruit orchards begin to clothe the hill sides that heretofore have produced naught but a poor quality of grass. The quality of the grapes and fruits are extolled by all acquainted with them. The vineyards of Lake are expected to render fertile many hills that have long "lain beneath the curse of God, and naught produced."

(237)

VIEW OF HARBIN SPRINGS.

CHAPTER IV.

TOWNS AND WATERING PLACES.

The mountains of Lake county are prolific of mineral springs. At several of these, hotels and cottages have been erected for the accommodation of visitors. The most prominent of these are, Bartlett's, Adam's, Caldwell's, and Sigler's. It is claimed that ten thousand persons visited these different resorts last Summer, (1872), and that as many as five hundred remained during the Winter. Wonderful cures have been effected, and as the report of a county official to a State officer remarks, "These springs are death on rheumatism." The proprietors of these different resorts claim to have effected cures at their springs for all diseases except those of a pulmonary nature. Their fame has gone out far and wide. Each season increases the number that come, and those who go away rejoicing. Good roads to all these resorts connect with the railroads at Calistoga and at Cloverdale.
(238)

––––––––

LAKEPORT.

Lakeport, the county seat of Lake county, is situated on the Western shore of Clear Lake, and in Big Valley. Distant from Calistoga, forty miles; from Lower Lake, twenty-five miles; from Cloverdale and Ukiah, twenty-five miles each. Its first name was Forbestown, from the fact that Mr. Forbes, who still resides here, had bought the tract of land on which the town was built, of Mr. Wm. S. Cook, who had purchased it of the United States in 1858. Mr. Forbes built a dwelling house and a blacksmith and wagon shop. As early as 1855, there was a store established about one-fourth of a mile below the present town, by Mr. Smith, now a merchant of Kelseyville, eight miles below. The county buildings add much to the place. Besides the splendid Court House, on a beautiful knoll is situated a fine Public School House, which is a credit to the district. The upper story, is used by the Odd Fellows and Good Templars as a Lodge Room. The population is about three hundred. There are six stores, two saloons, two hotels, one livery stable, two blacksmith and wagon shops, one gun shop, one jeweller, three churches, Lodges of the Masonic, Odd Fellow and Good Templar societies, and one public school building. During the past year there were erected in Lakeport eight dwelling houses, two stores and one saloon building, and one grist mill. The business of the town is steadily increasing, and real estate continually advancing in price. The Lakeport mills have now in operation one of the finest and most complete establishments North of San Francisco. This establishment, with the planing and moulding machines attached, is a well supplied long-felt want. A daily mail is in connection with Cloverdale, also express over same line, and tri-weekly with Calistoga and Ukiah.

LOWER LAKE.

Lower Lake is a beautiful village near five miles from Clear Lake at its Southern extremity. The population is about two hundred. There are here four stores, two saloons, one hotel, two livery stables, blacksmith and other mechanical shops. The office of the Superintendent of the Bensley Water Company was long situated here, and that officer still remains, but except in attending to the landed inter-
(239)
ests of the Company, his occupation, like that of Othello's, seems gone. Near this place still stands the first house built in Lake county, giving Lower Lake clear title to the claim of the first town in the county. The Masons, Odd Fellows, and Good Templars have each an organization. A substantial Public School building serves also as a church.

Lower Lake is thirty miles from Calistoga, and is connected with it by a tri-weekly stage line, which connects here with stages for Lakeport, Adams and Sigler Springs, Cobb Valley, and Bartlett Springs.

MIDDLETOWN.

This is a small town situated in Loconoma Valley, sixteen miles from Calistoga and about the same from Lower Lake. It gets its importance from the travel passing through to the various springs. Besides the usual number of stores, shops, etc., there is a neat school house, a lodge of Odd Fellows, and one of Good Templars.

GUENOC.

This is a small town on the main road to Lower Lake. It is situated in Coyote Valley and is surrounded by a fine grazing and agricultural country.

BARTLETT SPRINGS.

The repute of this place has become, during the last few years, wonderful. Such almost miraculous cures have been effected that the halt and lame, the wearied clerk from the counting-room and the mere pleasure and sight-seeker, have flocked here by the thousands. They are situated east of Clear Lake, about twenty-five miles from Lower Lake. They were first discovered by Mr. Bartlett, the present owner, in 1868. He was then a resident of Cobb Valley, and was much afflicted with the rheumatism, so much so that one of his legs had become quite emaciated. In 1870 he went out to these Springs for the purpose of seeking relief in hunting. The water, of which he drank freely, caused him at first to become swollen and to lose the use of his limbs more than before; but this soon wore off and he rapidly recovered from his ailment.
(240)

A correspondent of the Napa *Reporter* who visited these Springs in the Fall of 1872, thus speaks of them :

"A '49 miner would suppose, should he suddenly come in sight of this place from the top of some of the high peaks surrounding it, that some lucky miner had made a rich strike, and that a mining camp had sprung up here. Even after arrival in the camp, it reminds one forcibly of early days in the mining camps of California. The cabins are built with posts set in the ground three feet apart and sided up with shakes or driven rods, and are from 14 to 16 feet square, most of them having nature for their floors. Of these there are about 40 and can be rented for $2 per week where they have no floors. A few have rough floors laid in them and they rent for $2.50 per week. The livery and feed stables are about the best looking buildings in the camp, and our horses were well cared for on very reasonable terms. There are almost ice cold springs in the camp, one of which furnishes the finest soda water we think we ever drank, and the other is the one which Mr. Bartlett used and which has cured so many persons almost miraculously. The basin, which is cleaned out and walled up, is, we judge, about three feet long, two feet wide and probably two and a quarter feet deep. The water in it is about two feet deep, and although there is a continual run of persons from early morning till late at night carrying the water away in buckets, jugs, demijohns and other vessels, yet the volume of water is never diminished in the least, that we could see, and it certainly is the most pleasant mineral water we ever drank in our lives. Only a partial analysis of the water has been made. It is known to contain sulphur, carbon, magnesia, manganese, potassium and calcium. There are other springs in the vicinity. About 1 1/2 miles Westerly is one called the Soap Spring. It is about twenty-five feet long, twelve feet wide and six feet deep, with a natural wall of boulders on all sides of it, forming a splendid plunge or swimming bath. Its waters are known to contain borax, soda, salt and sulphur. The temperature is very pleasant for bathing. It is tepid. A few feet from it is another fine spring containing iron, soda and salt; temperature 85° Very near to this is a very cold spring of splendid water. One and a quarter miles in a Northerly direction from the Bartlett is a very singular spring known as the Gas Spring. The strong gas issuing
(241)
from it is the same as met with at the Sulphur Banks. No water flows from it, and the quantity of water never increases or diminishes, but is continually in motion, as if it were boiling. The

sound, as of escaping steam, may be heard for a considerable distance from the spring. The water is intensely cold. This spring is noted for the curing of corns."

––––––––

BEAUTIFUL SCENERY.

The same writer thus speaks of the road from Bartlett Springs to Upper Lake, on the way to Lakeport:

The country through which we pass is unsurpassably beautiful. The road is in good order and runs for the greater part through finely timbered country composed mostly of tall, straight pine trees, many of them 80 to 100 feet without knot or limb, and straight as an arrow. Mountain quail may be seen at almost every turn, and the large, handsome, graceful grey squirrel may be seen springing from limb to limb on these tall pines, and occasionally the fleet-footed deer is seen gracefully bounding over the hills. The picture is ever changing along this beautiful road. Here a beautiful, smooth, symmetrical hill, covered with tall stately pines or noble oaks with their wide-spreading branches, affording shade for the herds of cattle and sheep which roam over these hills, making the landscape all the more cheerful. On the other hand we behold bold, precipitous rocky peaks, giving wild romantic beauty. And again, we have presented to our view high cone-shaped hills or peaks covered with immense boulders, and in one or two instances we noticed a hill or peak of this kind on the very top of which was a large boulder surmounted by a beautiful green tree. Taken altogether, the scenery between Bartlett Springs and the upper end of Clear Lake is grand and picturesque in the extreme, and well repays the tourist a visit. From the mountains we came down into a very fertile little valley known as Clover Valley, through which we pass into the head of Lake Valley, where we find as rich land as can be found in California, with large corn and grain fields, while cheerful looking farm-houses greet us on every hand. Tall, straight oak trees may be seen from 30 to 40 feet without limb or knot. We noticed large farms or ranches (242) which had been fenced with rails made from this kind of timber, something not very common in California.

––––––––

HARBIN SPRINGS.

This is fast becoming one of the most pleasant and best patronized watering places on the coast. It is located about four miles from Middletown, and is well provided with all the conveniences for making guests comfortable. Not only are there suitable hotel accommodations, but also a plat of ground set apart and always kept clean for the use of those who prefer coming in their own wagons and camping out. The waters of the springs were used by the Indians long before the settlement of the country by whites, on account of the cures effected. The springs were discovered in 1852 by Messrs. Ritchie and Harbin. The land belonged to the United States at this time, and was entered by them. Some two or three weeks after the discovery of the springs they built a small house near them which was occupied by Mr. Harbin as a dwelling-house; he soon after bought Mr. Ritchie's interest, and in 1860 built a new house with five bath rooms in the lower part immediately over the springs used by the Indians for bathing. The building has since been removed and fitted up as a lodging house. In 1866 Messrs. Hughs & Williams purchased this property from Mr. Harbin for the sum of $3,000. Some years afterwards Mr. Williams bought the interest of Mr. Hughs. Since this time he has built several cosy little cottages and a commodious hotel capable of accommodating about one hundred and thirty persons comfortably. There are quite a number of springs of different temperatures, but most of them highly impregnated with iron, magnesia, and sulphur. The waters are much liked for drinking, and afford delightful baths. The climate about these springs is mild and pleasant. The thermometer rarely ever, even on the warmest days rises above 100^0, and generally stands much lower. The evenings are always cool and refreshing. Last Summer, (1872), 1000 people visited this retreat.

_____

ADAMS SPRING.

This spring is situated about four miles from Cobb Valley, and connected with it by a good road. There are rude accommodations
(243)
erected, like those at Bartlett Springs for the use of visitors., The water, on first tasting has a strong odor and taste of coal oil, though after a little use most persons become quite fond of it. There is only one spring here, but it furnishes a large quantity of water. The spring has been known for a few years only, but has now become a favorite resort, especially for those afflicted with the rheumatism. An analysis of the water shows that there is a large proportion of the carbonates of magnesia, lime, soda, and iron, also a considerable percentage of chloride of sodium and silica, besides traces of salt of potash and nitric acid. It contains a large amount of pure carbonic acid gas. Mr. Adams, the discoverer, sold the property in the Fall of 1872 to two of the Whitton brothers of Yountville, Napa county. These gentlemen have erected additional accommodations and expect a large travel to this place.

_____

SIGLER SPRINGS.

One of the oldest and most well tried of the many Springs in the lake region is Sigler Spring. These are situated about six miles Westerly from Lower Lake. The waters are highly recommended for their medicinal virtues, the surroundings for their beauty and the climate for its salubrity. Good accommodations are here furnished for tourists.

_____

CALDWELL SPRINGS.

These Springs are situated about eight miles from Lakeport, near the road towards Cloverdale. There are fifty or more of these Springs which burst from the banks of Limestone Creek. An analysis shows them to be impregnated with sulphate of magnesia, carbonate of magnesia, muriate sodium, carbonate manganese, potassium, silica and calcium, containing a trace of sulphur, and highly charged with carbonic acid gas. These Springs have been known for several years as a neighborhood resort for invalids afflicted with various chronic diseases, and many remarkable cures have been effected. No improvements or accommodations for the public had been made

until they were purchased last Summer by Dr. Caldwell. The baths are very invigorating, the water from some of the springs being warm enough for a pleasant bath, just as it flows from the springs. Visitors
(244)
can choose the waters that best suit individual cases, or as their feelings may indicate. The situation is a very pretty one, and the hills and mountains surrounding are very romantic and picturesque. Small game is quite abundant, and occasionally deer may be found in the hills and the fishing in the neighborhood is fine. These Springs may be reached daily from Cloverdale, Sonoma county, by stage, or from Kelseyville, Lake county. It may be remarked that an old bath tub at these Springs which has been in use for about ten years, is almost entirely petrified; the sides and bottom have become beautiful hard stone, having the appearance of quartz.

––––––––

SODA BAY.

Soda Bay is situated at the base of Uncle Sam Mountain. It consists of a considerable area covered by shallow water of the lake, over which bubble up great numbers of springs of the finest soda water. These Soda Springs are found both on the land and in the waters of the lake, and render this a delightful retreat. The bathing in this Soda Bay is fine and exhilerating. For sublimity and beauty of natural scenery it completely satisfies the beholder that he need look no farther to gratify his taste and imagination to the full. Nature seems here to have done her utmost to produce a scene combining all the elements of grandeur and beauty. A Bungalow cottage, surrounded with broad verandas, embowered in the shade of widespreading live oaks and rich-colored madronas, with their tropical verdure, rests on a gentle slope at the foot of a lofty mountain. In front is the silver-surfaced lake, with its many peninsulas and islands covered with green foliage. On the opposite shore the smooth brown sandstone mountain cones rise up in fanciful shapes, and beyond them are lofty mountains covered with an evergreen verdure. Taken as a whole, it is a scene of beauty and enchantment.

––––––––

COBB VALLEY.

As a pleasant place to enjoy the bracing mountain breeze, cool fresh water, and the best of facilities for hunting and fishing, there are few places of more importance than Cobb Valley. The elevation of this little valley is about 2,500 feet, and, twenty-eight miles from Calistoga, is surrounded on all sides by tall pine-clad moun-
(245)
tains. A hotel and cottages have been erected to accommodate visitors. The heat never is severe and the nights are quite cool. At least the recollections of the writer is to that effect, especially the part about the cold nights. His memory brings up a night several years ago, before there was any hotel in the valley, when he found himself there overtaken by the darkness (and it gets very dark there) with nothing to eat and nothing but a saddle-blanket to keep him warm. He attributes all of his subsequent nervous insensibility to the severe test this night's freezing gave. From this valley it is only about twelve miles over a good mountain trail to the celebrated Geysers. We know

of no place on the Pacific Coast where a few weeks during the Summer could be more pleasantly spent than in this quiet little nook, or where kinder, more accommodating, or more pleasant people could be found with whom to stop.

IN GENERAL.

Besides the attractions of watering places, Lake county offers the finest inducements to hunters and fishers. Game of all kinds abound in the mountains, and an occasional bear is to be found. The mountain streams are filled with trout and the Lake with various kinds of fish. There have been many "large fish stories" related about the wonderful shoals of fish that swarm up the creeks from the Lake at certain seasons of the year, but none of them that we have heard are larger than the facts will warrant. In the late Winter and early Spring these shoals of fish from the lake have been so great that the whole body of the water seemed a living, moving mass of fish; and the jam among these shoals so great that stock in crossing the creeks have been known to kill large numbers. This is the Indian's harvest season. They congregate on the banks of streams and by constructing a kind of net or trap catch immense numbers of fish and dry them for Summer use. The person who visited the sweat house mentioned in the chapter on Indianology at the commencement of this volume, speaks of the scents to which his nostrils were regaled, but had he visited one of these rancherias in the fishing season, he would have thought that the odors of the sweat house as compared with those here experienced, were sweet as the ottar of roses.
(246)

The roads in Lake county are all good. The toll roads connecting at Calistoga and running to Lower Lake, and through Cobb Valley to Kelseyville; also the one connecting Lakeport with Cloverdale, are fine structures, built at great expense. There are good roads constructed to all of the watering places, and a fine toll road is now projected from Bartlett Springs to Colusa. From Lower Lake a road passes down to Berryessa Valley, and from the upper end of the valley another one passes through the mountain by way of the Blue Lakes to Ukiah.

MORAL AND SOCIAL STATUS.

The moral status of Lake is of such character that the jail is seldom used. The County Court criminal calendar will not average over one indictment annually. The religious societies are working hard and continually, especially so at Lakeport and Kelseyville. At Lakeport the churches of the Methodists and Catholics are good substantial frame buildings, neat on the exterior, roomy and comfortable within. The Baptist church is rather small, but otherwise a very suitable building. This edifice is to be torn away this Summer and either enlarged or rebuilt entirely.

At Kelseyville are two churches, Methodist and Catholic, both ornaments to the town, while that energetic young place will this Summer try to erect a brick building for the Presbyterian denomination. At Lower Lake, at Upper Lake and throughout the county, the public school buildings are used for Divine worship and for Sabbath schools.

Of the benevolent societies, the Masons and I. O. O. F. have each a Lodge building at Lower Lake, the former also a building in Lakeport, which latter is used by both Odd Fellow and Good

Templar societies also; the latter have an organization also at Kelseyville. All of these societies are in a flourishing condition.

The educational facilities of the county are mostly confined to the public schools. There are quite a number of schools in the county, all well attended, and taught by able teachers.

The population of Lake county has, since its first settlement, been steadily increasing, and now numbers about seven thousand. The fertile valleys offer special advantages to the farmer. The hills,

(247)

covered with good grass, are well adapted to stock-raising; mountains, covered with pine and fir forests, furnish lumbermen with employment; dairying proves a remunerative business; mining one of the greatest sources of wealth; and, above all, the climate is both healthful and pleasant. The seasons are regular, and total failures in agricultural pursuits unknown.

FINANCIAL CONDITION.

The financial condition is sound, notwithstanding the many impediments and the trouble through which it has passed. It is calculated that the final settlement of the Tax Collector for 1872 will pay all warrants drawn on the General Fund to the first of October, 1872. The following are the tax levies since 1867:

1868-County,	$2.75 per $100.	State	$1.00	per $100.
1869, "	2.53 " "	"	.97	" "
1870, "	3.03 " "	"	.97	" "
1871, "	2.73 " "	"	.86	" "
1872, "	1.09 " "	"	.50	" "

In 1871 expenses incident to building and furnishing public buildings, and other internal permanent improvements, must explain the heavy county levy.

The Assessor's roll for 1872 shows the following facts:

Number of acres reduced to possession	150,614
Valued at	$871,708
Improvements on same, valued at	246,911
City and town lots, " "	31,270
improvements thereon, " "	67,093
Other improvements, " "	4,360
Personal property " "	580,484
Total valuation of Lake county	$1,801,826

From which the average value of land reduced to possession is five and seventy-eight one hundreth dollars per acre.

SONOMA COUNTY

(251)

CHAPTER 1.

GENERAL DESCRIPTION.

Sonoma is one of the most important and interesting counties in the State. Lake and Mendocino lie on the North; Lake and Napa on the East; Marin on the South and Southwest, and the Pacific on the West. It is about fifty miles in length by an average of twenty-five in breadth. By different branches of the main Coast Range, Sonoma is divided topographically into five sections. The valleys of Sonoma, Santa Rosa, Petaluma, and Russian River and the coast country. Considerable streams flow through all these. valleys. Sonoma and Petaluma creeks flow in a southeasterly direction, and empty into San Pablo Bay. They are navigable nearly as far as tide water extends for small crafts. In the former vessels go up to within a distance of about three miles from the town of Sonoma; in the latter to the city of Petaluma. These creeks flow through rich agricultural lands, and are of great importance in shipping. Russian River, after entering the county at the Northern extremity above Cloverdale, flows in a Southerly direction till it passes the town of Healdsburg. Here it begins to change to the Southwest, and after passing a few miles changes to almost due West, passes through a

(252)

gap in the Coast Mountains and empties into the ocean. The valley of this river varies considerable at different places in regard to width, but everywhere the soil is as rich as can be found anywhere.

Russian River, though a large stream, is not navigable. In the Summer season the water gets very low in it, and the bars and shoals prevent the passage of anything more than a light skiff or canoe, and frequently one of these only at considerable labor. During the Winter, when it is swollen by the rains, it looks as though it would float the *Great Eastern.* In the Spring, after the force of the waters from freshets is spent, a sand-bar is thrown up by the waves of the ocean across the mouth of the river. This causes the water to rise above the bar, and this back-water extends many miles up the main channel. Santa Rosa Creek rises in the Western slope of the Mayacamas Mountains, flows in a Westerly course through the Guilicos Valley, through a part of Santa Rosa Valley, and empties into the Mark West Creek. This latter creek rises in the same mountains, but farther to the North. It flows through a rich agricultural county and empties into Russian River.

The Northern part of the county is mountainous. Here the highest mountains in the whole section of country lie. This is the main dividing ridge between Sonoma and Lake and Napa. Sulphur Peak, near the Geysers, is the highest mountain, being 3,741 feet high. In this range is the volcanic region known as the Geysers, [to be elsewhere noted].

North of Cloverdale the mountains are very high and precipitous. Russian River passes a great part of the distance from Ukiah Valley in Mendocino to the valley around Cloverdale, through a deep gorge in the hills. Between Russian River, Mendocino county, and the Coast, is a series of bold, rocky mountains and deep gorges. Along the Coast, North of the mouth of Russian River, the country is much broken, in some places the mountains projecting into the ocean, and in others beautiful coves being formed. In this section there is very little land that is of any value save for pasturage. In the Coves along the Coast small farms are found, and vegetation grows well, but production is mostly confined to domestic necessities.

South of the mouth of Russian River extending to the Marin line on the South, and the valleys of Santa Rosa and Petaluma on the

(253)

East, the Coast country is composed mostly of a series of rolling hills, with small intervening valleys, among which may be mentioned Big Valley, in which the town of Bloomfield is situated, Green Valley, and other minor ones. Towards the Southern boundary many estuaries from the ocean put far out into the land. These are the homes of great numbers of water fowls, but are too small to be of service for navigation. Russian River, Santa Rosa and Petaluma Valleys are all closely connected, very little elevation existing between them. They extend in a South-southeasterly direction, and many form the idea that the river formerly flowed down the main depression, till by some convulsion of Nature the chain of mountains to the West was broken, and the course of the stream changed. Between the town of Bloomfield and Petaluma a marked depression exists in the chain of hills extending down into Marin. Petaluma and Sonoma Valleys are separated by a high range of hills. Between Sonoma and Santa Rosa the hills are much broken. The Guilicos, Rincon, Bennett, and some smaller valleys occur in this section, all of them of fine soil and beautifully located.

In the Northern portion of the county the mountains and hills are covered with pine, spruce, and various other species of conifers; also madronas, oaks, etc. In the section of country about the Geysers and across into Northern Napa and Lake counties, is found the California nutmeg. This is a beautiful tree, but the fruit, which bears considerable resemblance to the nutmeg of commerce, is not esteemed of value. The hills and mountains to the Northwest are heavily timbered with redwood, spruce, and other kinds of timber. The live oak here grows to a large size. The hills not densely covered with timber afford fine pasturage for large herds and flocks. Here the native wild oats are still to be found growing rank and vigorous over the hills. The hills South of the mouth of Russian River, except a small belt of heavy timbered country, are rich, fertile land, capable of being cultivated to the summits. This is one of the finest sections for dairies in the whole county. The country lying between the foot-hills West of Santa Rosa Valley and the town of Santa Rosa, is covered with a growth of low scrubby oak, and the soil is in many parts quite gravelly, in others rich and fertile. A low swale or slough, known as the Laguna, extends along the

(254)

Western side of Santa Rosa Valley and empties into Mark West Creek. During severe Winters this Laguna spreads out and overflows a large portion of the surrounding country.

Another section of gravelly soil lies between the town of Windsor and Healdsburg, known in the neighborhood as Poor Man's Flat. Although it is not well adapted to the cereals it could be made valuable for many other kinds of productions.

Bodega Bay is a small inlet in the Southwestern part of the county, and is a shipping point for the productions of the surrounding country. Tamales Bay, in Marin county, lies only a short distance South of Bodega Bay, and is formed between the same headlands, so that both Bays are reached through the same entrance. The harbor inside the heads of this Bay is poor. Water sufficiently deep for schooners is found near the shore, and it is well protected against any but a Southerly wind. The headland projecting down on the Westerly side of this harbor was selected by the Russians in 1812 for a settlement. They maintained the settlement here till 1841.

Knight's Valley, named after the first permanent settler in it, Mr. Thomas Knight, is situated Southwest of St. Helena Mountain, and the greater part of it is fine farming land.

Green Valley lies West of Santa Rosa Valley, and is drained by a small creek, named from the valley, which empties into the Laguna. This valley is one of the finest fruit growing sections of the county, soil is fine. The apples, plums, pears, and such fruits grown here, are not excelled anywhere; yet, the peaches, though of large and fine growth, have not the delicate flavor which those grown in parts farther removed from the coast fogs and winds have.

The greater part of Sonoma county enjoys a most even and agreeable climate. The Western portion, or coast country, is subject to the strong coast winds, but the interior of the county is sheltered by the hills so that it has a mild and pleasant climate. The whole Western portion of the county, during the Summer and Fall, is much visited by dense fogs, and those fogs, in a modified degree, extend over the whole county. By their influence in moistening the soil, a failure of crops on account of a dry season is unknown. The climate on the hill lands, both East and West of the main valley of the county,

(255)

is comparatively free from frosts. Tender flowers have been left exposed to the weather during a whole Winter, and received no injury.

(256)

CHAPTER II.

TOWNS AND WATERING PLACES.

The town of Sonoma is the oldest one North of the Bay of San Francisco. The name Sonoma is of Indian origin, and signifies the Valley of the moon. It was given to the valley of Sonoma on account of the great natural beauties of the place and for its shape as seen by moonlight. The name is peculiarly felicitous. This town is situated a short distance South of the base of the mountains, and about three miles from the place of shipment, the Embarcadero.

It is not our intention to enter into a history of this county, want of space prohibiting but a few notes historical may not be inappropriate. This was established as a Mission as far back as 1820. It was the chief pueblo of the native California population residing North of San Francisco up to the time of the settlement of the country by the Americans in 1846. Gen. M. G. Vallejo, acting under orders from the Mexican Government, in 1835 proceeded North of San Francisco Bay for the purpose of selecting a site for a town or pueblo, and locating said pueblo near the base of mountains or hills on which fortifications might be erected. On account of the beauty of the valley, the pleasant climate and fertile soil, Vallejo selected the present site of Sonoma. The establishment of the North-

(257)

ern Military Department was mainly caused by a desire to check the Russians and prevent them from encroaching farther South on the Mexican domain. The houses erected were built of adobe, around a plaza, after the old Spanish style. Many of these houses were abandoned by their owners, who had obtained grants from the Mexican Government, and retired on to the same, and furnished the main shelter for the immigrants of 1846. After the country was taken possession of by the United States forces, Sonoma was occupied for some time as a military post. Gen. Vallejo's palatial residence occupied the principal portion of the North side of the Plaza. The buildings were in the usual Mexican style, excepting on a large scale, the front, or main building was two stories high with a tower of four stories in the center of the building, the West wing of the front was not complete; in fact, the General had employed mechanics for years in finishing up the interior of the building long after the change of government. His brother, Don Salvador, had also erected a very large and commodious building on the West side of the Plaza, which has been built upon and occupied at times for various purposes, such as hotel, Masonic Hall, and at this time used for a wine cellar. Jacob P. Leese, the brother-in-law of General Vallejo, erected and occupied a large adobe building at the South-west corner, which still stands in good repair and is noted for being the headquarters of General Persifer F. Smith; General, or at that time Colonel Joe Hooker, Capt. Gibbs, Capt. Stone, Major Leonard. Paymaster, Major Phil. Kearney, Lieut. Derby *alias* Squibob, or John Phoenix, George W. Stoneman, Capt. Stone, afterwards General, of Ball's Bluff notoriety, Lieut. Davidson Williamson, and a host of United States officers. Many are still living and will long remember the happy hours they enjoyed while stationed at Sonoma Barracks. Many of these officers purchased lands and intended to make themselves beautiful homes for life. Among those who purchased land was General Persifer F. Smith. He selected 1000 acres on the West side of the valley at the foot-hills, which afterwards became the farm of Capt. Granville P. Swift, who erected on it the fine mansion now occupied by Col. Rogers. This building is of stone and cost some $60,000. Col. Hooker purchased a mile of land of Ernest Bufers, and improved it by substantial enclo-

(258)

sures and remained on it for some years, tilling the soil and laboring with his own hands, but being a better soldier than farmer, he did not succeed as well with the plow-share as he did in after years with the sword.

Sonoma was a favorite spot with the officers of the army. A great many of them besides those here mentioned, purchased lots or tracts of land and commenced improvements. But most had to abandon their homes to obey the call from the War Department.

The first American officer who raised the Stars and Stripes was Lieutenant Revere, from the sloop-of-War *Portsmouth*. This vessel, commanded by Captain Montgomery, entered the harbor of Yerba Buena early in 1846. Lieutenant Revere was dispatched to take possession of Sonoma, and arriving on the spot found the Bear Flag waving and the town in the possession of the Independent party. The oppressions of the Mexican authorities upon the citizens of the United States settled and traveling in California, had become exceedingly onerous, and to remedy their grievances a company of these citizens had united at Sonoma, and on the 15th of June, 1846, declared the country independent and hoisted the celebrated Bear Flag. This flag consisted of two stripes, one blue, the other white, with a picture of a bear on the upper portion. Several members of this party are still living, and have been mentioned elsewhere in this volume. Nine cannon and about two hundred and fifty stand of small arms fell into the hands of the insurgents. On the fourth of the following July, Fremont assembled all the forces at Sonoma, formally declared the independence of the country and was elected Governor. William B. Ide had been elected commander of the place by the Independent party on the hoisting of the Bear Flag. But when Lieutenant Revere arrived he pulled down this flag and hoisted the Stars and Stripes. He occupied the old Mexican barracks at the Northeast of the Plaza. After the country passed into the hands of the United States one Company under the command of Captain Bracket, of the well known Stevenson's Regiment of New York Volunteers, was stationed here.

W. B. Ide, while in command at Sonoma, appointed one John H. Nash, Alcalde. Nash proclaimed himself Chief Justice, and so exceeded his authority that after the establishment of the American

(259)

rule Gen. Riley had him arrested. Gov. L. W. Boggs, then a merchant in Sonoma, was appointed Justice or Alcalde. As an evidence of the importance of the office, it is only necessary to state that the limits of the District were Sutter's Fort on the East, the Oregon line on the North, the Pacific on the West, and the Bay on the South. Sonoma was the principal place of business and traffic on the North side of the Bay. The Rancheros came here to buy their goods. Governor Boggs, and one or two smaller dealers supplied the country around with goods, groceries, etc., taking in exchange hides, the circulating currency of the times. They kept small sloops or schooners plying between Sonoma and Yerba Buena, bought and sold many thousands of dollars worth of goods. Cargoes of flour from Chili were bought and disposed of by these country stores, also Chinese silks and many other goods, principally calicoes and domestics. It was not uncommon for a ranchero to kill a thousand head of cattle to get the hydes to pay a bill of as many dollars.

Sonoma soon became settled up by an American population, and Governor Boggs found it necessary to survey out the Pueblo lands in order to give the people who were settling all over the valley an opportunity to acquire titles to their land. Accordingly, he employed Jasper O'Farrel to run off a certain quantity of small lots, carrying out the original plan as started by General Vallejo; and also to survey outside of these small blocks, thirty and forty acres of land in squares, in conformity to the original design and granted the same to those who had settled on the land first and built homes at the rate of $5 per acre, and all others were sold to the highest bidder, and the proceeds placed to the credit of the Municipal Fund.

After the admission of California as a State, Sonoma continued to be for several years the important town in the county. It was the county seat, till in 1855 the people selected Santa Rosa. Since losing her importance as the county town she has not improved. While every other town in the county has been entirely changed by the hand of progress, Sonoma has remained almost stationary. We look at it to-day and a great part of it is the same old Mexican town it was in 1846. But this stagnation only belongs to the town, the valley is quite different. It is now probably one of the finest vineyard sections in the State.

(260)

Half a mile West of town is the present extensive and magnificent residence of Gen. M. G. Vallejo. This is property that has been highly improved, and is now one of the finest homesteads anywhere to be found. A large and copious spring near the base of the hills supplies an artificial pond, in which many varieties of fish are reared, and gives ample facilities for irrigating the pleasure grounds. Here nearly every variety of grape may be found, large fig trees nearly two feet in diameter throw their cooling shade over the grounds, and ornamental shrubbery adorns the surroundings. Here the orange, olive, lemon, pomegranate and other semi-tropical fruits grow and bear well, and form a beautiful contrast with the apple, quince, pear and other fruits. The walk or drive leading from the road to the residence was constructed at an expense of over $5,000. The residence is truly palatial, and supplied with fine paintings, etc., in fact, everything that go to make home attractive and comfortable.

———

DONAHOE.

The little town of Donahoe is purely an offspring of the railroad, and dates its existence only since Mr. Peter Donahoe took possession of the North Pacific Railroad. It is situated about a mile below the old landing known as Lakeville, on an arm of San Pablo Bay, where all the conveniences of water transportation may be had. It is connected by stage lines with Sonoma and Napa, and is surrounded by a rich agricultural district. The railroad passes up a country almost perfectly level fur several miles. Very little heavy grading is found anywhere on the road.

————

PETALUMA.

The largest town in Sonoma county, and, except Sonoma, the oldest, is Petaluma. It is situated on a creek of the same name at the head of navigation, and is an important shipping point for the county. The land to the East and Southeast is level, and of rich adobe soil. Much of that towards the Southwest is commonly called tule land, and overflows from the rise and fall of the tides. Across the valley to the East rise the high hills separating Sonoma from Petaluma Valleys. To the West of the town lie hills extending
(261)
back into Marin county. Most all of these hills are capable of being cultivated even to their summits. To the North opens the main valley. Good roads connect Petaluma with Tamales, Bloomfield, and other points towards the Coast, while the railroad passes through the Eastern portion of the town. The population is estimated to be near five thousand. It was incorporated in 1858. It has always been a progressive town, and the people alive to every movement of moral or material welfare. There have been several educational establishments started there. Some still survive and are doing well, while others have ceased. The public schools of Petaluma have been for many years among the best in the county. Most competent and experienced teachers have been employed, and the advancement of pupils marked. But more in regard to this in its proper place.

————

SANTA ROSA.

This town, the county seat of Sonoma, is most pleasantly and beautifully located on the creek of the same name, and near the center of the valley. It is distant from Sonoma, Northwesterly, twenty-two miles, midway between Petaluma and Healdsburg, and about seven from Sebastopol, which lies West, on the Western boundary of the valley. Six miles Easterly is Guilicos Valley, on the road to Sonoma. The railroad from Donahoe and Petaluma passes through the Western part of the town, and stages connect there for Sonoma, Sebastopol and the Coast country. A good road leads across the Mayacamas Mountains to Calistoga. The valley of Santa Rosa is about ten miles long with an average width of six miles, and the greater part of it is a perfect garden, so thorough is the cultivation. The town was first settled in 1852, but did not increase much for several years. In 1855 it was selected as the county seat, and soon after the Court House was erected, and the records of the county transferred there. This gave a great impulse to the prosperity of the place, and it has been steadily improving ever since and now stands second only to Petaluma in size and

business prosperity. Fine oak trees surround the town, and a well fenced and improved plaza, ornamented with shrubs and flowers, is situated near the center. The Court House, to the North of this plaza, is an imposing edifice of brick, and the Hall of Records near by is like-
(262)
wise a fine structure. The Methodist College was transferred from Vacaville to this place, and the building erected is one of the best that can be found. The Christian College was completed in 1872, and is a great acquisition to the town.

————

HEALDSBURG.

Healdsburg is another prosperous town on the line of the railroad, situated in the Russian River Valley at a point where that river deflects to the Southwest. It is situated near the confluence of this river with Dry Creek, a considerable stream flowing from the West, also with Knight's Creek flowing from the East, and having its source on the Western side of Mount St. Helena. In 1841 a large tract of land adjoining Healdsburg (eight square leagues of the finest of bottom land) was granted to a California family named Fitch. The country was principally used by them and others who settled in it for pasture lands for immense herds of cattle. Several of the members of this family still reside in the neighborhood of Healdsburg, but nearly all of their extensive and valuable landed possessions have passed to other owners. About two miles East of the town stands an isolated peak over five hundred feet high named after this pioneer family, Fitch Mountain. From the summit of this mountain a view can be obtained which, for extent, beauty and grandeur, is second only to Mount St. Helena. The town was named after Harmon Heald, who established a store there in 1846 for the purpose of supplying the hunters, trappers and herders. It is located on a plain, and is most beautifully surrounded. Russian River flows to the East, Dry Creek in the valley to the West, while to the North lie gentle rolling hills covered with oaks, madronas and other kinds of timber. This town is the natural trade center of a very large and fertile area of country. The rich and extensive valleys of Russian River and Dry Creek surround it, while Knight's Valley lies to the East. All the travel to Skaggs Springs, and a great part of that to the Geysers, pass through here. Since the completion of the railroad the town has greatly increased, both in population and in material wealth.

————

CLOVERDALE.

Situated to the West of Russian River in one of Nature's richest
(263)
and most attractive valleys, lies the small town of Cloverdale. This place is at the head of the main central valley of the county, and at the Northern terminus of the North Pacific Railroad. It is surrounded, except on the South, by lofty and picturesque mountains. There are good mountain roads connecting this place with Lakeport, Ukiah, Anderson Valley, and other points. The trade of the place consists mostly of agricultural and dairy products, wool, etc. Much of the trade to the Upper Lake passes through here. It is all important stopping place for travelers to Mendocino and Lake counties.

————

OTHER PLACES.

Windsor is a small place on the line of the railroad, between Santa Rosa and Healdsburg-ten, miles from the former place, six from the latter. The surrounding country is a fine farming section.

Sebastopol, seven miles West of Santa Rosa, is a small place on the Western side of the valley. On the East lies a fine section of rich alluvial land, through which passes the Laguna; to the West, extending across to Green Valley, lie low, sandy hills, covered with oaks, scattering pine and undergrowth. The sandy soil, when cleared of the timber, produces well.

Bloomfield is a place of considerable importance, situated in the great potato region of Sonoma county, and near the center of what is called Big Valley. It is surrounded by bald hills, but which are of rich soil and are cultivated in potatoes or the cereals to their very summits. This is in the section of county subject to the heavy fogs and winds of the ocean. It is closely connected with Petaluma and with Preston's Point, a shipping place on Tamales Bay.

Four miles down (West) the valley from Bloomfield, is a little place known as Valley Ford. From Valley Ford, three miles Northerly, lies Freestone, another small hamlet supplying the surrounding farmers, and the lumbermen in the redwoods a few miles North. The trade to the redwoods was formerly very great, but has fallen off much of late owing to the exhaustion of the timber from cutting; still a very considerable trade is carried on. The whole of the country in and about Big Valley and Tamales look to these woods for their supplies of fencing timber and fuel.

About four miles West of Freestone is Bodega Corners, the most

(264)

important town in that section. It supplies the farmers and dairymen in the surrounding country; also the lumbermen in the redwoods. It is a great resort for these lumbermen on Sundays. It is connected with Santa Rosa, Petaluma, and Duncan's Mills, at the mouth of Russian River, by lines of stages. Its main shipping point is Bodega Port, situated on the Bay of the same name. This latter place has a good wharf, at which vessels of considerable size can load and unload.

At the mouth of Russian River, Mr. Duncan, several years ago established a saw mill. Other buildings have gradually followed till now there is quite a little village. A short distance south of the mouth of the river is a little roadstead where small vessels come in and load with lumber, dairy, products etc. But only in fair weather will they venture into the place. Along up the coast to Mendocino are several other roadsteads and coves, but nowhere along this line is there found safe anchorage in time of severe gales. At Timber Cove, fifteen miles north of Russian River, considerable lumber and dairy products are shipped. Salt Point, Fisherman's Bay, Fisk's Mill are among the more important of these roadsteads. At the mouth of the Gualala is situated a large saw mill, and vessels come in with comparative safety. The Gualala River rises in the mountains between Healdsburg and the ocean, flows a north-westerly and westerly direction, and empties into the ocean nearly twenty-five miles north of the mouth of Russian River. It flows through a very heavily timbered country, and is a favorite resort for hunters who love tramping over steep mountains, and across deep gorges, and having a rough time generally. There is a moderately good stage road running up the coast, but travel into the interior is performed over trails, and either on foot or horseback. Most all of the country not heavily timbered is located for stock ranges.

Geyserville is a small place, near the line of the railroad, about seven miles North of Healdsburg. It is beautifully located, but is not favorably situated to amount to much as a business point. Knightsville is the name given to the hotel and surrounding houses in Knights Valley.

―――――

SKAGGS SPRINGS.

Connected with Healdsburg are two watering places resorted to
(265)

GOV. L. W. BOGGS

by large numbers of people. One is the Soda Springs about three miles Northwest of Healdsburg, where an excellent quality of medicated soda water may be had. It is bottled and shipped extensively and is well liked by most all who drink it. Closely connected with this soda spring is a seltzer spring, the waters of which are not exceeded for quality in the State.

About twelve miles Northwest of Healdsburg are the celebrated Skaggs Springs. The Waters of these springs are highly impregnated with sulphur, iron, magnesia, borax and soda, and are noted for their medicinal virtues. The temperature of the water is from 120⁰ to 140⁰. There are ample facilities for the accommodation of guests. A fine hotel and cosy little cottages have been erected, and visitors always speak well of the kind reception and generous treatment they receive here. Mr. Skaggs, the owner of the property, has spent a great amount of money here, and deserves the success he has attained. The mountains surrounding, bound in game, and the streams in trout. The roads to these springs, and in fact all leading out of Healdsburg furnish excellent drives. The climate is pleasant, never disagreeably warm and the nights always cool.

————

THE GEYSERS.

Next to the Yosemite Valley, the greatest of curiosities in the State is the collection of springs in Sulphur Creek Cañon, known as the Geysers. They are extraordinary both on account of the chemical composition of the waters, and for the different appearances the spot presents, at different times. There are two localities of hot springs, the Geysers and the Little Geysers. The name was given to these springs from their imagined resemblance to the Geysers of Iceland; though it must be confessed that the person who could see any marked resemblance had a vivid imagination. The Springs are situated in a deep gorge known as Pluton Cañon, though really one main branch of Sulphur Creek, that empties into Russian River near the town of Cloverdale. The Geysers are about 1,700 feet above sea level, are surrounded by lofty and rugged mountains, and are situated about half way between Healdsburg and the lower end of Clear Lake. The locality of this strange subterranean chemical

(266)

MOONLIGHT ON PLUTON CANYON.

laboratory is wildly picturesque, and can only be reached by passing over roads that present to the view scenes of loftiest grandeur.

There are two roads leading to the Geysers, one from Healdsburg, by way of Foss Station and the Hog's Back, called the old road; the other from Calistoga, Napa county, by way of Knight's Valley, known as the new road. The road from Healdsburg passes over a gently rolling country for a few miles, and thence across Russian River Valley. Near the foot-hills East of the valley, about eight miles from the town, is Foss Station, where the stages change horses. Bayard Taylor thus speaks of this piece of road:

"This is certainly the last created portion of our planet. Here the divine Architect has lingered over his work with reluctant fondness, giving it the final caressing touches, with which he pronounced

(267)

it good. Our further journey seemed to be through some province of dreamland. As the valley opened again, and our course turned Eastward toward the group of lofty mountains in which the Pluton River lies hidden, visions of violet peaks shimmered afar, through the perfect trees. Headlands, crowned with colossal redwood, were thrust forward from the ranges on either hand, embaying between them the loveliest glens."

The scenery from the road from Foss Station up the mountains is gorgeous and picturesque. Pines, oaks, madronas, and other trees shade the road, while there is a thick undergrowth of buckeye, manzanita, and other brush. High up the sides of the mountains are densely covered with chaparral. The road winds around mountains and deep cañons, till the highest point on the road is reached, called the Summit. This point is 3,200 feet high. Before reaching the Summit the road winds around Sulphur Peak, which is, next to Mount St. Helena, the highest peak in this part of the Coast Range. It is one of the stations of the primary triangulation of the Coast Survey, and affords a view of great extent and grandeur. The greater part of Russian River Valley, clothed in a misty violet bloom, lies far below, while peak beyond peak covered with the purple chemisal, rises to view. All around is a seemingly endless region of mountain waste divided by deep gorges and cañons. From the Summit the road passes along the celebrated Hog's Back. This is a ridge connecting two ranges of mountains, and from which on either side deep ravines put off. It is covered with a heavy growth of chemisal and chaparral brush. This part of the road has been compared to riding along the roof of a gothic church, but the person who drew the comparison either had never visited the spot, or had no regards for his character for veracity. One describing this ridge, after speaking about the road being only seven feet wide, says:

"On each side the mountain plunges sheer down thousands of feet to the ravines below, the bottoms of which are invisible from the steepness of the sides." We passed over this famous Hog's Back with our own conveyance, and took ample time to note the surroundings. We have seen few prospects so wildly beautiful as the one here presented, but we protest against the steepness of the sides, the thousands of feet, and the invisibility. The description is a lit-

(268)

tle more than the facts warrant. The descent down from the Hog's Back to the hotel at the Geysers is very tortuous, and in some places rather steep.

The road from Calistoga over, presents much of the same character of scenery as this one, but not so wild. The road is a much better grade, but the magnificence of the view from the Summit and the Hog's Back is lost.

At the Geysers is a fine hotel, where everything is done to make visitors comfortable. The hotel stands on the Western bank of Pluton River, facing the side cañon in which are the more notable springs. Along this cañon for a distance of quarter of a mile or more, and covering an area of several acres, numerous hot springs and steam jets occur. There are over three hundred of these springs and jets. The water varies from 200^0 to 210^0. The springs are of various sizes, and the color of the matter emptied or deposited varies from that of the snow flake to the blackness of night. The waters hold in solution a great variety of salts. The sulphates of iron, lime and magnesia predominate. Epsom salts, tartaric acid, alum, magnesia and sulphur are found in great quantities incrusted on the rocks. These salts give the rocks a peculiarly vivid coloration. Farther down the cañon are extensive deposits of sulphur known as the Sulphur Banks. It would seem that Nature has here instituted a grand chemical laboratory. All colors can be seen along the orifices of these springs and steam jets. The names given to many, of the springs are peculiarly suggestive. One spring, called the "Devil's Inkstand," contains dark precipitate of sulphuret of iron, that is used to write the registries at the hotel. Another is called the "Devil's Gristmill," from which spouts clean boiling water, and makes a noise precisely like the grinding of a mill. And many other places will be found, that both in appearance and name remind one of his Satanic majesty. Then, there is a continuous subterranean roar, and in many places a tremulous sensation of the ground nearly all the time is experienced. Besides, the stifling sulphurous steam jets, each making a sound peculiar to itself, and the noxious gases emitted, all combine to impress the visitor with the idea that he is near the confines of Tartarus. From one of the large vents in the ground, one that is about two feet in diameter, the steam escapes with a loud

(269)

sound not very unlike that from the escape pipe of an engine; from which it is called the Steamboat Geyser. The amount of steam ejected from this aperture is very great. The steam is quite hot, and often rises several hundred feet high; and it is ejected in regular pulsations, as by an engine at work, each pulsation sending the steam up fifty to seventy-five feet. On the same side of the ravine as this Steamboat Spring and some fifty rods below, is the greatest attraction of this land of volcanic wonders-the Witch's Cauldron. It is an unfathomable pool, near seven feet in diameter, filled with a viscid, Stygian fluid, which, at a temperature of 200^0, is continually boiling and splashing, seething and roaring, with a most unearthly smell and appearance. The rocks that form the back wall to this infernal fount are for many feet begrimed by the heat and sulphurous gases, and ornamented above with crystals of sulphur. The fetid odor of the sulphuretted hydrogen gas issuing from this Stygian bowl makes the visitor think that the stench from a whole wagon load of putrid eggs, suddenly mashed, would be a relief. There are other wonders here to be found, such as springs only a few feet apart, one cold and the other seething hot; and other springs issuing apparently from the same orifice, of waters of different color, smell, taste and chemical composition; some fissures through which steam will be issuing with a gentle murmuring sound, and one close by emitting a loud and terrible wheeze; one spring out of which spouts pure clear water, while one close by is seething with a vile, miry, inky compound; one place where the visitor can get a breath of fresh air, another near by where he is suffocated by noxious, mephitic vapors; and many similar contrasts. "Here we would turn up a patch of brown, crumbly soil, and find a clay that looks like blue vitriol; near by under a shelving ledge, is a brisk, bubbling pool, overhung with verdigris encrustings; a few feet off spurts a beaded jet of hot water which sheds a dismal brown casting over the surrounding earth; a little way further still, is a spring that looks like pure hot ink; then we discover a rock of alum that weighs two or three hundred pounds; then a small fountain of Epsom salts; not far off, again, a basin apparently of boiling soap-suds; then iron

springs, soda springs, white, red, and black sulphur springs; and soon a foul Stygian sluice, close to the wall, from which a steam exhales that covers the overhanging
(270)
earth with a slimy deposit which eats your clothes, if you touch it, as ravenously as aqua fortis."[*]

Yet, it is not at all times that these phenomena can be seen. At times, the steam is not rising from any of the apertures except in small quantities; at other times the various vents puffing away, and the steam rising three or four hundred feet; at times very little commotion is experienced, and the subterranean forces seem slumbering; at others the din and tumult is deafening. It is stated that the hot water and acids are decomposing the rocks around some of the most active Geysers, and the ground is gradually sinking.

About four miles up Pluton Cañon are situated the Little Geysers. They consist of a number of hot springs along a hillside. Many of the effects seen at the Geysers may here be witnessed; but the water is pure. Several forms of vegetation are seen growing in this volcanic region. Some low forms of growth, such as algae and conferva, grow on the surface of the water that stands at a temperature of from 190^0 to 200^0. Ample bathing facilities are provided at the Geysers, and the baths are very exhilerating.

The Geysers were first discovered in 1847, and have since been visited by tourists and pleasure-seekers in great numbers from almost every part of the world. Those who see it in favorable times, when the Grand Chemist has his works in full operation, are sublimely impressed with the scene. The surrounding hills furnish excellent hunting and fishing to those who enjoy this kind of recreation. The stage line over the road from Healdsburg to the Geysers was, until late years, owned by the world renowed Foss. His line was put on during the era of stage driving (there is a story afloat about the late Horace Greeley, on his trip to California, experiencing some of the delights of this era) and he was second to none in the handling of horse, whip and lines. He now drives on the road from Calistoga, but is the same driver as formerly. Previous to the completion of the new road most of the travel passed through Healdsburg, but now Calistoga gets the greater part.

TO TOURISTS.

To tourists seeking either pleasure or health, Sonoma presents

------

[*]T. Starr King
(271)
many attractive features. Besides the watering places mentioned above, there are innumerable other places in the hills and mountains, where many of the attractions of these places may be found, and where the quiet and solitude of the surroundings add a charm not found at these great centers of fashionable resort. If the pleasures and excitements of fishing and hunting are the incentives for travel, let the mountains and vales remote from these places be chosen. If the desire is to get large game, and no fears are harbored about the severities of a few weeks "roughing it," let a party be formed and take a trip into the mountains about the head waters of Austin Creek and the Gualala. But, if a venture is made off here, the heart must be nerved to the possibility of a tussle with a bear, or a jaguar. All through this section of country, deer, brown or cinnamon bear abound, grizzleys are frequently found, the jaguar or California lion, the wild cat, and other animals are frequently met with. If the ambition does not lead to so venturesome a journey, the

hills nearer the valleys may be selected. Here small game with an occasional deer abound, while the streams are filled with trout.

THE WITCHES' CAULDRON.

A journey up the coast North of Russian River is one of the finest that can be had for those who enjoy coast scenery, spiced with a sufficient amount of roughness to prevent monotony. Along the coast at various places sea lions congregate in large numbers and form an interesting feature. A drive from Santa Rosa to Calistoga and the
(272)
Petrified Forests forms a pleasant day's journey, and well repays the fatigues in making it. From Cloverdale the tourist may take the good road across the mountains to Lakeport, well assured that if he enjoys fine scenery, that here he can have it in the highest degree. One view that is obtained some twelve miles from Cloverdale of the Lake region is grand as heart could desire. After toiling up a steep mountain, the traveler sees laid out before him the beautiful Clear Lake, surrounded by its grand amphitheater of mountains extending away into the purple distance, tall, rugged, and heaped together in wildest confusion. From Cloverdale to Ukiah, or Anderson Valley, the road passes over a mountainous country. On the way quite a number of fine mineral springs occur. One noted spring supplies a large quantity of soda water, said to rival the famed Napa Soda.
(273)

CHAPTER III.

SOURCES OF WEALTH.

The resources of Sonoma are varied, and are capable of being developed to an indefinite extent. Agriculture is here chief, and of all its branches wheat raising is principal. Nearly all the land in the county, except some of the gravelly hill land, is admirably adapted to wheat raising. Here, as in Napa county, a succession of wheat crops have been reaped off of the same land until the soil has become impoverished. Russian River, Santa Rosa and Petaluma are the principal wheat producing sections. Sonoma Valley, Big Valley and the hilly country along the Coast are also excellent sections for wheat. Barley is also extensively grown. In the Coast country oats are more generally grown than in any other portion of the county.

The country about Bodega, Bloomfield, and down to Petaluma, is the renowned potato district. The potatoes grown in this section

(274)

were formerly by far the best that could be had in the market, and the crop was the most remunerative to the growers. But many severe losses were sustained by reason of such quantities being raised that a market could not be had; and a continual cropping for so many years has to some extent exhausted the soil, and the quality of the potato has slightly deteriorated. But, when the farmers, learning the benefit of rotation of crops, began to sow the cereals on their potato land, they found the result a great success.

As a fruit producing county Sonoma has few equals. The apple, pear, plum, and in fact all kinds of fruits, grow finely and produce abundantly, in all parts of the county, save in the immediate vicinity of the ocean. In the hills, where frosts are rare, the orange and other semi-tropical fruits thrive well. Some years ago, the writer experimented in growing some of the wild fruits common in the Eastern States. On the hills West of Santa Rosa Valley the persimmon was found to grow luxuriantly, but the fruit lacked the flavor common to it in the Mississippi Valley. The Papaw was also grown, but never produced.

All the remarks made in regard to the adaptability of the soil and climate of Napa for various kinds of production, are equally applicable to Sonoma. Hops, flax etc., have been grown here, and are no longer experiments. During the war between the States, while prices were high, an attempt was made to introduce the culture of tobacco into this county, and much interest was taken in its cultivation. But the curing of it was not a success, owing probably wholly to the difference in the soil and climate between this country and the States East of the Rocky Mountains. But some of it was cured sufficiently well, that when a foreign brand was put upon it there was a considerable demand for it, and it gave general satisfaction. The culture, however, declined, and very little attention has been paid to it since. Parties about Santa Clara have, it is said, discovered a process for curing the California tobacco, so that even experienced tobacconists cannot distinguish it from the best Havana brands. All the experiments made in Sonoma and Napa counties proved that the tobacco grew admirably and we may yet expect this section to become an important tobacco producing district.

Berries of various kinds grow luxuriantly and bear well all over the

(275)

county. The fogs from the Coast so thoroughly bathe the land that many kinds of fruits and berries can be grown here which cannot in other places on account of the drouth. There are several kinds of wild berries, but they are not, except blackberries, much esteemed. There is a gooseberry common along brooks and in the bottoms in timbered portion of Sonoma, but it is much smaller than that found in other States. Wild strawberries are abundant in some sections, and are very fine. There is a kind of raspberry, commonly called thimbleberry from its shape when plucked, found along creeks and in moist places. It has a good flavor, and would be much esteemed only that it is so scarce. The huckleberry is found in great abundance in some of the Western parts of the county. The berry is some larger than that found in other States, and is much esteemed. The wild blackberry is the most abundant of any of the native berries, and is best liked; the vine is a creeper and is rarely found except in timbered sections and along water courses. The berry is of fair size and luscious; the vine resembles that of the dewberry of the Mississippi Valley. All of the cultivated varieties of berries grow and produce well.

Next to the cultivation of the soil the greatest source of wealth is stock-raising the Northwestern part of the county is principally devoted to this industry. Large herds and flocks occupy the hills. The herder's only care is to guard the stock from straying too far off the range, and to attend to the shearing of the flocks in proper season. Most of these stock ranges are so far removed from roads and markets that no attempt is made at dairying. This is about the only section of the county where the wild oat, that formerly covered the whole county, is now found. Along the Northern Coast where the roadsteads offer shipping facilities, considerable attention is given to dairying, but it is not till we get to Russian River that we come into the chief dairying districts of the county. All along down the Coast from this point into Marin are large dairies, where nothing else is attended to but butter and cheese making. Along a great part of this belt of country the land is quite cheap, the hills are well supplied with grasses and springs, and the expense of keeping stock light, so that it is found very remunerative. The natural grasses common to this section, in fact to the whole county, consist of burr clover

(276)

alfilerilla, bunch grass, and wild oats, which are very nutricious, and, excepting the last, quite abundant. Alfalfa is being extensively cultivated for feed for stock, and is fast becoming a favorite. The mezquit grass, the cultivation of which was lately commenced by Mr. Hudspeth of Green Valley, bids fair to be an important addition to the grasses found and grown here.

The wool product of Sonoma is very large. The stock has been greatly improved of late years by importing fine blooded sheep, and more attention is continually being given to this industry. The sheep require little attention, markets are convenient, and fair prices have always been obtained for the wool. In the hills remote from markets the wool is carried on pack animals to places where transportation can be had.

Among the chief sources of wealth are the forests of redwood, fir, and other timber. The redwood forests cover a very large portion of Western Sonoma, extending in an almost unbroken line from near Green Valley North to Mendocino. Mills have been established at every available point, and immense quantities of lumber have been shipped, and the business still goes on unabated. As the convenient forests become exhausted, roads are built to others, and every road-stead on the Coast is occupied as a shipping point for lumber. The mill at the mouth of Russian River and of the Gualala are supplied with logs from the forests far above by floating the same down the rivers in rafts.

A considerable trade has been carried on for several years past in charcoal from Sebastopol. Large kilns have been burned, the coal obtained from the wood in that section being found to be of excellent quality. A ready market is always found for it.

MINERAL WEALTH.

There are few mines being worked in Sonoma, though there are fine prospects for valuable lodes of ore in several parts of the county. Fair specimens of auriferous quartz have been found on Mark West Creek and in the hills near Cloverdale, but nothing yet sufficient to warrant working. Gold has been found in small quantities near the Geysers. In 1862-3, considerable excitement was created on account of the discovery of what was thought to be rich sil-
(277)
ver bearing ore near Healdsburg. Many claims were located and companies formed for working these mines. Copper was also found associated with the silver, and in many instances it was the chief metal sought. Much work was done, and considerable sums of money expended in prospecting. Many specimens of rich copper ore were found, but no well defined ledge. The excitement continued till in 1864-5, when it waned. The cost of smelting and transportation was so great, and the quality of the ore found so low, that operations were most all suspended in 1865. Yet there is little doubt of the existence of rich copper mines here. The outcroppings and the character of the rock obtained from the shafts and tunnels run into the hills are sufficient guarantee that there are rich lodes of ore somewhere near by. The excitement on account of rich copper discoveries extended to other parts of the country. Fine prospects were reported in the mountains Northwest of Sebastopol. Among the persons who became suddenly rich by this discovery was Mr. O. A. Olmstead. This gentleman owned a saw-mill and a small tan-yard on one of the small creeks tributary to Russian River, but had not been very successful. On the breaking out of the copper mania he became greatly interested. He prospected long and faithfully, and though he failed to find copper, succeeded in finding mines that are destined to be of great value. These are paint mines, in which deposits of variously tinted ochres, and other mineral colors are found. The colors are of superior quality, and after being long and thoroughly tested, these mines are found to yield a paint in many respects better than any other found in market. The deposits appear to be almost inexhaustible, and the quality to increase the more the mines are worked.

Mercury in a pure state has been found about the Geysers, the severe heat having sublimated it from other ores. A few miles from the Geysers, and near the little Geysers, rich cinnabar prospects have been found, but no work has here been done sufficiently extensive to test the value of the deposits. Fine prospects for cinnabar have also been found in the mountains between Guilicos Valley and the town of St. Helena. Coal has been found, of fair quality, at several points along Russian River Valley. Near Cloverdale a body of coal has been found some seven feet wide, that is nearest a
(278)
valuable discovery yet made of this mineral. Several tons of coal have been put on the market from this mine, but it is not now worked.

Extensive quarries of a fine stone suitable for building are found extending all along from Petaluma to the redwoods. This stone is soft and easily worked when taken from the quarry, admitting of a good polish, but it becomes quite hard after being subjected to the air. It has been used-considerably in building and as it is found in exhaustless quantities and convenient to market, it only awaits a test of the pressure it will bear, for this rock to become of great value. Limestone and gypsum, though existing in various parts of the county, are found most plentifully along the Northern coast.

————————

VINEYARDS.

Next to wheat, the vine engrosses more attention in Sonoma than any other agricultural production, The main locality or center of the grape interests is Sonoma Valley. The soil, especially along the foot-hills, seem peculiarly adapted to the grape, and has a decided resemblance to some of the famed wine districts on the Rhine. It was in this valley that the vine was first planted, and here the first important measures were taken to make of the grape and wine interests an important branch of industry.

To the old Fathers of the Missions in California must the credit or blame be given of in inaugurating this business in the State. They planted the vines about the Missions, and in a crude way made wine. The grape planted by them was our common Mission variety. This grape is peculiar to California, and is thought to be a seedling from seed sent out from Spain. The Fathers made their wines and added spirits to the same to keep them sweet. This gave rise to the sweet liquor called Angelica wine. But the product of the vine must have been very small at this early day as none of the Missions had but a small number of acres planted. The the early settlers from the United States in the few vines they planted, followed the example of the Fathers, both in regard to the kind and number of grapes planted, and in the location. At this early day it was thought impossible to raise any kind of vegetation without irrigation. It was only where the conveniences of water could be had

(279)

that vines were set. It was also thought essential to select for grapes a rich alluvial soil. The first person who doubted the correctness of this old maxim about the importance of irrigation, and was willing to test the validity of his doubts, was Colonel Agoston Haraszthy, of Sonoma. In the Winter of 1858 he planted a vineyard of one hundred and forty acres, or about 80,000 vines on a high tract of land East of the town of Sonoma, where irrigation was impossible. Many were the predictions of failure of this experiment. It was watched with interest by all favorably disposed to the building up of the wine business in the State. The success of this experiment was the commencement of a new era in vine growing in the State. The rich and heavy bottom lands were abandoned, and the hill side lands selected.

About this time another interesting subject came up-that in regard to securing a finer wine, by means of raising foreign grapes. Our wines were not esteemed by connoisseurs and habitual wine drinkers. The wines were, it was said, either earthy and fiery, or sweet and insipid. This was unquestionably, in a great measure, owing to the quality of the soil and the irrigation of the vine, and also to the inexperience of the persons engaged in the business. Since more experience has been had, and more suitable soil adopted, even the Mission grape is found to make a wine of good quality. Still, the excellency of foreign wines could not be obtained from that made of this grape so that efforts were put forth to get foreign varieties. It has been proved that the fine bouquet, so common and so much liked by wine drinkers of the best European wines, is a result of the species of the grape. In 1861 the Legislature appointed Colonel Warner, Mr. Schell and Colonel Haraszthy as a committee to inquire into, and report upon, the best means of promoting and improving the growth of the vine in California. Warner reported upon the condition of viniculture as then existing in the State, Mr. Schell upon the viniculture of the South American States, while Colonel Haraszthy visited Europe and made selections of different varieties of grapes and imported the same. He selected over three hundred different varieties of grape, and imported near 200,000 rooted vines and cuttings. These vines were distributed to various parts of the State, and every variety produced and matured its peculiar grape to perfec-

(280)

tion. Some have been found far superior to others, and hence have been very generally selected, but none have been found that in our soil and climate do not maintain their distinctive European qualities; and the modes and conditions of wine-making being equal, produces a wine here identical with what it does in Europe. At the present time most all the new vineyards are being set with the best foreign varieties of vine.

In the *Overland Monthly* for January, 1872, Arpad Haraszthy thus speaks on some of the advantages of our State as a wine-growing country:

"California has one advantage over any wine-producing country on the globe, and that is the certainty, constancy, and duration of her dry season. The grape is a fruit that needs, above all others, a warm sunshine, without interruption, from the time that the blossoms set forth their tender flowers, until they gradually develop into its rich, luscious fruit in October. This advantage has always existed here, as far back as our record extends, and no rain or hail ever destroyed the tender fruit. The sure and uninterrupted duration of this dry weather secures a crop without a chance of failure, and ripens the grape to perfection. One of the most serious drawbacks in all other parts of the world is the uncertainty of the seasons and entire variance from preceding ones, thus creating a great difference in the quality of the wine produced in successive vintages. This difference in quality is so great that it is quite common to find the prices vary from one to two hundred per cent. in the same district. The products of the renowed vineyards are known to have fluctuated even to a greater extent. In Europe, they only reckon to secure in ten years one good crop of fine quality, but small quantity; while seven vintages are reckoned as being of poor quality, small quantity, and total failures. In our State, the variation in quality seldom amounts to five per cent., while the most disastrous years have not lessened the crop below the ordinary yield more than twenty-five per cent. in quantity. This very variation in quantity can be fully known three months previous to the vintage, thus allowing the producer ample time to secure his casks, and furnishing him positive knowledge as to the number required. In other countries, even fourteen days before the vintage, there is no certainty of a crop; a

(281)

wind, a rain, or a hail-storm is apt to occur at any moment and devastate the entire vintage. All is uncertainty there; nor has the vintner any possible means of positively ascertaining how many casks he must provide. In abundant years in the old countries the exchange has often been made of so many gallons of wine for an equal number of gallons' capacity of casks. The disadvantages of being forced to secure such immense quantities of casks in so limited a period are too easily perceived, and we certainly can not appreciate our own advantage too much in being very differently situated. Another great benefit derived from the long continuance of the dry weather, is the exemption from weeds in our vineyards after the final plowing. Thus all nourishment and strength of the soil go wholly to their destination, the vine, and hence the vigorous appearance that even the most delicate imported varieties acquire even in our poorest soils. They necessarily bear much more. This circumstance will also explain, in a measure, why our cultivation does not cost as much per acre as that in European countries, though our labor is so much higher. The advantage of our dry weather does not end here: it precludes the possibility of continued mildew, and allows the vintner to leave his vines unstaked, the bunches of grapes actually lying, and securely ripening upon the very ground, without fear of frost or rotting. In this condition, the grapes mature sooner, are sweeter, and, it is believed, possess more flavor.

*   *   *   *   *   *

"Above and beyond the ability and advantage we have of producing all kinds of grapes to perfection, of making from them wines that are pleasant, inviting to the taste, and which will keep, with but little skill and care, for years, whose limit has not yet been found we still have a greater advantage over European vintners in the cheapness of our cultivation. Labor, material, and interest are all very high with us; but, nevertheless, the setting out and cultivation of an acre of vineyard costs less in California than it does in France. For this we are as much indebted to our improved means of cultivation as to the nature of our climate. All labor, in the majority of the wine districts of Europe, is done by hand. We use the horse and plow, while they use the prong-hoe and spade, and they actually dig and hoe up their entire vineyards, with few exceptions. After

(282)

our Spring cultivation is over, we need not go into our vineyards, and, having no Summer rains, weeding is not necessary, and still their freeness from weeds and clean appearance strike the stranger with surprise. Owing, on the contrary, to the wet season of Europe, the vine-dressers are constantly kept among the vines, trying to give them a clean appearance; but, in spite of all their efforts, they but imperfectly succeed, and their vineyards never possess that appearance of high and perfect cultivation that is so apparent in our own."

No clearer idea can be given of the extent of the grape culture, than by reference to the statistical tables at the end of this volume. What the future of this great and rising interest shall be is yet a matter of speculation, but the present prospects are that it will be very important. New vineyards are continually being planted, extensive cellars erected and the confidence of those engaged in the business in its future value increasing.

(283)

CHAPTER IV.

HISTORICAL AND BIOGRAPHICAL.

It is beyond the possible limits of this volume to give a biographical sketch of even a tithe of the pioneers and citizens of worth of Sonoma. We will, however, arrange a few niches for some, not because they are more deserving the honor than others, but because the necessary notes are more conveniently obtained.

CYRUS ALEXANDER.

A correspondent to the Healdsburg *Flag* gives the following notes of one of the oldest and most respected pioneers of Sonoma. It is quite lengthy, but owing to Mr. Alexander's being so long and so intimately identified with the history and progress of that part of Sonoma, we reproduce it entire.

Cyrus Alexander was born in Pennsylvania on the 15th of May. 1805, and was consequently in his 68th year when he died. When he was about six years of age his parents removed with him to St.

(284)

Clair county, Illinois, a short distance from St. Louis, which, at that time, was a great trading post for the fur companies, and also the headquarters for those brave, rude trappers and mountaineers-those rough diamonds of hardy civilization that sparkled so brilliantly in the diadem of the then Great West. Frequent intercourse with these men, and their thrilling tales of flood and field stirred up the spirit of adventure in the breast of young Alexander, and at the age of sixteen, with no other capital than a stout heart, and trusty rifle, he bade his parents, relatives and friends farewell, and left to seek his health and fortune in the wilds of the unknown West, saying at the time he would never return until he had made his fortune. His health at this time was quite delicate, and his frail constitution, one would naturally suppose, would quickly succumb to the hardships unavoidable in the career he had chosen; the contrary proved to be the case however-he gained strength rapidly, became possessed of an iron constitution, and, when under certain severe trials some of his comrades would die from want and exposure, his power of endurance brought him safely through all.

From St. Louis he first went to Galena, the lead mines having then been but recently discovered, and this point was then almost without the pale of civilization. Remaining here but a few months his restless spirit whispered, Onward! And making arrangements with Sublett, then one of the famous trappers of the day, he penetrated to the Rocky Mountains, where, for a year, his efforts resulted quite favorably to his employer's interest. Mr. Alexander then resolved to hunt and trap on his own account and lay the foundation of wheat he hoped would prove to be his fortune. At three different times, with unflagging energy and a determination to overcome every obstacle, he thought he had accumulated furs and peltries enough to realize his moderate idea of a fortune; but reverses would overtake him, and disasters sweep away everything he had in the world, with the exception of his original capital, which he had at the start, and which, happily, never diminished, *viz*: a stout heart and a trusty rifle.

On one occasion whilst returning to the settlement in a boat laden with the fruit of his year's labor, the boat upset on the Yellowstone and everything was lost. At another time a large amount of pel-

(285)

tries which he had "cached" or hidden in the mountains, was stolen from him by one of his comrades whilst he was off on a short expedition.

On several occasions he and his companions did not live as luxuriantly or fare as sumptuously as one would expect in a wild region where game should be plentiful, for boiled moccasins and dried skins, he relates, was once their entire bill of fare; and at another time, after several days of fasting, the decaying carcass of a deer floating down the stream was considered a God-send-hastily taken out, roasted and devoured without the assistance of any sauces whatever to give it a relish.

After several years passed in the mountains with indifferent success, he determined to push still onward towards the Pacific, and arrived in San Diego about the year 1827. He spent several months hunting otter and seal in the Gulf of California: here he had a very narrow escape with his life. He was out in a boat with three or four others, when a sudden squall upset it and the occupants were drowned with the exception of Mr. Alexander, who strange to say, was Providentially saved, although unable to swim a particle, whilst those who were drowned, were expert swimmers. At San Diego Mr. Alexander became acquainted with Captain Henry D. Fitch, a leading merchant then of Alta California, a man of sterling qualities of head and heart, who having come here from Boston several years previous to Mr. Alexander, had already established an enviable reputation among the natives. His acquaintance with Captain Fitch seems to have been the turning point in his fortune, and cast his lot in this section of the country, for the Captain, being a shrewd judge of human nature, selected him at once, as the proper person to take charge of his immense and valuable grant, the Sotoyome. Shortly afterwards Captain Fitch sold to Mr. Alexander a goodly portion of the grant, the main part of which is now known as Alexander Valley. On two occasions Mr. Alexander could have obtained a grant of land from the Mexican government, but as the oath of allegiance was required, he refused to take it. He said the times looked very squally to him for a while, upon the breaking out of the Mexican war, and, as an American, the excitement against him was intense.

(286)

When the discovery of gold took place, and the great American hegira commenced to this our favored Mecca, the early Pioneers of '49 found Mr. Alexander peacefully living under his own vine and fig tree; and even then, in these comparatively early times, he was an old settler. The gold fever proving contagious, he, also, left his ranch for awhile, and in company with Nathan Coombs and others, spent several months in the placers; but his keen judgment soon showed him-what California farmers have ever since been slowly finding out-that every acre of the virgin soil of our glorious State was a mine in itself and liberally repaid the laborer for all the toil bestowed upon it. His cattle, fruit and onions found a lively, ready market, and were liberally paid for by the hard-working miners.

In 1844 he married Rufina Lucero, a fine looking young lady, a native of New Mexico, who had come to this State on a visit with her sister, the wife of William Gordon. As was customary in those days, and still is in many European countries, he was first married by the Alcalde, a Civil Magistrate, and then by the Church at the old Catholic Mission of Santa Clara. His wife and five children survive him, his daughter Margarita, the oldest of his children now living, was married several years ago to William Mulligan of Healdsburg.

When he first settled in this portion of the country his nearest Post Office was Sonoma, and his nearest point for family supplies was Yerba Buena, the embryo San Francisco.

Mr. Alexander always looked forward with pleasure to the completion of the Pacific Railroad, anticipating a visit to his old home and the scenes of his boyhood days, after so many years of absence, for he was now in good circumstances and could well afford to enjoy himself and reap some of the pleasures justly earned by years of labor and industry. This fond hope of his, however, was never realized, for long before the railroad was completed he was stricken with paralysis, and it was with difficulty that he could go over the ranch and superintend his affairs. A few years later, a second stroke, more severe than the first, confined him to the house, and thus silently and gradually passed away one of the fathers of our new State--a self-made man, who, reared amid the storms and solitude of the mountains, laughed at danger and discouragement, and alone and unbefriended, carved out his fortune.

(287)

A person to take a look, to-day, at the beautiful, thriving village of Healdsburg would think it strange, perhaps, that bears and panthers were once the only inhabitants within its incorporate limits, but such was the case after Mr. Alexander moved here, and he used, frequently, to refer with pleasure and with a glow of his youthful fire, to an exciting incident of lassoing a wild bear, with some comrades, at a place about where the Healdsburg plaza is now situated.

Mr. Alexander was very plain and unostentatious, but his hand and heart were always open to the needy. As a member of society his character was unblemished, and his word was always considered as good as his bond. The only enemies he ever had were ejected squatters who had settled on his land, but this was no fault of his, being an unfortunate misunderstanding which has occurred in almost every county in the State; but even the majority of these, after the heat of passion had died away, have acknowledged him to be a worthy, honest man. His character for hospitality was widely known, and in early times, as many as twenty strangers would often meet at one time at his table and partake of his cordial generosity.

'Tis the memory of such men as these that we should cherish in this, our adopted State, and while now, enjoying here all the luxuries of civilization, we should often take our grandchildren upon our knees and relate to them the adventures and the sterling qualities of our noble Pioneers.

COLONEL AGOSTON HARASZTHY.

The subject of this sketch, by the important services rendered to the State, deserves more than a passing notice. Colonel Haraszthy was born in the year 1812, in the Comitat of Backsa, Hungary. His family was one of the oldest and most influential of the old nobility-his name appearing frequently in the history of that country over a period of 760 years. He was educated to the law, as was the custom there. At the age of 18 he was a member of the body guard of the Emperor Ferdinand, which was composed of nobles. Then he was Chief Executive Officer of his State. He then became the Private Secretary of the Viceroy of Hungary.

When the Liberal movement began, he at once took the lead of

(288)

that party in his State, but was afterwards, upon the failure of that movement, compelled to leave his country. He came at once to New York, and after travelling over the United States he wrote and published a book upon their resources. The work was designed to invite emigration from Hungary, and was the first work upon that subject ever printed in the Hungarian language.

Soon after he made the State of Wisconsin his home, purchased large tracts of land, founded several settlements, built bridges, constructed roads and established ferries.

Having in his possession valuable State papers, the Austrian Government opened negotiations for their surrender. The question was referred to General Cass, who succeeded in gaining permission for Colonel Haraszthy to Hungary and remain for one year. This he did, settling up his affairs; and although his landed estates were confiscated, he succeeded in saving $150,000, which he brought with him to this country, together with his family plate and paintings.

Returning to Wisconsin, he engaged in mercantile pursuits- built and owned steamboats, and also engaged extensively in agricultural pursuits. He was the first to plant the hop in the State, and encourage its cultivation. The Commissioner of Agriculture report that the product of this crop, in the county where it was then introduced, for the year 1866, amounted to over two millions of dollars.

He was at this time also at the head of the Emigrant Association of Wisconsin, which brought over large colonies of English, Germans and Swiss, and settled them upon the fertile lands of that State. He gave to the Catholic Church a tract of 640 acres of land, upon which has since been erected an extensive monastery.

When news came of the revolution in Hungary, he was the leader of those who gathered arms and ammunition, and sent them to his countrymen-also expending large sums from his own private purse for the same object.

In 1849 he removed to California-settled at San Diego-was elected Sheriff of the county, and rendered valuable aid in suppressing the Indian war of that period. He laid out what is known as "Middle San Diego," and in 1852 was elected a member of the legislature. Being a working member, he had a place on the
(289)

J. R. SNYDER.

principal Committees, and distinguished himself by his opposition to all schemes of fraud and monopoly.

In 1852 he removed to San Francisco, and devoted himself to agriculture and horticulture upon his property at Crystal Springs, in San Mateo County. He was appointed by President Pierce as Assayer in the United States Branch Mint, and at a later period was made smelter and Refiner. After his resignation of these positions, serious character charges were made against him, but upon a thorough investigation they were proved to be wholly without foundation, and he was honorably acquitted. During this time he built the present Metallurgical Works which have rendered such important service, and also he received patents for improved processes for the refining of gold.

In 1856 he removed to Sonoma, and devoted his whole attention to viniculture. He founded a Horticultural Society, and began importing vines from abroad. He was the first to advocate the raising of vines without irrigation-planted the most extensive vineyards, and at once put himself at the head of the wine interest. He may with propriety be called the Father of Viniculture in California.

In 1858 he wrote a treatise on the culture of the vine and the manufacture of wine, which was published by the State for gratuitous distribution. This publication gave the first impulse to this interest, and from that time California became the Wine State of the Western Continent. He was the first to employ Chinese labor in his Vineyards, and the first to adapt the redwood timber to the making of casks for wine.

In 1861 he was appointed by the Governor of California as a Commissioner to visit the wine countries of Europe, which resulted in the importation of 300 different named varieties, of grapevines, which have now been planted quite extensively in most of the vineyards in the State, from which are made the most valuable wines we now produce.

The book written by Col. Haraszthy, entitled "Grape Culture, Wines and Wine-Making," is conceded to be one of the best yet written. Upon his return from Europe in 1862 he was chosen President of the State Agricultural Society-having been Vice-President for three terms prior thereto. In 1863 he organized the Buena Vista
(290)
Vinicultural Society, to which Society he conveyed his 400 acres of vines in Sonoma.

In 1868 Col. Haraszthy went to Nicaragua, with the intention of engaging in trade; but his active mind and talent for improvement, would not let him rest. He became interested in an extensive sugar plantation, and began clearing new lands and planting more canes. Having procured from the Government of Nicaragua valuable privileges for distilling, he erected an extensive distillery for the manufacture of spirits for exportation. He also turned his attention to the textile fibers of the country, and was waiting patents for improved machinery for their cleansing and preparation for market.

In the winter of 1870 he returned to California to purchase machinery, and to charter a vessel with which to open the trade between San Francisco and the ports of Nicaragua. It was his desire to make the rich products of that country tributary to the wealth and material progress of California. He returned to his plantation in Nicaragua; and on the 6th of July, 1869, mysteriously disappeared. On that day he left his home to go to where he was having a saw mill erected. His footsteps were traced to a river. It is supposed that he endeavored to cross this river by climbing the branch of a tree, and that the branch broke, letting him fall into the water, where he was devoured by an alligator.

Colonel Haraszthy's whole aim was to introduce new elements of wealth, to search out new fields of industry and thus to lead the way to a wider field of material progress in whatever country he lived. He was a man of good and generous impulses. He was hospitable and liberal almost to a fault. His hand was ever ready to help those who stood in need. He was full of ambition, but only in the line of being useful to his fellows. Those who knew him intimately loved and admired him, and all acknowledged a charm in his presence which they felt, but could not explain.

RANSOM POWELL.

Among the genial whole-souled spirits of Sonoma, few rank higher than the subject of this notice. Mr. Ransom Powell was born in Robertson County, Tennessee, in 1826. He traveled ex-
(291)
tensively through Tennessee, Kentucky and Missouri. In 1845 he enlisted in the Mexican war, under Congrave Jackson, of Donathan's Regiment. His regiment was sent to Santa Fe and thence

to El Paso and into the State of Chihuahua. They had several engagements with the Mexicans, and in one, near the city of Chihuahua, among other trophies taken from the enemy, captured twenty-one pieces of ordnance. After the war he returned to Missouri, and in the Spring of 1849 started overland for California. He was principally engaged in the mines till in 1856, when he came to Sonoma, arriving there just in time to vote for James Buchanan. He now lives upon a fine homestead near the town of Healdsburg. Since his settling in this county he has, though paying considerable attention to farming, been chiefly engaged in speculating and general trading.

———

A. P. PETIT.

Mr. Petit, the well know architect and builder, is a native of Bucks County, Pennsylvania, migrated to this State in 1849, and settled in Santa Rosa in 1864. He has followed the business of architect and builder since he has been in the State, and has won an enviable reputation for his excellent designs and masterly workmanship. He has erected some of the finest and most substantial houses, both public and private, found in this section of the country.

———

WILLIAM ROSS.

The subject of this sketch has long been known throughout the county and this judicial district as one among the ablest of attorneys. He was born in Mifflin County, Pennsylvania. His family emigrated to Ohio when he was an infant and he resided in the latter State until he started for California. From 1840 to 1849 he served the County of Perry, Ohio, as Auditor, and no better evidence could be given of the esteem in which he was held than this long continuance in one office. He studied law and was admitted to the bar in Ohio. In 1849 he joined an ox train, and came overland to California. The company left Zanesville April 3d, and after a severe and perilous journey of seven months reached Sacramento in November. He settled in El Dorado County, and commenced the
(292)
practice of his profession. He attended the first court ever held in the county, and there defended his first client, a man charged with stealing gold dust. He filled an unexpired term as District Attorney in that county. In 1852 he removed to Sonoma County, where he has since resided, engaged in his professional practice. In 1860 he was elected to the Legislature. Since then he filled an unexpired term as District Attorney, and was afterwards twice elected to the same office. He has always taken a deep interest in the prosperity of the county. In his official career, and his professional practice, he has acquitted himself with credit, and won the esteem of a host of friends.

JOHN MATHEWS.

This gentleman was born in Kentucky in 1828. His family removed to Indiana in 1832, and in 1847 went to Missouri. He enlisted in the Mexican War, and served in Arbuckle's Regiment under Col. Gilpin. Was thirteen months in the war, then returned to Missouri, and six months after, on the 26th of April, 1849. started for California "the plains across," reaching Lassen's on the 3d of October, 1849.   Came to Sonoma county in 1865, where he has since remained.

ELISHA L. DAVIS.

Born in 1823 in Marengo County, Alabama, Mr. Davis removed to Texas in 1840.   Left Texas in 1846 for the Mexican War under Jack Hayes.   He was engaged with the Indians in several battles. Remained in Mexico principally till peace was declared.   He then returned to Texas, and in March, 1849, left for California, coming through Mexico, and reached San Diego in July, 1849. Came to Sonoma County, to live in April, 1862, and has been farming here ever since.

ATTILA HARASZTHY.

The subject of this brief memoir is a son of Colonel Agoston Haraszthy, whose biography is elsewhere found.   He was born in Hungary in 1835, settled in Wisconsin in 1844, and came overland through Arizona and New Mexico to San Diego in 1849. ln 1851
(293)
settled in San Francisco, where he resided till 1856, when he removed to Sonoma where he has ever since resided, engaged in the of vineyard and wine interests. He has assisted in the planting near seven hundred acres of vineyards in Sonoma Valley and now has charge of three hundred acres, the property being owned by a company of five individuals who confide their several interests to his care. He superintends the manufacture and sale of all the wines from this extensive property. He was Superintendent of the vineyards of the Buena Vista Vinicultural Association and held an interest in the lands until the incorporation of that society. Since the incorporation and during the absence of the Superintendent, Colonel Haraszthy during, two years in Europe, he acted as Superintendent. He is a pioneer not only in the State, but in viniculture here. He has done much to advance this interest, and by his fair and courteous dealing has won the esteem of a host of friends and acquaintances.

DAVID COOK.

David Cook was born in Lincoln county, Kentucky, in 1804, and when quite young his parents removed to Rock Castle county. Here he lived till 1831, when he removed to Missouri, and in 1833 settled with his family in Cass county. In 1848 he removed his family to Bates county and he engaged in business in the Indian Territory. In 1849 he emigrated across the plains to California. He arrived in the Sacramento Valley the first of October of that year but did not stop long. He came on to Sonoma, where he arrived the latter part of October. He has ever since been a resident and of the valley, and has occupied several positions of trust.

ALBERT G. LYON.

Is a native of Patrick county, Virginia, but at the age of twelve moved to Missouri. He was among the emigrants to California in 1846, arriving in the Sacramento Valley in October of that year, and spent the Winter with William Gordon, near Cache Creek, in Yolo county. In the Spring of 1847 he purchased land of Manual Vaca, on what was afterwards known as Vaca Plains. Here he raised one crop, when the excitement on the discovery of gold break-
(294)
ing out, he left for the mines. Not succeeding well at mining he left and came to Sonoma in the Fall of 1848 where he has since resided. He has been extensively engaged in farming and in the vineyard and orchard business. He is an active member of the Order of Odd Fellows, and a much esteemed citizen in the neighborhood.

CHARLES V. STUART.

Mr. C. V. Stuart, a lineal descendant of the old house of Stuarts of Scotland, was born in Lycoming county, Pennsylvania, 1819, and there spent his early years. In 1834 he removed to New York and engaged in mercantile business. In 1848 a company was formed to emigrate to California, and he joined it. Independence, Missouri was made the rendezvous for the party, and there all the supplies were shipped. In April, 1849, all things were ready and his train started on the perilous journey. The company had no wagons, all their supplies being carried on pack animals. Mr. Stuart was elected Captain of the company, which position he held till they arrived in California. From Independence the train passed on to the Arkansas River, following that river up to Pueblo thence Northerly to Snake River, thence to Salt Lake, where they remained three weeks. From Salt Lake they proceeded through Tejon Pass to Los Angeles. At the latter place Mr. Stuart left the company and proceeded to San Francisco, and has since been engaged in the real estate business. In 1859 he purchased his present valuable property in Sonoma Valley. It was the Northern part of the Agua Caliente Ranch. He has on it a large vineyard of bearing vines. Mr. Stuart has made very extensive and costly improvements on his place, and now has one of the finest and most convenient homes in the valley.

WM. B. READ.

Wm. B. Read was born in Harrison county, Ohio, in 1824, and has seen much of the world and its reverses. He worked at his trade, blacksmithing, for some time in the Shenandoah Valley; in 1845 he started for New Granada, but brought up in Rio Janeiro; 1845 thence he went to Chili and remained several months in Santiago.
(295)

In 1846 he left for San Francisco. Here he joined the Government forces and served six months in Los Angeles. He was then employed in the Quartermaster's Department at Monterey under Captain Marcy. He was one among the first miners in the cañon of the middle fork of the American River and followed mining in different places for considerable time. In 1848 he made a trip to the Sandwich Islands, but soon returned. The Winter of 1848-9 he spent in Sonoma and Pope Valleys. He was principally engaged in mining from that time till in 1862, when he came to Sonoma and located a tract of land on the East side of Agua Caliente Rancho. Here he has since resided, following the business of general farmer.

WILLIAM HOOD.

The subject of this sketch was born September 9th, 1818, in St. Andrews, county of Fife, Scotland. Here he learned his trade of carpenter, cabinet maker, and ship joiner under his father. At the age of 19 he left his father and went to Dundee, where he worked at his trade for three years. Afterwards he went to London, where he followed his business for a short time. Thence he sailed to Fort Nicolson, New Zealand, where he remained about three years, but work becoming scarce and the great fire at Valparaiso having just occurred, he sailed for that place, remaining there till 1845, when he left for the purpose of coming to California, but first going to Peru to buy a vessel there in which to make the voyage. On the road between Callao and Lima he was robbed by banditti, which deprived him of the means of purchasing a vessel. After remaining two months in Peru he took passage with Captain Juan Cooper in the bark *Hover Gipasquanna* and landed in Monterey eight days after the American flag was raised there. He started from there overland to San Francisco with Dr. McGee, arriving, in May, 1846. Here he found the Mormons, Samuel Brannan among the number, all encamped between Jackson and Clay Streets, they all having landed in San Francisco the same time as he had landed in Monterey. He followed his trade in San Francisco for some time, building several launches and scows. When the mining excitement broke out in 1848, Mr. Hood had the American bark *Annita* under repairs, and
(296)
he had to raise his men's wages to $10 per day in order to keep them at work. In the Fall of 1849 he bought, in company with Wm. Pettit, Los Guilicos Rancho, and has made it his permanent home ever since, buying Mr. Pettit's interest therein shortly after they bought it. In 1861, after the Frazer River excitement broke out, he took two ship loads of horses, mules, cattle and sheep from his ranch to Victoria with the intention of disposing of them in the mines. This enterprise failing, he took a contract from the British Government to build about forty miles of road between Lytton and the Junction. In this enterprise he used his stock to some purpose.

Having finished this contract, he put his force of men and animals on the Bentick Arm road which he brought into such condition as to admit of its use by pack trains, the first of which, his own, he drove through himself. At this time the Indians became troublesome and put an end to his operations by murdering his drivers and stealing his animals, so that he was glad to return to Sonoma, where, having had enough of adventures in other countries, he is content to rest and enjoy the beautiful home his individual exertions have made for him on Los Guilicos Rancho, where he has 160 acres of grape vines and cellar room for 200,000 gallons of wine.

JAMES A. SHAW.

Born in Hobart Town, Australia, in 1818, he spent his early years in that country. In 1842 he removed with his family to Valparaiso. Thence in 1846, in company with William Hood, he went to Peru, and came to California. In 1850 Mr. Shaw came to Sonoma and took charge of Mr. Hood's stock ranch, and continued in this business till 1858, when he purchased of John Gibbs the claim to 1,000 acres of land lying in the mountains between Guilicos Valley and St. Helena. During the great Cariboo mining excitement of 1861, he became affected, and went up to Salmon River. Four weeks satisfied him, and he went to Vancouver's, where he remained about three months. He then returned to Sonoma, and took up a lot of cattle to Vancouver's for slaughter. In 1867 he purchased 265 acres of the Guilicos Rancho, and has since made this his home, pursuing the varied branches of industry of a general
(297)
farmer, fruit grower, and stock raiser. In 1869 he was placed in charge of the property of the Sonoma Land Association, and now has under his care the property of Mr. H. K. Miller, of Virginia City, consisting of eight hundred acres of fine land lying in the center of Guilicos Valley. Mr. Shaw is a man of great energy, and has done much for the permanent welfare of this portion of the county.

N. J. S. LONG.

Mr. Long is a native of St. Louis county, Missouri, where he was born in 1815. He lived there till 1849, when he came to California, and to Sonoma the following year, and has ever since resided there. At the election of 1853 he was elected constable, and with one exception has been re-elected at every succeeding election.

LOUIS ADLER.

Born in Prussia in 1820, Mr. Adler there received his education and spent his early years. In 1846 he came to California. He lived in San Francisco for two years, and in Sonoma ever since. He was twice Councilman in Sonoma under Alcalde Fuller. He has been engaged in merchandising, farming and grape growing.

O. W. CRAIG.

Mr. Oliver W. Craig was born in Rumney, Grafton county, New Hampshire, in 1809. He was educated there, and followed the business of mechanic till he came to California. On the breaking out of the gold excitement in California he took passage on a vessel bound for San Francisco. He came through the Straits of Magellan, and landed in San Francisco July 6th, 1849. He went into the placers, and followed the fortunes of a miner for near two years, when he settled in Sonoma. His fine farm, situated on the West side of the Valley, contains three hundred acres of land. There is a large vineyard and orchard on the place, and an extensive cellar.

HOWARD CLARK.

Mr. Howard Clark is a native of Essex county, Massachusetts, where he was born in 1827. He came to California in 1849, and
(298)
for a time followed mining, but afterwards went to San Francisco and followed his trade, that of carpenter and builder. In 1863 he settled permanently in Sonoma.

THE CARRIGER BROTHERS.

Among the valuable and highly esteemed citizens of Sonoma are to be numbered the Carrigers. They are all natives of Tennessee, but lived for a few years in Missouri and came overland to California in 1849. Solomon Carriger enlisted at Johnson's Ranch under Colonel Fremont, served seven months in Southern California, and was honorably discharged at San Gabriel in the Spring of 1847. Since then he has resided in Sonoma. Caleb C. Carriger, the youngest of the three, followed much of the fortunes of his brothers. He purchased land in Sonoma in 1846; moved to Napa in 1852, but soon returned to Sonoma, and in 1856 purchased his present home of one hundred and eighty acres, in which he has highly improved. Nicholas Carriger, the oldest, was born in Carter county Tennessee, in 1816. In 1835 he joined a company of mounted volunteers mustered into the United States service by General T. E. Wool. He was honorably discharged the following year, and still holds the land warrant for one hundred and sixty acres of land issued to him in 1855 for that service. After arriving in California he served five months under Lieutenant Revere. He also served for a while under Lieutenant Maury, while the latter was in command at Sonoma. Mr. Carriger built the first redwood house and put up the first fences of that wood in Sonoma. The house was regarded with much interest by the Mexicans and native Californians in the valley. They came in great numbers to see the house, and brought pitchers and other vessels in which to bear away water from the well sunk near the house. Mr. Carriger was among the first to go to the mines after the discovery of gold, but soon returned to Sonoma. In 1849 he moved to his present home, and has since resided here, improving his valuable property. In Missouri he was engaged in growing tobacco, and as a miller and distiller. He was the first American who planted a vineyard in Sonoma. He has now over 1,050 acres of land, 130 of which are planted in vines. He has a large cellar, and manufactures his own grapes into wine. He is
(299)
likewise extensively engaged in growing the cereals and in stockraising. He was for a long time President of the Pioneer Association, and is one of the most esteemed citizens of the valley.

CHARLES W. LUBECK.

Mr. Charles W. Lubeck is a native of Sweden where he was born in 1814. His early years were spent in his native country, and he engaged in mercantile pursuits. In this business he visited various countries. In 1849, being in China, he sailed for California, landing in San Francisco in 1850. In the following year he purchased property in Sonoma Valley, making that his home. He has been engaged in San Francisco in mercantile pursuits, and in ship brokerage.

L. W. MEYER.

Mr. L. W. Meyer is a native of Germany and was trained to the business of vine grower. He emigrated to New York in 1840, and in 1846 enlisted in the United States service for the Mexican War. He was stationed at Monterey, and at the close of the war went to the mines. In 1866 he came to Sonoma, and for five years was Superintendent of General Williams' property. He then purchased property of his own, and has since been engaged in vine growing in and wine making.

FRANKLIN SEARS.

Born in Orange county, Indiana, in 1817. When quite young he emigrated to Missouri where he followed farming for many years. Started for Oregon and California in 1844, and reached this country, in the Spring of 1845, celebrating the Fourth of July of that year at Red Bluff. In 1846 he came to Sonoma and joined the forces under Fremont and served through the war. He was in the battalion that captured Los Angeles. He was afterwards stationed for a few months at San Diego under Colonel Gillespie. From San Diego the battalion went over to Aguas Calientes to meet General Kearny. They had an engagement here with the Spaniards and lost twenty men. After being discharged from the service at the close of the war, Mr. Sears went to the mines. For many years he followed
(300)
mining experiencing to the fullest the fortunes and vicissitudes of a miner's life. In 1861 he came back to Sonoma and purchased his present property Southwest of Sonoma, and has since been extensively engaged in stock raising and farming. He has about two hundred and seventy acres of land, thirty of which are planted in vineyard and orchard.

G. T. PAULI.

Born in Austria in 1827, and lived in his native country and Hamburg, Germany, till 1848, when he went to Rio Janeiro. From the latter place he went to Valparaiso, thence to San Francisco, where he arrived in the Spring of 1849. He immediately went up to Sonoma, where he has ever since remained, engaged in merchandising. In 1869 he was elected Treasurer of Sonoma county, which position he still holds. He belongs to the association of Pioneers, and is honored and respected by all who know him. _____

EDWARD NEBLETT.

Born in Prince George county Virginia, in 1818. Lived in Virginia and Kentucky till the great rush of 1849 for California, when he came to this State. He crossed the plains in company with Mr. Bryant, author of "What I saw in California." He was engaged in mining and in business in the mining counties for nearly twenty years. He was Sheriff of Trinity county from 1855 to 1857, and served one term in the Legislature. In 1868 he settled in Santa Rosa, where he has since remained, engaged in merchandising. _____

THOS. HOPPER.

Mr. Thomas Hopper was born nine miles West of Lexington, Lafayette county, Missouri, in the year 1821. His parents moved to Indiana in 1825. Then back to Missouri in 1839. On the 9th of May, 1847, he started from the town of Lone Jack, Missouri, for California. He reached Sutter's Fort September 5th, 1847. From there he went to Santa Cruz. On the 1st of June, 1848, started for the mines on the American River, working near Sutter's Mill. Remaining in the mines but a short time he returned to Santa Cruz, and from there moved his family to Napa Valley, settling near the
(301)
residence of George C. Yount. Leaving his family here he returned to the mines, but in the Winter came back to Napa. In the Spring of 1849 he joined a party for a prospecting tour to the Yuba River, but at Sacramento fell in with Joe Walker, or "Mountain" Walker, who persuaded the company to go with him to King's River, representing, that gold could be literally shovelled into bags there. Reaching the locality specified, and finding nothing, the party came very near hanging "Mountain" Walker in part payment for having sold them. The company returned to Sacramento, when Mr. Hopper left them and moved his family from Napa to Sonoma, purchasing a thirty-acre lot near the city of Sonoma, and building a house thereon. In the Fall of 1850 he moved to the head of Green Valley, Sonoma county, where he took up a claim of 160 acres. In the Spring of 1852 he sold out there and moved on to a portion of his present farm of 2,000 acres, close to the spot whereon stands his present residence.

_____

JOHN BROWN.

The subject of this sketch was born April 13th, 1826, in Wheeling, Va. When at the age of two years his parents moved to Tennessee. In the Spring of 1846 Mr. Brown enlisted in the United States Army for one year to serve in Mexico, and with the Tennessee troops landed on Brazos Island on the 1st of June, 1846. When his time expired he again joined the service and was elected first Lieutenant of his Company, and was then appointed Quartermaster's Deputy, which office he retained till the close of the Mexican War in 1848, when he returned to his home in Tennessee. Early in the Spring of 1849 he started for California across the plains in a "prairie schooner,"

which, on the little Blue River was literally capsized in a storm. The lightning was so vivid during this storm that the earth presented the appearance of a net-work of flames, and in one instance a flash went through a pillow and melted the hammer of a revolver under his head, exploding the weapon at the same time. The trip was to Mr. Brown one of pleasure, as being well provided and equipped for hunting and fishing, it devolved on him to furnish the party with meat, so that it was to him only a protracted hunting and fishing excursion barring the light-
(302)
ning. Brown arrived in California in June, 1849, and engaged himself in the mercantile business in El Dorado county. In 1850 he was appointed by Governor John McDougall Quartermaster and Commissary, for the Northern Division of California in the war against the Indians, and served all through the El Dorado Indian war, resigning in May 1852 at Sacramento City. In 1854 he went into business in Sacramento on I street, and was burned out, losing everything. From there he went to El Dorado county and opened a hydraulic claim. This was not a very successful venture, for after erecting the necessary sluices, flumes, and all other things necessary, their sale became necessary in order to liquidate the wages of the miners employed. As mining refused to be remunerative, Mr. Brown went to a small mining village in the same county, called Brownsville, which had been an old camping ground of his during the time he was Quartermaster in the Indian war. Here he taught a five months' term of school, when, concluding he was not intended for that avocation, he made his way to Sonoma, reaching here in 1855, and on the day of his arrival was appointed Deputy County Clerk, a position he retained for four years. While Deputy Clerk he studied law, and in 1858 was admitted to the Bar. He has resided in Santa Rosa ever since, following his profession.

_____

W. S. M. WRIGHT.

Mr. Wright was born in Boone county, Missouri, August 5th, 1822. He left Missouri for California in 1849, crossing the plains by the Northern route, and reached Lassen on the Sacramento River October 13th, 1849. The following Winter he spent in the mines at Stringtown, on the North Fork of the Feather River. He made a visit to Missouri in 1850, returning in 1853, and came to Sonoma and purchased a portion of his present property, which now consists of 6000 acres, on which he resides. He is a farmer and
stock raiser, a business he has followed all his life, and in which he has been eminently successful.

_____

E. LATAPIE.

This gentleman, was born in Louisville, Kentucky, in 1830. On the discovery of gold he embarked at New Orleans in the ship _Ar-_
(303)
chitect for San Francisco. In 1852 he came to Sonoma, and has resided in the county ever since. His home is in Petaluma. In 1871 he was elected Sheriff of the county but had been deputy for fourteen years previous thereto. In all his relations as private citizen and public officer, he has maintained the character of an exemplary man whose efficiency is unquestioned and whose integrity is above suspicion.

JOHN INGRAHAM.

Mr. John Ingraham was born in Casswell county, North Carolina, in 1813, where he spent his minority. From 1833 to 1848 he lived in Tennessee and Missouri, working at his trade of wagon making. He joined in the great overland rush for California in 1849. After few years spent chiefly in the mines he came to Sonoma in 1852 where he has since resided. He is now acting undersheriff.

WM. R. MORRIS.

Wm. R. Morris was born in Moniteau county, Missouri, in 1835, and lived in his native State till 1849, when he came overland to California. He arrived in the Sacramento valley in October. Thence he came to Napa, where he spent a few months, and then went up to Cache Creek. In the Spring of 1850 he went to the mines, but soon returned to Cache Creek, and remained there till 1857, when he removed to Sonoma county, where he has since resided. He located near Healdsburg, and was engaged in farming and merchandising. On the 4th of October, 1865 he, in company with W. A. C. Smith, then principal of the Healdsburg Public School, commenced the publication of the *Democratic Standard*. These two gentleman continued the publication of the paper till in October, 1866, Mr. Smith sold out to Mr. Morris. Soon after a half interest was sold to J. B. Fitch, and in January, 1867, the latter became sole proprietor, Mr. Morris taking a portion of the fine land east of the river in exchange for his interest. He then followed farming till in 1869, when he was elected County Clerk, which position he still holds.

WILLIAM MACPHERSON HILL.

This gentleman first saw the light of day, on the 22d of October,
(304)
1822, in Montgomery county, Pennsylvania, sixteen miles from Philadelphia. The first thirteen years of his life were spent on a farm; then he was sent to a boarding-school for two years, when he entered a College in Newark, remaining two years, where he was fitted for the University of Pennsylvania, at Philadelphia, and there was graduated in 1840. For fifteen months he was engaged in teaching at an Academy in Berks county. He then commenced the study of law, but abandoned this profession after a trial of six months' duration, on account of poor health. Was next engaged as first clerk in the Naval Office in the Custom House, Philadelphia, under Polk's Administration, for the next two years, when he resigned January 1, 1849, and started for California January 16th; *via* Cape Horn, arriving in San Francisco on August 3, 1849. Mr. Hill, in the course of a few days after his arrival in California, was appointed first clerk in the Custom House, and retained the position for one year, when he resigned, and started for the East by the Panama route. Returned again to California in May, 1851. At this time he was a partner in the firm of Burling & Hill, commission merchants, and returned after the May fire, which had destroyed their place of business. He was in business at the time of the June fire, but did not suffer

much loss. In June, 1853, his health being very poor, he took a trip to Manilla, during which he was absent four months. After returning to San Francisco, he immediately set out for Philadelphia, married, and returned to California in 1854. On his return he established his home on his present property in Sonoma, which he had acquired in 1851. It consists of 1400 acres, 60 of which are in vines, and 15 acres of fruit trees of all varieties. Mr. Hill was Supervisor of the county of Sonoma for three years. He was nominated for State Senator in 1862 on the compromise ticket, but shared defeat with Douglas & Breckenridge. He has always taken an active interest in all that pertained to the general welfare, and no gentleman stands higher in the respect and esteem of the community.

———————

JOEL P. WALKER.

This venerable citizen was born November 20, 1797, in Goochland county, Virginia. His family migrated in 1801, and settled in
(305)
Tennessee, where they remained till 1819, when they moved into Missouri. On the 1st of May, 1840, he started across the plains with the families of some missionaries, and found his way into Oregon the following year. He left for California, September 20, 1841, and reached Sutter's Fort on the 22d of October. In 1842, came to Napa Valley, remaining one year, and started from Cache Creek the following year for Oregon, with cattle and horses. Returned to Napa in 1848, and in 1853, moved into the neighborhood of Santa Rosa. Accompanied Commodore Wilkes' Scientific Corps in 1841 and served under Lieutenant Emmons, a grandson of General Putnam. The notorious Admiral Semmes was one of the corps. Mr. Walker was a delegate to the Convention which assembled at Monterey in 1849.

———————

T. M. LEAVENWORTH.

This gentleman, who claims to be the worst abused man in California, was born in Litchfield, Connecticut, in 1803. He graduated in the same class with James Buchanan. He sailed from New York in 1846 as Assistant Surgeon in the United States Army, and arrived in San Francisco. For eighteen months, ending in August, 1849, he was Alcalde in San Francisco. In the latter year he came to Sonoma, and has since resided here on his farm, the Agua Caliente Ranch, engaged in cultivating the soil. The Agua Caliente Ranch, of which various portions have been sold, was originally purchased as an endowment of the first organized College in California for $10,000, the College receiving a further endowment of $150,000. The trustees were John W. Geary, A. D. Cook, and John McVicker.

———————

JOSEPH WRIGHT.

Mr. Wright was born on the 22d of January, 1827, in Boone county, Missouri. Left there in 1849, to come to California, and reached Lassen on the Sacramento River, October 12th. Came to Sonoma Fall of 1851, and lived here ever since. Has been a farmer all his life.

————

CHARLES HALL.

Mr. Hall was born in Garrett county, Kentucky, May 18th, 1826. When a child his family moved to Missouri. He served in Mexico during the war in Col. Gilpin's Regiment. At the close of the war he went back to Missouri, but left there for California in 1848, reaching Lassen on the 30th of October, 1849. He settled in Sonoma county in 1860, and has been there ever since.

————

JACOB R. SNYDER.

The reminiscences of the early pioneers and adventurers on the Pacific Coast must ever possess a peculiar interest for the Californian. Green in their memory will ever remain the trials and incidents of early life in this land of golden promise. These pioneers of civilization constitute no ordinary class of adventurers. Resolute, ambitious, and enduring, looking into the great and possible future of this Western slope, and possessing the sagacious mind to grasp trite conclusions, and the indomitable will to execute just means to attain desired ends, these heroic pioneers by their subsequent career have proved that they were equal to the great mission assigned them-that of carrying the arts, institutions, and real essence of American civilization from their Eastern homes and implanting it upon the shores of another ocean. Among the many who have shown their eminent fitness for the important tasks assigned them, none merit this humble tribute to their characteristics and peculiar worth more fully than he of whom we now speak.

Jacob R. Snyder was born in Philadelphia on the 23d of August, 1813, at an early day he was apprenticed to a house carpenter, but his keen foresight showed him there was in the broad and beautiful West a great hidden destiny, a destiny that only required the hand of industry to consummate; and, abandoning the luxuries of civilization and the comforts of a well settled country, he left for the land of primeval forests and untutored savages. At the age of twenty-one we find him emigrating West. He settled at the Falls of the Ohio River, in what then was an almost unbroken forest, but where now stands the city of New Albany. Here Mr. Snyder remained for several years, but in 1845, being thoroughly imbued with the spirit of adventure, he determined to push forward to the Pacific. In the Spring

of that year he formed one of a party of nine who made Independence, Missouri, their rendezvous preparatory to the arduous journey across the plains. All necessary preparations being made, the party on the 5th of May struck camp and started on their hazardous and tedious undertaking. Besides Major Snyder, there were in the company Judge Blackburn, George McDougal, W. F. Swazy, John Lewis, Hiram Rhenshaw, (afterwards lieutenant in the California Battalion), and Messrs. Wright and Hohen. The party crossed the Sierra Nevada Mountains by what was afterwards known as the Truckee route. At that time, however, there was no trail, and they spent many days in these rugged hills seeking a proper route, but after suffering almost incredible hardships, on the 23d of September they reached Johnson's ranch on Bear River, and from there went to Sutter's Fort, where the company dispersed. Major Snyder traveled down to Yerba Buena, then numbering less than two hundred inhabitants, whence, after stopping a short time, he passed down to Santa Cruz. Owing to a disposition on the part of the natives to check the immigration from the United States, and not only to prevent the ingress of new comers, but to drive out those already in the country, Major Snyder, in the Spring of 1846, in connection with others, attempted to get a grant of land from Pio Pico, on the San Joaquin, where a fort might be erected and aid and protection granted to immigrants. But Pio Pico distrusting the movement refused the grant. Soon after the word reached him of the Bear Flag party. He was subsequently deputed by Lieutenant Gillespie from Santa Cruz to communicate in regard to public affairs with Colonel Fremont, then at Pacheco Pass. He united with Fremont's forces and returned to Monterey, prior to the latter starting on the Southern campaign. Owing to his knowledge of the country and the customs of the people, Mr. Snyder was of much service in bringing this campaign to a successful issue. He was next detailed to duty in a company of mounted riflemen under Captain Fontleroy, at the Mission San Juan, where he remained till Commodore Stockton returned to Monterey. He was then entrusted by the latter to organize an artillery company. He was afterwards commissioned Quartermaster of Fremont's Battalion, which office he filled until the close of the war. He was then appointed by Gov-

(308)

ernor Mason Surveyor General for the Middle Department of California, where his services were called into frequent activity in settling disputed questions of boundary, but he so discharged his arduous duties that he gained the esteem and confidence of the people. In the organization of civil government he was chosen a delegate from Sacramento, where he was then in business, to the convention called by Governor Riley to form a constitution. His course in this body was firm and decided, his suggestions clear and pertinent, and his attachment to the interests of the people marked and commendable. His labors were manifestly for the interests of the State, and he allowed no party trammels to swerve him in the least. None quitted that convention with more honor and more general esteem than did he.

In January, 1850, Mr. Snyder was married to Miss Susan H. Brayton, an accomplished lady, formerly of Massachusetts. He has since had the grievous misfortune of losing her.

In 1851 Mr. Snyder received the Senatorial nomination from the city of San Francisco, and was elected by a large majority. In the Legislature he proved himself admirably adapted to the position he held. He was cool and practical in all in views, untiring in his perseverance, and devoted to principle.

In 1859 he moved to Sonoma and purchased his present property. He purchased seventy-four acres from Colonel Haraszthy, and one hundred and twenty-five acres from the city of Sonoma. He has now a large vineyard and an extensive wine cellar. He has, since its organization, been President of the Grape Growers' Association and has done much to make the industry of viniculture a success.

In politics Major Snyder is a Democrat, firmly attached to the principles of that party. At every point of observation, and in all in his varied pursuits and positions, he has ever commanded the respect and esteem of all parties. He has so identified himself with the State, that her history, in a great measure, is his. He watches her progress and her extending fame with tender solicitude. He is a citizen of whom California is justly proud. Frank, courteous and confiding in his manners, liberal in the encouragement of every enterprise of moral or material worth, a man of extensive reading and

(309)

scientific acquirements, he is in all the relations of life a worthy citizen of a great and growing State.

————

MARIANO DE GUADALUPE VALLEJO.

Among the estimable citizens of Sonoma, who, owing to their services in connection with the early history of California deserve a niche in our Sketch Book, few rank higher than he of whom we now speak, General M. G. Vallejo. He is descended from an old Castilian family, and was born in Monterey July 7th, 1808. His father, who had moved from Spain to the State of Guadalajara while yet a youth, took an active part in exploring and settling California. Mariano was educated in the schools of Monterey. These schools were intended to impart an education not only intellectual and religious, but also civil and military. In 1829 he removed to the Mission at San Francisco, where he remained until 1835, acting as Commandante of the Presidio, Collector and Alcalde. In the latter year he was sent to establish a colony at Sonoma. This he did, and took a very prominent part in all the affairs of State and the revolutions of the country till the ascendancy of the immigrants from the United States. In June, 1846, he was taken prisoner by the Bear Flag party, and was for a few days confined at Sutter's Fort. He was then released by command of Commodore Stockton on his parole. General Vallejo favored the Americans in California, and seems never to have placed a high estimate upon the Mexican people. He, with the other Californians, readily acquiesced in the rule of the conquerors. He was, in 1849, elected a member of the convention to form a constitution. He has since occupied many honorable positions, and has in all acquitted himself with credit.

In 1832 he was married to Señorita Benicia Francisca Filipsa Carrillo, daughter of one of the most influential families. Fourteen children have sprung from this union. As a soldier and states-man he commanded universal respect for his marked ability, and now, as a polished gentleman, retired from the scenes of active political life, he enjoys the esteem of all who know him.

————

WM. M. BOGGS.

Mr. Wm. M. Boggs, though at present a citizen and property
(310)
holder in Napa, has in the past held so prominent a place in the annals of Sonoma, that we here notice him. He came out to California with his father in 1846, and acted as captain of the train most of the way. The ill fated Donner party was for the greater part of the journey attached to his train, and had they so continued would have escaped the horrible fate that overtook them in their snow-bound camp. Mr. Boggs crossed the Sierra Nevada some two weeks in advance of the Donner party, and reached the valley in time to secure shelter for all. He served three months in the Mexican war on this coast as a non-commissioned officer in a battalion of mounted riflemen, recruited by himself and A. F. Grayson. The battalion was attached to the command of Lieutenant Maddox of the Marine Corps under Commodore Stockton, and was honorably discharged at Monterey. Mr. Boggs settled in Sonoma with his family, and resided there seventeen years. He was a large dealer in real estate, some of the finest places in the valley having been at different

times owned by him. His eldest son, now twenty-six years old, was born in Sonoma, and is the first American born in California under the national Party. Mr. Boggs moved to Napa in 1863, and has since resided in that city. _____

WM. J. REYNOLDS.

Born in Southwark, England, in 1816 and lived in his native country, following the business of ship carpenter, till 1838. In this year he left for Valparaiso. The year following he took passage at Valparaiso for San Francisco. In California he went into the shipwright and blacksmithing business with Messrs. John Rose and J. C. Davis, under the firm name of Davis & Co. They built and launched two vessels from the point of land in Napa City now owned by G. N. Cornwell, above the stone bridge on First street.

One was a schooner, launched in 1841, the other a barge, launched in 1845. In the barge Mr. Reynolds traded up and down the streams emptying into San Francisco Bay, exchanging general merchandise for the circulating medium of the time, hides and tallow. In 1847 this same company took a contract from Salvador Vallejo, and built a mill on the East side of Napa River near seven miles above the city. Some of the timbers of this mill are still standing. The firm built

(311)

some other vessels in the State for the river and coast trade. In 1852 he settled in Sonoma, where he has ever since resided. _____

DAVID CHAMBERLAIN.

Mr. Chamberlain was born in Deerfield, Oneida county, New York, July 5th, 1819. After traveling through Louisiana, Mississippi and Ohio, and after spending the Winter of 1846-7 in Missouri, set out for Oregon on May 9th, 1847. Mr. Chamberlain arrived with the "Chicago Company," which made the first settlement in Oregon, on the 3d of October 1847. In August of the following year he emigrated to California and mined on the Feather River, getting provisions at Sutter's Fort, and paying such prices as this- flour, $25 per hundred weight. He then went to the American River as a miner. Here beef cost an ounce ($16) a pound. The same for beans, sugar and tea; and for tobacco, an ounce and a half per pound. Thence he went to Kelsey's dry diggings, since called Oregon City, and Hangtown, since grown to be the city of Placerville. Mr. Chamberlain returned to Oregon in 1849, leaving San Francisco, February 3d-fare $100 to Astoria, and thence to Portland, by canoe, $150. In April '49 he again came to California by the ox-team method. In July '49, paid, in Sacramento, $3,000 doctor bill for three month's sickness. Again he returned to Oregon in 1850. In 1851 he went East, returning to Oregon in 1854, crossing the plains a second time. In 1857 he came to Sonoma county, California, settled down, and has had a home here ever since. Visited the Sandwich Islands in 1864; returning, went to New York, by way of Panama, in 1871; again returning to California, this time via Central Pacific Railway. Mr. Chamberlain is now a resident and solid member of society in Santa Rosa.

MATHEU ENGLER.

This genial Teuton was born in Baden, Germany, 1816. In 1844 he moved to Massachusetts, and has since passed an eventful life. He remained in Massachusetts three years, then moved to Ohio, where he remained the same length of time. In the Spring of 1850 he started overland for California. His trip across the plains was romantic, though not very desirable. He traveled on foot:
(312)
started bringing his provisions on a wheelbarrow, and carrying his blankets on his back, trusting to fortune and his rifle for meat. After traveling about two hundred miles from St. Joseph, Missouri, his wheelbarrow gave out. From Green River he traveled eight hundred miles without anything to eat except what he killed. After a journey of over four months, the character of which may be judged from these incidents, he arrived in Sacramento, August 15th. He was employed as cook at Sutter's Fort with the promise of $150 per month. But the cholera breaking out one of his employers died of this epedemic, the other was hanged for horse stealing, so that his remuneration failed to appear. He then took up a 160 acre tract of land near Sutter's Fort, and erected thereon a small house, 8 x 10 feet, and called it the Eight Mile House. After stopping here four months he sold out and started by water for Gold Bluff. He took provisions and pack mules for making the overland journey after landing. He took steamer at San Francisco, but after being out at sea four days a severe storm came on, and there was for a time little hope but that the vessel would go down. Owing to the severe rolling of the vessel the mules were so badly injured that one hundred were thrown overboard. Most of the sails had been blown out of the bolt ropes, and the passengers were so thoroughly convinced of the unseaworthiness of the vessel that they compelled the Captain to put back into port. Eight days after they started they got back to San Francisco. He left San Francisco at once and started for Gold Bluff overland, with a pack train. The Winter of 1851 he spent in Weaverville and engaged in mining. His second day's mining was rewarded by his finding a two ounce nugget of gold. He was one of a company of twenty who went out to prospect the country towards the head of the Sacramento River. On account of the hostile demonstrations of the Indians, all but four of the party, three besides Mr. Engler, turned back. The remaining four were lost on the old Oregon trail, finally gave up the project and turned back.

Another expedition was formed for going out to Rogue River, but it too was given up on account of the Indians. He traveled over a great part of the rough mining country during 1851. In the fall of that year he left for Australia, and there met with severe financial
(313)
reverses, and returned the following year. He was afterward engaged at various occupations till 1858, when he came to Sonoma and purchased his present property Southwest of the town from Wm. M. Boggs. He has since devoted his attention to viniculture and general farming. He has a beautiful farm and a cellar, and manufactures his own grapes into wine.

JOHN KINDER SMITH.

This staunch and substantial citizen was born in Adams county, Illinois, 1830. In 1849 he started for California. He remained two months in Salt Lake, and reached California late in the Fall of 1849, and in 1851 moved to Sonoma county, where he has principally resided since. He was raised a farmer in his native State, and has, since coming to California, been chiefly engaged in farming and working in the lumber business. He now has a large saw-mill in Coleman Valley, in the coast country South of Russian River. He has seen much of the eventful career of a pioneer, and in all his relations in life has acquitted himself with credit and gained the esteem of all who know him.

(314)

CHAPTER V.

NEWSPAPERS OF SONOMA.

Sonoma county has been peculiarly blessed with newspapers, both as regards number and intrinsic merits. The first paper in Sonoma. The Sonoma *Bulletin,* was started by A. J. Cox, in 1850, and had a sickly existence till in 1855 it ceased to be published. It was a diminutive affair, and was issued as circumstances permitted, some times regularly, at other times with intermission, rarely ever prompt on the day announced for publication. The subsequent history both of Mr. Cox and of the press upon which the *Bulletin* was printed, are elsewhere briefly noted.

August 18th, 1855, Mr. Thomas L. Thompson issued the first number of the *Petaluma Journal and Sonoma County Advertiser.* He continued the publication of this paper till in the Fall of 1856 he sold out to H. L. Weston. Mr. Weston has been associated with

(315)

the paper a greater part of the time since. It was afterwards known as the Petaluma *Journal*, and was afterwards consolidated with the *Argus,* and has since been known as the *Petaluma Journal and Argus*. This paper has always been conducted with marked ability, and proved a paying concern. It has been a firm advocate of all matters of local and general interest, and the prosperity of that part of Sonoma county is in no small degree due to its influence. It is now published by Weston, Scudder & Co., and is one of the ablest country papers in the State. Connected with the paper is an excellent job office.

The *Petaluma Argus* was started by A. Guilliard in 1858. J. J. Pennypacker and A. J. McNabb succeeded him, and after conducting it a few years, consolidated it with the *Journal*. At the time Mr. Thompson issued the first number of the *Journal*, Sonoma county included all of Mendocino, yet the total population did not exceed 4,000.

In October, 1857, W. A. Russel, now of southern California, issued the first number of the Sonoma County *Democrat*, published at Santa Rosa. He kept the paper a year or more, and was succeeded by Budd & Pinkham. Mr. Budd soon became sole proprietor, and in April, 1860, transferred the establishment to Mr. Thos. L. Thompson. The latter gentleman continued its publication till in 1868, when he transferred it to Peabody, Ferral & Co., but resumed again in

1871, and still continues. Sonoma has for many years been the great stronghold of the Democracy in the coast counties, and the *Democrat* has always been the party paper. Yet, while it has been an earnest and zealous advocate of the principles of Democracy, it has not been behind any in its guarding the local and general interests of the people. Ever ready to assist in works of enterprise and local improvement, and ever earnest in advocating whatever would tend to better the social and moral status of the community, it has become a power in the land.

In January, 1860, Mr. A. J. Cox, the pioneer printer, commenced the publication of the *Review* at Healdsburg. This was a small five column four page paper. Mr. Cox continued the publication with varied success till in February, 1863, when an extra was issued announcing the paper's suspension. In May, 1864, Messrs.

(316)

Fenno & Warren, with Mr. Cox as editor, commenced the publication of the *Advertiser,* a sheet smaller than its predecessor. In 1865, after a suspension of some time, the paper was revived and called the *Weekly Advertiser,* J. E. Fenno, publisher, A. J. Cox, editor. But only a few numbers were issued.

On the 4th of October, 1865, the first number of the *Democratic Standard* was issued at Healdsburg. It was edited and published by Wm. R. Morris, now Clerk, and W. A. C. Smith, then principal of the public school at that place, later of St. Helena, under the firm name of Wm. R. Morris & Co. This was a six column paper. It was a local paper in its policy, taking more interest in the material welfare of that section of the county than in politics; yet, during the whole existence of the paper, it strongly advocated the principles of the Democratic party. On the 3d of October, 1866, Mr. Morris became sole proprietor, who, a few weeks thereafter transferred a half interest to John B. Fitch. In January 1867, Mr. Fitch became sole proprietor, and the following month sold out to Messrs. Boggs & Menefee. A few weeks thereafter Mr. Boggs retired, and W. A. C. Smith purchased an interest, the paper being published under the firm name of Menefee & Co., with C. A. Menefee as editor. After Boggs & Menefee purchased the establishment, the paper was enlarged, and printed on paper 26 x 40 inches, the present size of the *Napa Reporter.* Under the editorial management of Mr. Menefee, it gave a warm support to the Democratic ticket during the gubernatorial campaign of 1867. In the Winter of 1867-8 the office was transferred to Messrs. Fitch & Davis. Soon. after the transfer, the subject of voting a subsidy to a railroad company to build a road into the county came up. Two routes were to be voted upon, one to build a road connecting with the Napa Valley road near Soscol, running through Sonoma, Guilicos Valley, Santa Rosa, Healdsburg and on to Cloverdale; the other from some suitable point on the river south of Petaluma, and follow up the main valley. Messrs. Fitch & Davis were strong advocates of the former route, but a visit to Petaluma completely revolutionized their ideas, and made them strong advocates of the latter route. This compelled a change in the paper, and it was run by several parties, till in the Fall of 1868, the material was purchased by John G. Howell, its

(317)

publication discontinued, and the *Russian River Flag* started. This latter paper has always been strongly Republican in politics, but eminently local. It is still under the control and management of Mr. Howell, assisted by his brother, S. S. Howell. The *Flag,* contrary to the *Standard,* has, ever since its commencement, been a paying concern. It was for a considerable time regarded as the most wide awake local paper in the county.

In 1860 a paper was started in Petaluma called the *Republican.* It breathed awhile and then died.

In the Summer of 1870, Messrs. Woods, McGuire and Edwards commenced the publication of the first daily paper in the county, the *Daily Petaluma Crescent.* Mr. C. B. Woods was editor. The paper was Democratic in politics. It was issued by various persons, but most of the time by Mr. A. McGuire, till in the Spring of 1872 it passed into the hands of H. M. Woods. It gave a warm support to the Greeley electorial ticket, and soon after the result of the election was announced, suspended publication. In addition to its daily, it also issued a weekly edition.

At the opening of the political campaign of 1872, the *Argus* commenced the publication of a daily and has kept it up since.

In the Spring of 1872, Mr. W. J. Bowman commenced the publication of the Cloverdale *Weekly Review,* but after issuing a few numbers, declining health compelled him to give up the enterprise. Short afterwards Mr. J. B. Baccus, Jr., took the material of the *Review* and commenced the publication of the *Bee.* This was continued till in the Fall of the year, when he removed his office to Lakeport and commenced the publication of the Lakeport *Bee.*

The influence that these papers exerted upon the social, moral and material welfare of the people has been, and still is very great. The general prosperity of the country, and the superior educational and social status of the people is due, more than to any one thing, the influence these papers have exerted.

SCHOOLS AND SCHOOL FACILITIES.

Sonoma county has been pre-eminently blessed in regard to schools and school facilities. The county is divided into eighty-six school districts, and Petaluma has been set apart as a school city, (318)
with her own school regulations. In the districts in the county there are ninety-six separate schools maintained, and there are 6,127 school children in the county. The public school buildings in Santa Rosa, Petaluma, and several other places, are elegant structures, and well supplied with all the appurtenances for thorough teaching. The grade and character of the teachers has for many years been far above the average. The thorough systematization of the schools and their efficient management are in a great measure due to Mr. C. G. Ames, who for six years was active County Superintendent, and to the gentleman, Mr. G. W. Jones, who at present occupies that position.

Several high schools and colleges in embryo were at different times started in Petaluma, and for a time bid fair to become permanent institutions of the place, but after accomplishing much good, were compelled to suspend. Some of these institutions were presided over by some of the ablest educators the county afforded. But the thoroughness of the Public Schools, that were financially backed by the State, was so great, that patronage was not sufficient to these schools to warrant a farther continuation. There are in the town now two private institutions of learning, one of which, St. Vincent's Seminary, is a Catholic school under the management of the Sisters of Charity. Both of these schools are in a flourishing condition, and are doing an excellent work.

There were several attempts to make Santa Rosa the location for the establishment of a fine school. A large and imposing edifice was erected in the Northwestern portion of town by a Mr. Scott, and several unsuccessful attempts made to establish here an institution of learning. A great deal of capital was expended, but the enterprise was finally abandoned and the building sold to assist in liquidating the debts. It was moved and placed in position on Main street, and now forms the commodious Kessing Hotel. A few years after this the managers of the Pacific Methodist

College at Vacaville became dissatisfied with the latter place as an educational point, and determined to move the college and establish it at Santa Rosa. They completed in 1871 one of the finest buildings for school purposes to be found in the State, and have now one of the largest and best schools to be found in the whole country. The course of study is

(319)

complete, discipline is rigid, and thorough proficiency in studies unfalteringly exacted. It is an endowed institution, and is destined to become a great and superior resort for those wishing a complete education.

In 1872 Elder Johnston completed an elegant and commodious building to be used as a college. As soon as completed school was opened. Mr. Johnston is a member of the Christian Church, and it was his design to erect a school under the auspices of that denomination, but owing to the excellent school at Woodland he has been compelled to rely solely upon local support. This, however, notwithstanding the presence of the Methodist College and the superior Public Schools, has been very fair, and his school promises to become valuable and permanent.

Healdsburg was at an early date, owing to its beautiful location and pleasant surroundings, selected as a site for a collegiate institution. A large building was erected by Mr. Scott on a beautiful spot on the Eastern boundary of the town. Colonel Matheson, who fell at the head of his men almost at the commencement of the war between the States, opened a mechanical and agricultural school here. It was the design of the founder to build up a large institution here that should not only confer a collegiate education, but prepare those leaving it for active work in life. But the design was too comprehensive for the times, and ample support could not be had. So at the commencement of the great struggle, becoming infused with patriotic enthusiasm and a desire to lend his services to protect the unity of his country, he joined a California regiment, was sent into active operations on the Potomac and fell at the head of his men. One or two other unsuccessful attempts were made to establish a school here, till in 1863 Messrs. J. W. Anderson and S. E. Stockwell took charge of the concern and established what they called the Sotoyome Institute. the first term of this Institute opened in January, 1864, with the most flattering prospects of success. In February of the same year W. A. C. Smith was received as a partner in the adventure and took charge of the mathematical department. It continued in this management for some time, and the reputation of the thoroughness of the instruction went abroad, and it was fast growing in general favor and esteem. An unfortunate difficulty be-

(320)

tween the proprietors occurred in the Fall of 1864 that blasted the fair prospects of the institution, and it gradually declined, till in 1867 it suspended, and the building was sold to satisfy an outstanding mortgage. Thus ingloriously ended a concern that for some considerable time after incipiency promised soon to become second to none other in the State. The building was purchased by the mortgagor, Mr. Cyrus Alexander, and afterwards donated to the Presbyterian Church. There has since been a school conducted here, known as the Alexander Academy. It has able and experienced educators at the head of it, and will doubtless, backed by the Presbyterian denomination, become a permanent and useful institution. In the Spring of 1870 Mr. W. A. C. Smith opened a private school in the building owned by the Christian Church, but it lasted only a short time, when he closed it and went back to his former place of work, St. Helena, Napa county, where he still remains as principal of the school.

Several schools of importance were at different times started at Sonoma. That town, being the oldest one in the county, received the earliest attention as an educational center. As early as 1857 the foundation for a magnificent college edifice was laid. The building was afterwards completed, and is an imposing and commodious school building. A high school was commenced known as the Cumberland Presbyterian College. It was at different times conducted under different managers, but a few years since closed. The building is not now occupied. Many other attempts were made at different times and places with private schools, but the efforts produced nothing permanent. Under the present able management of the Public Schools, private institutions must be much more than mediocre to be at all successful.

CHURCHES, ETC.

For church facilities Sonoma has few superiors, and for her benevolent orders she stands in the front ranks. In the towns large and commodious churches are erected, while in the country, school houses are most frequently used. In Petaluma there are several churches, four of which, Episcopal, Baptist, Congregational and Christian, have edifices assessed at $1,200, and over, the last, for (321) over $6,000. In Santa Rosa there are Catholic, Advent, Methodist (South), Methodist (North), Presbyterian, Baptist and Christian churches, each of which have an edifice assessed at from $1,400 to $2,800. In Windsor there is a large building known as the Anti-Sectarian Church, which was erected in 1867 chiefly by the labors of one Kirkpatrick for the purpose of having a place where all kinds of worship, or speaking, could be held free. It has never been finished but is used. The Methodists (South) also have a building here. At Healdsburg the Christians, Adventists, Baptists, Catholics, Methodists, North and South, and Presbyterians, all have separate houses of worship. Besides these, Sebastopol, Bloomfield, Sonoma, Bodega and other places have edifices dedicated to church purposes.

The Masonic Order is the oldest in the county, and has seven subordinate Lodges, and two of Royal Arch Masons. The Lodges are as follows: Temple Lodge, No. 14, Sonoma; Santa Rosa Lodge, No. 57, Santa Rosa; Petaluma Lodge, No. 77, Petaluma; Sotoyome Lodge No. 123, Healdsburg; La Fayette Lodge, No. 126, Sebastopol; Curtis Lodge, No. 140, Cloverdale; Vitruvius Lodge No. 145, Bloomfield; Arcturus Lodge, No. 180, Petaluma; Russian River Lodge, No. 181. Windsor; Bodega Lodge, No. 213, Bodega. The first Chapter of Royal Arch Masons, No. 22, was established at Petaluma. The second one was established and the first meeting held by dispensation at Santa Rosa on the last Wednesday in March, 1873.

The Order of Odd Fellows was not established till a later date, but they have spread rapidly, and now number nine Lodges in the county, as follows: Sonoma Lodge, No. 28, Sonoma; Petaluma Lodge, No. 30, Petaluma; Santa Rosa Lodge, No. 53, Santa Rosa; Healdsburg Lodge, No. 64, Healdsburg; Evergreen Lodge, No. 61, Sebastopol; Osceola Lodge, No. 215, Windsor; Relief Lodge, No. 196, Stoney Point; Cloverdale Lodge, No. 193, Cloverdale; Valley Ford Lodge, No. 191, Valley Ford. In addition there is one Encampment, Relief, No. 29, at Petaluma.

The Order of Red Men established their first Lodge in Healdsburg in 1870. Another one has since been established in Windsor. The most numerous Order in the county is that of the Good Templars. Their first Lodge, No. 32, was established in Healds-

(322)

burg, May 12th, 1861. For several years the Order made little progress. Up to 1870 there were but three Lodges in the whole county, but in that year it commenced to grow, and now numbers fourteen Lodges. They are as follows: Star of Hope Lodge, No. 32, Healdsburg; Valley Ford Lodge, No. 156, Valley Ford; Young America Lodge, No. 162, Bloomfield; Enterprise Lodge, No. 356, Guerneville; Cloverdale Lodge, No. 357, Cloverdale; Melissa Lodge, No. 374, Coleman Valley; Santa Rosa Lodge, No. 370, Santa Rosa; Phoenix Lodge, No. 371, Windsor; Buena Vista Lodge, No. 373, Bodega Corners; Evergreen Lodge, No. 375, Sebastopol; Two Rock Lodge, No. 378, Two Rock; Star of the West Lodge, No. 380, Petaluma; Liberty Lodge, No. 381, Stony Point; Bethel Lodge, No. 382, near Petaluma.

There are six banking houses in Sonoma county-three at Petaluma, two at Santa Rosa and one at Healdsburg. In Petaluma are the Savings Bank, 0. W. Walker, Cashier; the Sonoma Bank, J. L. Van Doren, Cashier; and the private house of I. G. Wickersham Co. in Santa Rosa there are the Savings Bank, F. G. Hahman, Cashier, and the Santa Rosa Bank, C. G. Ames, Cashier; and in Healdsburg the private house of Canan, Hutton & Smith.

The Sonoma and Marin Agricultural Society has property assessed at $8,000; the Sonoma Water Company of Petaluma, $16,256; the Sonoma and Marin Beneficial Association, $18,000; and the Washington Hall Association of Petaluma, $10,000.

In the county there are fourteen saw mills having a capacity of from 10,000 to 30,000 feet of lumber per day; eight grist mills of different capacities: ten brickyards, two potteries, six tanneries, and two planing mills.

THE RAILROAD.

The railroad history of Sonoma is brief but expressive. In the Spring of 1868 the subject of voting a subsidy of $5,000 per mile to some company who would construct a road through the county, came before the people, the Legislature having acted on the question. At the election authorized for the decision of this question, the vote was not only as to the giving of the subsidy, but as to the line of the proposed road. Two routes were proposed, one from Vallejo by

(323)

way of Soscol, Sonoma, Guilicos Valley, Santa Rosa, Healdsburg, and up to Cloverdale, with branch leading West from Santa Rosa, if desired; the other from some suitable point below Petaluma up to Santa Rosa and along the same route, with branch leading from above Petaluma out through Two Rock and Big Valleys. At the election the Petaluma route was selected, and the subsidy voted by large majorities. In 1868 the San Francisco and Humboldt Bay Railroad Company was organized to build a railroad from Saucelito to Humboldt Bay, on the route through Sonoma county as selected by the popular vote. The Company did nothing but grade a few miles of road between Petaluma and Santa Rosa. Affairs here rested till the following year, when all the rights, franchises, etc., of this company were transferred to the San Francisco and North Pacific Railroad Company. Nothing was done by the new Company until August, 1870, when Peter Donahoe, of San Francisco, purchased the stock and commenced operations. This person commenced one of the most vigorous prosecutions on record for individual capital. He commenced work about the first of September, and in no less than four months had the road

running as far as Santa Rosa, a distance of twenty-two and a half miles. Mr. Donahoe built this road entirely with white labor, no Chinese being employed, and paid for the same as the work progressed out of his own private resources. In the spring of 1871 the California Pacific Railroad Company began grading between Santa Rosa and Healdsburg, ostensibly with the intention of building a road between these points, and finally extending up to Cloverdale, before Mr. Donahoe could complete his, and thus claim the subsidy. But their real designs were to make Mr. Donahoe sell his works and franchises. They succeeded, and the latter transferred to them all of the road, right of way, depot buildings, rolling stock, etc., for the sum of $750,000. The California Pacific then pushed the work along, and early in 1872 had the cars running into Cloverdale. When this Company transfered all their property and franchises to the Central Pacific Road, this road through Sonoma likewise passed. It continued under the control of the latter Company till early in 1873, when it was transferred back to Mr. Donahoe, under whose management it still remains.
(324)

The road has been of inestimable benefit to Sonoma County, especially to that portion through which it passes. Santa Rosa, Healdsburg and Cloverdale have had new life infused into them, and have made most rapid strides in progress and improvement. The population has steadily increased, both in the town and in the country. The communication with the City is so convenient and so direct, that people in the metropolis come up along the road to select pleasant residences. The value of land has increased very much, and business has more than doubled.

———

ELECTION RETURNS OF SONOMA.

Not pretending to give a detailed history of Sonoma, we omit all the election returns up to 1865. In this year the following officers were elected: Senator, George Pearce; Representatives, O. H. Hoag, J. L. Downing, A. C. Bledsoe; Sheriff, James P. Clark; County Clerk, Wm. L. Anderson; County Recorder, Murray Whalon; County Treasurer, E. T. Farmer; District Attorney W. Ross; Assessor, G. W. Huie; Surveyor, J. B. Wood; Superintendent of Public Instruction, C. G. Ames; Public Administrator, R. G. Baber; Coroner, L. D. Cockrill. Supervisors, J. K. Smith, Z. Jackson, A. B. Aull. On November 5th, 1866, G. W. Frick was appointed to fill the unexpired term of Z. Jackson, resigned.

At the election of 1867 there was a total vote of 4,201 cast, Out of which H. H. Haight for Governor had a majority of 940. The following officers were elected members of Assembly, S. M. Martin of Two Rock Valley, Wm. Caldwell, of Cloverdale, and J. B. Warfield, of Sonoma Valley; Sheriff, Samuel Potter, of Bodega; Clerk, Wm. L. Anderson, of Santa Rosa; Recorder, W. H. Bond, of Santa Rosa; Treasurer, E. T. Farmer, of Santa Rosa; District Attorney, A. P. Overton, of Petaluma; Surveyor, J. B. Wood, of Healdsburg; Assessor, A. J. Gordon, of Healdsburg; Superintendent of Schools, C. G. Ames, of Santa Rosa; Public Administrator, L. D. Cockrill, of Bloomfield; Coroner, Wm. Mead; Road Commissioner, Z. Jackson; County Judge, C. W. Langdon; Supervisors, J. K. Smith and J. D. Grant.

At the Presidential election of 1868 there were 4,201 votes cast with a majority of 603 for Seymour.
(325)

At the general election of 1869 there was no regular Republican ticket run, but a ticket made up of compromise men from both Republican and Democratic candidates in opposition to the regular Democratic nominations. The vote was not so large as in 1867, and the majorities for the regular Democratic ticket not more than half so large. It resulted in the following choice, all Democrats: Senator, Wm. Burnett, of Petaluma; members of Assembly, Barclay Henley, of Santa Rosa, B. B. Munday, of Petaluma, and T. W. Hudson, of Healdsburg; Sheriff, Samuel Potter; Clerk, Wm. R. Morris, of Healdsburg; Recorder, Wm. H. Bond; Treasurer, G. T. Pauli, of Sonoma; District Attorney, A. P. Overton; Assessor, A. J. Gordon; Superintendent of Public Instruction, G. W. Jones; Public Administrator, Geo. A. Noonan; Road Commissioner, R. Head; Coroner, S. Larrison; Surveyor, J. B. Wood. At the judicial election in the same year, out of a total vote of 2,444, W. C. Wallace, of Napa, received a majority of 590 over J. B. Southard for District Judge. James M. Palmer was elected Supervisor.

At the general election of 1871, the vote was, considering the number of registered voters, very small. Out of a total vote of 4,393 for Governor, H. H. Haight received a majority of 631. Geo. Pearce, of Petaluma, received a majority over J. M. Coghlan for Congress, of 589. The following county officers were elected: For Senator to fill the unexpired term of Wm. Bennett, deceased, B. F. Tuttle, of Petaluma; members of Assembly, B. B. Munday, Wm. Caldwell, and E. C. Henshaw, of Big Valley; Clerk, W. R. Morris; Recorder, W. H. Bond; District Attorney, Barclay Henley; Sheriff, Edward Latapie, of Petaluma; Treasurer, G. T. Pauli; Assessor, W. C. Gaines; Superintendent of Schools, Geo. W. Jones; County Surveyor, J. B. Wood; Public Administrator, L. B. Hall; Coroner, Charles Humphries; Road Commissioner, R. Head; County Judge, A. P. Overton.

For President in 1872 there were but 3,301 votes cast, and a majority of 99 for Grant; while for Congressman there were 3,365 votes cast, of which Luttrell had a majority of 63.
(326)

VALUE OF LAND.

Real estate is generally rated high in Sonoma as well as in Napa county. The county is divided into thirteen townships. Petaluma, including the city of Petaluma, and extending North; Vallejo, including the hill country lying East and Northeast of Petaluma; Sonoma, including the town and valley of Sonoma; Santa Rosa, including the town of that name and surrounding country; Anally, including towns of Sebastopol and Bloomfield, and intermediate country; Mendocino, including town of Healdsburg, the rich surrounding country, and extending down the valley of Russian River; Cloverdale, including the town of that name and country surrounding, to the Lake and Mendocino county lines, and a great part of the mountainous country West; Washington, lying between Mendocino and Cloverdale townships, and extending East to the Napa and Lake county lines; Salt Point, lying along the ocean South of the Mendocino line; Ocean, lying South of Salt Point township and extending down to Russian River; Bodega, lying along the coast South of Russian River, and including Coleman Valley and the towns of Freestone, Bodega Corners, and Bodega Port; Redwood, lying in the great redwood district of the county, and Russian River, lying along that river South of Mendocino township. The land in these townships is divided by the Assessor into four grades, called respectively First, Second, Third, and Fourth Quality. The first quality land is assessed at from $75 to $150 per acre, according to location; second quality from $50 to $75; third quality, from $25 to $50; fourth quality, $1 to $25. Santa Rosa, Sonoma, and

Mendocino, are the principal Townships having large quantities of land of the first and second quality; of the third quality, Vallejo, Petaluma, and Anally are principal; of the fourth quality, Mendocino, Santa Rosa, and Annally have the largest quantities, though Salt Point and Ocean have no other kind. The Assessor's returns show the following: First quality, 5,589 1/2 acres; average value per acre, $107.14 3/4; second quality, 11.869 3/4 acres, average per acre, $56.32; third quality, 119,801 3/4 acres, average per acre, 30.32 3/4; fourth quality, 485,344 acres, average per acre, $9.08 1/4. The land of the fourth quality is principally hilly and mountainous, suited only to grazing and to growing the vine. The third comprises the lands

(327)

along the foot-hills, and the greater part of it is excellent vineyard land, and well adapted to growing many other kinds of productions. The first and second qualities comprise the great body of agricultural lands of the county, and those convenient to market. Here is the home of the cereals, the fruits, etc. Here are located the towns of the county, and are established the most wealthy and substantial citizens.

CHARLES HOPPER

MENDOCINO COUNTY

216

(331)

SCENE AT THE MOUTH OF THE ALBION RIVER.

CHAPTER I.

GENERAL DESCRIPTION.

We now come to the last and the largest of the four counties of which this volume treats. Mendocino county lies along the shore of the Pacific Ocean from the mouth of the Gualala River to the fortieth parallel, and is bounded on the East by Lake county almost entirely, and North by Humboldt and Trinity counties. The line between Mendocino and Lake follows the dividing ridge between the waters of Russian River and the waters of the Sacramento, until it reaches a point at about thirty miles Northeast of Ukiah, when it crosses one branch of Eel River in a line due North, and then takes the divide between the waters of Eel and Sacramento Rivers.

(332)

The length of the county North and South is about eighty miles, having an average width of about sixty miles. It has an area of more than 2,000,000 acres, of which nearly half is suitable for cultivation, about one-tenth good grazing land, and the remainder rugged hills and mountains. Two almost parallel ranges of the coast mountains extend through the whole length of the county. The range on the East is a continuation of the Mayacamas Mountains. In this range, near Potter's Valley, rise the two largest rivers of this section, Russian and Eel; and between it and the Western range are the valleys of the county. In the Western range rise quite a number of streams, some of them of considerable volume that flow Westerly into the ocean. None of these little streams are navigable, but many of them are made serviceable by lumbermen, both in floating logs down to the mills and also in furnishing power to turn the machinery. Many of these streams form estuaries where they flow into the ocean, and these estuaries afford fair shipping places. Many other streams rise in the slopes East and West of the chain of valleys between the main ranges and flow into either the Eel or Russian River. Thus it will be perceived that Mendocino is one of the best watered counties in the State. Along the whole Western slope for over one hundred miles, and extending back from ten to thirty miles, lies the great redwood district of the county. This whole vast area is covered by one dense and almost impenetrable forest of giant trees from two to four hundred feet high, and from ten to sixty feet in circumference. East of this timbered section is a tract of open country of great value as a pastoral district.

The county is divided into three geographical sections: That consisting of Sanel, Ukiah, Redwood and Potter Valleys, from which flow the waters of Russian River southerly; that consisting of Little Lake, Sherwood, Long Valley and Round Valley, from which the water flows Northward through Eel River to Humboldt Bay, and that consisting of a strip of country from twelve to twenty miles wide lying immediately upon the coast, intersected by the Garcia Nevarra, Albion, Rio Grande, Noyo, and Ten-Mile Rivers, all running nearly West into the ocean. The first named division is ag-

(333)

ricultural and pastoral, the former predominating. The second is agricultural and pastoral, the latter predominating.

————

THE COAST DIVISION.

The third is agricultural, pastoral, and lumbering, the latter being by far the predominating industry. This latter section is mainly heavily timbered with redwood and fir, interspersed with pine, laurel, madronas, live oak, burroak, etc. Along the immediate bank of the ocean is a strip of open land of great fertility, from one to three miles wide. The shore is generally a bluff rock fifty feet high, there being not more than twenty-five miles of beach in the whole stretch of over one hundred miles.

The principal shipping points are Noyo, Caspar, Mendocino, Albion, Nevarra, Little River, Salmon Creek, Cuffey's Cove, Point Arena, and Gualala. There are numerous other places where the shipping of railroad ties, bark, posts, wood, etc., is carried on, but they are mostly dangerous except in the calmest weather. Little River, Cuffey's Cove and Fish Rock are the safest roadsteads, while Albion and Novo offer safe anchorage for vessels that are taken up the river. The other shipping places are only protected from wind and waves in one direction. At nearly all the shipping points mentioned are situated sawmills with a varying capacity of from ten to twenty-five thousand feet per day. Over three hundred thousand feet were once sawed in one day at the Mendocino mill, on an extraordinary occasion, in twelve hours. The same mill once sawed eighty-six thousand feet of lumber from one redwood tree. At the Noyo mill a plank twelve feet long and seven feet wide was sawed for the Mechanics' Institute. The average annual production of lumber from these mills has been over forty-five million feet for the last two or three years. These mills are grand concerns. Most of them cost from $20,000 to $60,000. The one at the mouth of the Albion was erected at a cost of $35,000; at the mouth of the Gualala, $30,000; at the mouth of the Nevarra, $30,000; at Mendocino City, $60,000. When driven by a press of work they sometimes run night and day, and at such times it requires a very large force of men to work them.

The agricultural productions of this section consists principally of
(334)
hay, oats and potatoes; plums, pears and apple do well, but the softer fruits and corn, tomatoes and melons do not grow well nor ripen. The temperature is very equable, but inimical to persons troubled with throat and lung difficulties and rheumatism. At Fort Bragg, near the Noyo River, the mercury remained between 65^0 and 75^0 Fahrenheit for eighteen months. The rushing wind and driving fogs are the only disagreeable features.

THE RUSSIAN RIVER DIVISION.

The first geographical division, comprising that portion lying upon the waters of Russian River, is particularly favored in respect to climate; the lowest range of the mercury in twelve years having been 16^0 and the highest 112^0. The upper valleys, particularly, have afforded a residence for asthmatic persons, almost entirely relieving them of any return of the disease. The climate of these valleys is quite humid, and being so elevated, and more subject to the coast winds and fogs, is colder than the valleys further South and East. In Summer the forenoons are warm, but the sea breeze springs up near the middle of the day and tempers the air to a delightful coolness. Snow sometimes falls upon the hills surrounding the valleys, but rarely to lie upon the ground more than a week or less, and seldom falling in the valleys at all. In this division is situated Ukiah City, the county seat, with a population of about 1,000. The town is situated upon a gravelly bench sloping gently towards the main valley on the East, backed by a high chimisal mountain on the West, with the Valley of Ukiah (Indian, To-ky-zah) stretching North and South for about ten miles, and in the East beyond the Clear Lake range rising in broken, bushy masses, to guide the eye grandly up to the blue horizon. This valley was covered with the Zokaya Grant, owned by Hastings, Curry & Carpentier, of eleven leagues, and was surveyed and sold in lots to suit purchasers. The land brought higher prices than were ever before realized from a grant of its size and location in the State. The soil along Russian River, which flows through its center, is a sandy loam, and produces all the small grains, hops, tobacco, corn and fruit, in the greatest perfection. The best land now commands fifty dollars per acre. Ukiah, the county seat, has one shoe store, one grocery and provision store, two drug stores, two stationery and
(335)
fancy stores, six dry goods and grocery stores, two furniture stores, two livery stables, seven saloons, four churches, Masonic, Odd Fellows' and Good Templar Halls, several milinery shops, etc.

South of Ukiah, fourteen miles, lies the town of Sanel, in Feliz Valley, named from the valley being covered by a grant owned by a family of that name. This town contains two stores, one saloon, one blacksmith shop, and seven or eight dwellings. From its vicinity was sent the first deed recorded in the county. The deed was from Louis and Beatrice Pena to Richard Harrison, of 500 acres of the Feliz grant, for consideration of $2,000. The first mortgage was from Wm. Heeser to W. H. Kelly, mortgaging what now constitutes a good part of the town of Mendocino, for the penal sum of $4,000.

North of Ukiah, twelve miles, lies Potter Valley, so called from the Potter brothers who first settled there in August, 1853. This valley is seven miles long from Northeast to Southwest, and an average width of two miles. In it is about 4,000 acres of good corn land and several thousand more adapted to small grains. Fruit and grapes do well, and the climate is about three degrees cooler than in Ukiah. Asthmatic persons are almost entirely cured by a residence there. The East branch of Russian River rises in this valley. The North end of the valley reaches to within one and a half miles of the South branch of the North Fork of Eel River, and the low gap affords the best route for a railroad to connect San Francisco Bay and Humboldt Bay. Two small towns are laid out in this valley three miles apart -Centreville and Pomo- each consisting of a store, blacksmith shop, saloon, hotel, and four or five dwellings. The soil of the valley is sandy loam and black loam, tapering off to light sand soil or adobe as you go up the hills surrounding the valley.

Directly North of Ukiah, eight miles, on the West branch of Russian River, lies Redwood Valley. At its Southern foot is the town of Calpella. This place was laid out by Col. Veeder and his son-in-law, James Pettus, and for a time was a rival of Ukiah. Between these two places was quite a contest for the honor of being selected for the county seat. Ukiah triumphed, and Calpella fell into decay. It is now owned in great part by Mrs. Capt. DeWolf, widow of the gallant Capt. DeWolf who was lost with the Brother Jonathan. She

(336)

has surveyed and marked out streets, plazas and squares, and is offering great inducements for settlers. It now contains two hotels, one blacksmith shop, and four residences.

———————

THE EEL RIVER DIVISION.

The second division, comprising the Eel River valleys, is probably the best pastoral country in the Coast Range. The soil is generally dark and rich, yet not much of the adobe, and is covered with a rich growth of clover, wild oats, bunch grass, rosin weed or wild sunflower. For timber it has all the varieties of pine known to California, several kinds of oak, laurel, redwood, some little cedar on the higher ranges, and maple. Most of the mountain part is as yet unsurveyed, and is held by brush fence titles in large ranches counted by square miles. Round Valley is the largest valley, and is about seven miles in diameter in any direction; the soil mostly rich loam, but approaches the adobe on the East side and rather gravelly on the West. It was first settled in 1856 by Government employes from the Nomo Calkee Indian Reservation, as an Indian farm or station. From fear of the wild tribes surrounding the valley, many settlers were induced by the authorities to accompany the Government train, and from this time the valley rapidly filled up. Much trouble was experienced with Indians, usually nothing more serious than wholesale destruction of stock, though occasionally a house would be burned and a lone settler or hunter waylaid. At the present time the valley contains about forty families, and will soon afford room for many more. Improvements have been at a standstill for years on account of the declared intention of the Government to take the whole valley for an Indian Reservation, and consequent ejectment of the settlers. By a bill passed at the last session of Congress, about two-thirds of the valley will be thrown into market and the controversy forever settled. This alone will add near $400,000 of taxable property to the assessment roll of Mendocino county. Up to the year 1870 all supplies were packed into the valley on the backs of mules. Wagons were brought in from the Sacramento

over a difficult natural road, but not of such a nature as to admit of freighting. In 1869 the people, with the assistance
(337)
of an appropriation from the county, built a road of forty miles in length to connect with the county seat, and now a road has been commenced to connect the valley with Humboldt Bay. Long Valley and Sherwood are hardly entitled to the name of valleys, as they are but one farm wide, though the former stretches Northwest and Southeast for several miles. Cahto is the postoffice and business place for Long Valley, for here are the store, saloon, blacksmith shop, saddler shop, postoffice, and express office. It is a high but beautiful valley, owned by Robert White and John P. Simpson, and was settled in the early days of the county. Long Valley lies a little to the East of it and is the head of one branch of Eel River: Cahto is the head of stage travel on the route from San Francisco to Humboldt, the mail being packed from this point to Hydesville on mules. Sherwood Valley was first settled by A. E. Sherwood, from whom it took its name. It is more a settlement on the hills than a valley, though Sherwood has a fine valley farm, as also L. Tuttle and one or two more; but the "valley" is made up of numerous detached glades dotted around through the timber and hills. Little Lake, lying about eighteen miles North and six West of Ukiah, is a fine mountain valley containing about forty farms in the valley proper, and numerous others in the detached valleys surrounding it. Martin, Henry and Samuel Baechtel were the first permanent settlers of whom we have any knowledge. They commenced erecting buildings of split redwood in 1853. Alvin Potter, Wm. Roberts, and James Rawlison, Fulwider brothers, and others, soon joined them and are still residents in the valley. Little Lake retains her original population to a greater extent than any other settlement in Mendocino county. The valley is nearly round, and in Winter has quite a lake in the North, or lower end of the valley, from which the waters join those of Long Valley, and Sherwood.

These three last named valleys are quite elevated, and are sometimes visited by frosts as late as June, yet most of the fruits of a temperate climate, including peaches, rarely fail of producing a good crop. The hills afford excellent pasturage, and the timbered portions offer better feed, in the shape of nuts, for hogs, than the lower valleys of the county.
(338)

CHAPTER II.

HISTORICAL SKETCH.

Mendocino county was originally organized by Act of the Legislature approved March 11th, 1859, having been up to that time attached to Sonoma county for civil and political purposes. Jos. Knox, F. Nally, H. Baechtel, G. W. Brown and Wm. Heeser were appointed Commissioners to locate polling places for the first election. On the first Monday in May of that year the following county officers were elected and entered upon the discharge of their several duties: Sheriff, J. B. Price; Clerk, G. Carminy Smith; Surveyor, J. J. Cloud; Treasurer, John W. Morris; School Superintendent, A. L. Brayton; District Attorney, Wm. Neely Johnson; County Judge, Wm. Henry; Assessor, John Burton; Assemblyman, J. B. Lamar; Supervisors, O. H. P. Brown, J. F. Hills, Daniel Miller.

February 20th, 1860, Dan Miller resigned and H. Willitts was elected Supervisor.
(339)

September 4th, 1861, H. Willitts, M. T. Smith, and John Gschwind were elected Supervisors. Clerk, G. Carminy Smith; Sheriff, W. H. Tainter; District Attorney, Wm. Neeley Johnson; Superintendent of Schools, E. R. Budd; Public Administrator, W. H. Kelly; Treasurer, J. W. Morris; Assessor, J. Burton; Coroner, J. D. McGann. Total vote, 1,345.

September 3d, 1862, Supervisor, O. H. P. Brown; County Judge, R. McGarvey. Total vote, 1,040.

September 2d, 1863, Assembly, L. Wilsey; District Attorney, R. McGarvey; Sheriff, L. M. Warden; Clerk, F. W. Watsons; Treasurer, J. W. Morris; Assessor, E. S. Reed, removed and S. W. Haskett appointed; Coroner, E. M. Pierson; Superintendent of Schools, J. S. Broaddus; Surveyor, C. A. Conkling. Judicial election October 21st, 1863, County Judge, E. R. Budd. Votes cast, 1034. At the Gubernatorial election the month previous, 1203 votes were cast.

September 6th, 1865, Assembly Wm. Holden; Sheriff, L. M. Warden; Clerk, Jas. Anderson; District Attorney, T. B. Bone; Treasurer, S. Orr; Assessor, B. J. McManus; Coroner, T. J. Cooley; Surveyor, J. S. Heiser; Superintendent of Schools, C. C. Cummins; Supervisor, O. H. P. Brown.

Special election November 6th, 1868, D. B. Holman elected Supervisor in place of Willitts, resigned.

September 4th, 1867, Assembly, W. H. Cureton; Sheriff, D. C. Crockett; Clerk, James Fowzer; District Attorney, T. B. Bone; Treasurer, S. Orr; Assessor, J. A. Jamison; Coroner, J. McNeil; Surveyor, T. P. Smythe; Superintendent of Schools, C. C. Cummins, resigned and T. B. Bond appointed; Supervisor, J. Shoemaker. Total vote, 1412.

November 3d, 1868, L. F. Long, T. W. Dashiells elected Supervisors. Vote cast 1623.

September, 1869, Assembly, G. W. Henley; Sheriff, D. C. Crockett; Clerk, J. Fowzer; Assessor, J. A. Jamison; District Attorney M. A. Kelton; Treasurer, Wm. Ford; Surveyor, T. P. Smythe Supervisors, T. W. Dashiells, Wm. Handley.

September, 1871, Assembly, Geo. B. Mathurs; Sheriff, S. J. Chalfant; Clerk, H. J. Abbott; Treasurer, Wm. Ford; District

(340)

Attorney, M. A. Rilton; Assessor, J. H. Donohoe; Superintendent of Schools, J. M. Covington; County Judge, R. Harrison; Coroner, S. W. Haskett; Supervisors, W. J. Hildreth.

November, 1872, H. Willitts elected Supervisor.

The first permanent white settlements in the county were made in 1852 on the coast. In the first week of April of that year, Captain Peter Thompson, one of Carson's old trappers, Geo. Raney, afterwards mate of a Panama steamer, and Steve ---, clerk for American Consul at Callao, passed down through Anderson Valley, and on to the coast, reaching it worn out with fatigue and hunger. At Little River Thompson shot an elk and plenty crowned their festive board. Thompson settled at Pine Grove, four miles above Big River, and was the first known permanent white settler of Mendocino county. He is a native of Ayershire, Scotland, and is now 72 years of age. He went through the Apache country with Walker in 1836; was with Carson in several expeditions in South America in 1848. In 1844, in command of a company, he attempted to go down the Upper Colorado Cañon on the ice with fifty horses. Starting in February they were soon caught in the Spring thaws, and the breaking ice compelled them to climb the mountains where they were so rugged that their horses were often lowered from one bench to another with ropes. He is still hale and hearty, and leads as wild a mountain life as this county will afford. In the Fall of 1852 the sawmill at Big River in Mendocino was commenced by Henry Meigg, J. B. Ford and others. This enterprise was soon after succeeded by the building of the Novo, Albion, Nevarra and Caspar mills. In 1852 Wm. and Thos. Potter, M. C. Briggs, Al. Strong, J. L. Anderson, and Cestos Feliz, went up Russian River to Potter. In August, 1853, the Potter brothers moved their stock up there. In 1856 Thomas Henley, as Indian Agent of Nome Lackie, established a farm in Round Valley; he was accompanied by Denman Brothers, Martin Corbett, C. H. Bourne, G. E. White, and some others. In 1859 John Parker and John Turk settled in the lower end of Ukiah Valley with cattle belonging to Jerry Black of Marin county, also Truman. In 1851 L. B. Arnold and three others came up through Ukiah Valley and across to Anderson and back to Cloverdale, killing twelve or fourteen grizzly bears on the route.

(341)

Ukiah City, has since the organization of the county, been the county seat. The town was incorporated in September, 1872, by the election of T. L. Carothers, S. Orr, R. N. Wellisey, J. R. Moore and E. W. King as Trustees; Thos. Charlton, Marshal; J. L. Wilson, Assessor. The original Court House was built by E. Rathburn for $7,000, in the Fall of 1859. A new Court House was built by A. P. Petit in the Fall of 1872 for $40,000. County Court was convened in the new building for the first time on the first Monday in March, 1873.

RESOURCES OF MENDOCINO.

As noted in various places along through the descriptive sketch of this county, the resources are varied and extensive. At present the chief business is lumbering. Mendocino City, situated on a bay of the same name, at the mouth of Big River, is a town of considerable importance in the center of this lumber trade.

Grazing and stock-raising is of much importance and increasing. Agriculture, owing to the distance from market, is chiefly confined to domestic necessities. Farmers find it more remunerative to feed their stock with their surplus grain and drive the stock to market, than to attempt to transport the grain.

Mendocino affords evidence of the presence of various minerals, but not as yet discovered in quantities to pay for working. Virgin copper has been found, and its sulphates in numerous places, Gold has been washed out near Calpella by means of rockers. Traces of silver and gold in quartz have caused excitements from time to time, and lately some excellent cinnabar veins are said to have been found near Ukiah. A very large vein of coal, forming a bar eight feet thick across the river, exists four miles above the forks of Eel River, between Round Valley and Eden Valley. I. Friedlander has entered 30,000 acres of land around the vein. It was first located and steps taken to interest capitalists in it by B. S. Coffman, formerly a Lieutenant stationed at Round Valley, but it was first discovered and coal brought out by H. L. Hall, many years a resident in Eden Valley. The vein is but four miles from the proposed railroad route.

Many springs abound, the virtues of which are as various as the

(342)

diseases of man. Near Ukiah is one peculiarly efficacious in skin and rheumatic complications, and has materially improved several bad cases of asthma. On the head waters of Big River, fifteen miles from Ukiah, is the Hot Sulphur Springs. At either end of Potter Valley are soda and sulphur springs, each possessing their peculiar virtues. On the ranch of the late Dr. Sargeant, in Long

Valley, is a mineral spring of large volume, but of unknown properties, which afford almost water enough to run a small mill.

Mendocino county offers peculiar inducements to tourists and pleasure seekers. The Eel River section is one of the finest hunting and fishing countries to be found. In all parts of the county, save the immediate settlements in the valleys, game of all kind amounds. Some of the scenery in this county is unrivaled for beauty and grandeur. Especially is this true of the coast country.

ADDENDA

226

STATE ASYLUM FOR THE INSANE, NAPA.

(345)

BIOGRAPHIES.

JOHN YORK.

The main portion of this volume had gone to press ere we were able to get a notice of this old and highly esteemed pioneer. Therefore, the few lines notice of him found on page 167 are so unsatisfactory that we here give a more extended notice.

Mr. York was born in Granger county, Tennessee, in 1820, and lived with his family in that State till in 1840 he removed to Missouri. Here he lived till he started for California. Two years after he went to Missouri he was married. On the 15th of April, 1845, he, with his wife and one child, started overland for California. At Independence he joined a company of which the following were members: Benjamin Duell, now of Lake, John Grigsby, David Hudson, Wm. Hudson, W. B. Elliot, now of Lake, Wm. Ide, Mrs. Delaney and sons, Messrs. McDowell, Ford, and others. John Brown was elected Captain and served as such till the company reached Fort Laramie, where John Grigsby was elected successor. The company having experienced no unusual events on the way, arrived at Sutter's Fort in October, 1845. Later in the Fall he, in company with David and William Hudson and W. B. Elliot, came to Napa Valley, stopped a few days at Mr. Yount's ranch, moved to near the present site of Calistoga, where he erected a log cabin, the first building in that part of the country, and also put in the first crop of wheat. The valley abounded in all kinds of game, and the Indians were numerous. In 1848, on the discovery of gold, he went to the mines. Before leaving for the mines he had purchased his present ranch near St. Helena, and after an absence of six weeks in

(346)

the mines, where he had been at work making sometimes as much as $150 per day, returned and erected a house. Until 1860 he had confined his business to stock-raising, but in that year he commenced setting out vines, and has continued till the present, till he now has one among the best vineyards in that section. In early times bears were so numerous in that section that he many times stood in the door of his house and killed them. He had many thrilling adventures with these animals. When he first came into the valley it was hard to get bread, and after harvest it was some time, very difficult to get wheat ground. Many times has he found his house for weeks without bread. He is now blest with a fair share of this world's goods, and is one of the most respected citizens of his neighborhood.

J. B. WARFIELD.

J. B. Warfield, M. D., was born in Tuscarawas county, Ohio, in 1819. His father was a merchant, and both parents were natives of Baltimore, Maryland. When the War of 1812 broke out, the father, Basil H. Warfield, was one of the enlisted of the Maryland draft, and participated in the battle of North Point, where the Americans were victorious, and the British General lost his life. He then removed (having a large family), to a place remote from the seat of war and settled in Ohio. In 1831, the father, with his family of twelve children, removed to Indiana. At the age of twenty-four the subject of this sketch commenced the study of medicine, and in 1849 he graduated in his chosen profession at Cincinnati. He had for some years prior to his graduating been engaged in practice in the town of Weston, Missouri, and after he graduated returned to this place, intending there to locate. But on his arrival he found many of the people wild with excitement over the discovery of gold in California, and in August of the same year, after a trip of ninety-six days, he found himself in the mines of El Dorado county. After following the adventurous life of a miner for some time, he settled in Marysville and commenced the practice of his profession. He was eminently successful here. In 1854 he visited his parents, they having returned to their native city. His father died in 1856, at the age of seventy-five. His mother, now in her eighty-fourth

(347)

year, still lives and enjoys excellent health. In 1856 Dr. Warfield removed to North San Juan, El Dorado county, and was elected a member of the Assembly to the Legislature of 1858. He was for some years engaged in mining, merchandising, and the practice of his profession. In 1860 he removed to San Francisco and engaged in the exciting business of the day-incorporations, quartz mining, and mills. In 1864 he married the eldest daughter of Dr. C. T. Overton, formerly of Nevada county, but who died some years since in Napa. In 1867 he located in Sonoma Valley, purchased his present excellent property, where he has since resided cultivating the soil and practicing his profession. In 1867 he was elected a member of the Assembly from Sonoma county, and ably represented his constituents in the Legislature.

In politics Dr. Warfield has always been a firm Democrat, but his public services have ever been characterized for their fairness and statesmanlike ability. Ever watchful of the interests of the people, he has made many political friends, and by his courteous and fair dealing in his private relations of life, has surrounded himself with a host of warm personal friends.

CHARLES M. HUDSPETH.

This highly esteemed citizen and pioneer was born in Overton county, Tennessee, in 1800. When ten years old emigrated with his family to Alabama. In 1816 he emigrated to the territory now known as Mississippi. After remaining here ten years following the business of farmer, he moved to the territory of Arkansas. In 1849 he came by the Southern route overland to California, and settled in Sonoma county. He served as a volunteer Captain under Lieutenant-Colonel Gray in the Mexican War. After coming to California he tried mining for a time, but this proved financially disastrous, and he returned to his home in Sonoma county. He now resides near Santa Rosa. He has been elected to many offices by the people, and always acquitted himself with credit. He was married in 1821, and is the father of twelve children, only three of whom are still living.
(348)

JAMES M. HUDSPETH.

The subject of this sketch was born in Madison county, Alabama, in 1812. In 1816 his family removed to Mississippi, where he resided till 1842, when he emigrated to Oregon. In 1843 he came to California and settled in Sonoma county. He was a member of the Bear Flag party, and

served as Lieutenant under Fremont in the liberating of California from Mexico. In 1851 he was elected Assemblyman from Sonoma, and the following election was chosen Senator. He owns a fine tract of land West of Sebastopol, where he devotes his attention to farming and stock-raising. He lost one arm by an inflamation of the hand. He is highly esteemed by his neighbors and the people of the county.
(349)

_____

THE BAR OF NAPA.

The following compose the Bar of Napa: W. C. Wallace, W. W. Pendegast, Robert Crouch, Thos. P. Stoney, C. Hartson, R. Burnell, F. E. Johnston, T. J. Tucker, D. McClure, R. N. Steere, Dennis Spencer, R. M. Swain, G. W. Towle, J. E. Pond, C. A. Menefee, Charles A. Gardner.

Mr. Wallace is a native of Missouri, and has been long and favorably known in Sonoma, Napa, and adjoining counties, as one among the ablest of practitioners. In 1869 he was elected Judge of the Seventh Judicial District to succeed J. B. Southard, and still occupies that position.

W. W. Pendegast is a native of Kentucky. Attended the Hesperian College at Woodland in the early days of that institution, studied law under Wallace & Rayle, of Napa, was admitted to the bar in 1864, and has been in practice in Napa since. He served the county one term as District Attorney, and has been twice elected to the Senate.

T. J. Tucker was born in Toledo county, New York, in 1833: came to California in 1852; studied law and was admitted to the bar of the Supreme Court at Sacramento in 1860, and has since been engaged in practice in Napa. In 1869 he was elected District Attorney, and served one term.

R. Burnell was born in Chautauque county, New York, in 1825. He was admitted to the Bar in the Common Pleas Court in 1847. He represented Amador county one term in the Legislature, and was in 1871 elected District Attorney for Napa county.
(350)

David McClure was born in Clark county, Illinois, in 1842. Studied law and was admitted to the Bar in Napa county before J. B. Southard in 1869. In 1871 he was admitted to the Supreme Court of Illinois, and in the following year to that of California. He is now partner in the firm of Crouch & McClure.

G. W. Towle was born in Franklin county, Maine, in 1823. At the age of twenty-three he was admitted to the Bar in Massachusetts, and in 1853 to the Supreme Court of California. He has long been a resident of Napa City, where he has filled many positions of trust.

F. E. Johnston was born in Green county, Missouri. Taught school for some time in California. Studied law and was admitted to the Bar in 1869. He has since been practicing in Napa, and is now partner in the firm of Pendegast & Johnston.

Dennis Spencer was born in Jackson county, Missouri, in 1844. Studied law in the office of Pendegast & Stoney, and was admitted to the Bar in 1870, and is now attending the law school at Albany, New York.

R. N. Steere was born in Rhode Island, in 1839. Studied law in the office of Wallace, Rayle & Pendegast, and was admitted to practice in 1866. In 1867 he was elected District Attorney and served one term.

R. M. Swain was born in Michigan in 1839, and was raised a farmer. Attended the College at Santa Clara, and was for a time engaged on the press. He studied law and was admitted to the Bar in Napa county in 1870. In 1871 he was elected Justice of the Peace for Napa Township, but resigned. He was appointed Under Sheriff by Mr. Zollner, and still occupies that position.

T. P. Stoney, was born in Charleston, South Carolina, April 25th, 1835. He arrived in California in December, 1856. Studied law in the law office of Hartson & Edgerton, and was admitted to the Bar in Napa county in 1859. In 1871 he was elected County Judge of Napa county, which position he still holds.

Charles A. Gardner was born in Iroquois county, Illinois, in 1843. He was admitted to practice in Los Angeles county in 1870. Located in Napa in the Winter of 1872.

Robert Crouch and C. Hartson are noted in the chapter on biographies of Napa county. (351)

TABLE SHOWING THE CONDITION AND PROGRESS OF NAPA CITY.

————

The following shows the business condition in 1856 and 1872. The first is that of 1856:

Miscellaneous stores, 9; hotels, 2; restaurants, 3; blacksmith shops, 3; wagon makers, 3; shoe-makers, 2; tailors, 1; butchers, 2; saddler, 1; tin smith, 1; sewing machine, 1; apothecary, 2; express offices, 2; printing offices, 1; billiard saloons, 2; bakery, 1; steam mills, 2; store-houses, 2; livery stables, 3; barbers, 1; churches, 1; bar rooms, 12; physicians, 2; lawyers, 4.

Within the period between 1856 and 1858 was organized the Napa County Agricultural Society, Napa Jockey Club, Napa Dramatic Club, Napa Brass Band, and a Minstrel Troupe.

Business houses, &c., in Napa City, November, 1872: Book, stationery and fancy goods store, 2; stationery stores, 3; general merchandise stores, 7; grocery stores, 5; fruit and confectionery stores, 4; dry goods stores, 3; clothing stores, 1; hardware and agricultural implement stores, 5; drug stores, 2; shoe stores, 3; bakers, 3; millinery stores, 3; butchers, 3; dress makers, 3; watchmakers, 3; land and insurance agents, 3; insurance agents, 2; law firms, 8; dentists, 1; physicians, 5; undertakers, 2; hotels, 9; bars, 27; wine depots and manufactories, 2; wine cellars, 2; coopers, 1; plow and wagon manufacturers, 4; marble works, 1; marble dealers, 1; machine shops, 2; blacksmiths, 6; bakeries, 3; tailors, 2; boot and shoe shops, 8; barbers, 5; saddlers, 4; feed stables, 2; livery stables, 3; furniture stores, 2; tanneries, 2; wood-workers, 1; gunsmiths, 2; breweries, 1; photograph establishments, 1; carpenter shops, 5; grain warehouses, 4; restaurants, 4; wagon makers, 1; vegetable dealers, 2; tinsmiths, 4; printing offices, 2; billiard saloons, 5; steam mills, 1; lumber yards, 2; paint shops, 3; public halls, 1; schools, 4; churches, 7; congregations, 8; glove factories, 1; whip factories, 1, gas works, 1. (352)

STATISTICS OF THE FOUR COUNTIES

	Sonoma*	Napa*	Lake[r]	Mendocino[r]
Land enclosed, acres..................	500,000	107,650	59,596	250,000
Land cultivated, "	312,800	40,620	12,227	24,000
Land cultivated in Wheat..........	165,200	32,530	5,591	31,000
Land cultivated Barley..............	15,340	3,725	3,068	9,000
Land cultivated Oats.................	23,380	750	235	40,000
Land cultivated Rye..................	159	40[r]	9	--------
Land cultivated Corn................	3,873	1,700	467	250
Land cultivated Hay..................	21,510	8,650	3,565	30,000
Land cultivated Potatoes...........	3,543	30[r]	31	3,000
Land cultivated Hops................	26[r]	15[r]	--------	200
Butter, pounds..........................	762,400	145,000	30,896	117,600
Cheese, "................................	356,207	7,350	65,600	9,800
Silk Cocoons, pounds...............	--------	100	--------	--------
Wool, "	272,925	51,610	56,488	274,000
Honey, "	1,200	3,750	6,245	--------
Apple trees.............................	29,086	61,500	11,143	25,000
Peach trees..............................	62,300	25,800	6,002	22,000
Pear trees................................	16,175	19,025	1,791	3,060
Plum trees...............................	44,890	7,115	2,431	2,100
Cherry trees............................	8,321	12,340	362	640
Orange trees (other fruits omitted)	56	70	15	--------
Mulberry trees.........................	2,877	58,250	129	--------
Grape vines.............................	4,798,348	2,324,545	30,979	25,000
Gallons of wine........................	876,328	464,320	--------	--------
Distilleries..............................	4	11	--------	--------
Gallons of Brandy....................	1,250	13,999	--------	--------
Breweries................................	4	2	--------	5
Gallons of Beer........................	85,010	38,000	--------	15,000
Grist Mills--Water power..........	2	2	1	5
" " Steam " ...	6	2	1	2
Bbls. Flour made......................	75,063	14,370	21,600	27,000
Bushels Corn ground................	6,399	5,650	2,000	600
Saw Mills-Steam power............	13	2	3	18
Saw Mills-Water "	1	0	2	0
Lumber sawed-feet...................	14,693,327	60,000	--------	70,000,000
Shingles made..........................	4,286,890	--------	500,000	3,000,000

* Report of 1872;   [r] Report of 1871

(353)

VALUE OF PROPERTY IN NAPA COUNTY.

Napa county is divided into eleven Road Districts. No. 1 comprises the Soscol county; No. 2, Napa City and vicinity; No. 3, Berryessa Valley; No. 4, country between No. 2 and Sonoma county line; No. 5, country West of Napa River and North of Nos. 2
and 4; No. 6, country East of Napa River and North of No. 2; No. 7, country North of Yountville; No. 8, St. Helena and vicinity; No. 9 Calistoga and vicinity; No. 10, Pope Valley; No. 11, Knoxville and vicinity.

The following is the assessed value of the lands in these several Road Districts:

	Real Estate	Personal Property	Total
Road Dist. No. 1	$ 567,335	$ 160,103	$ 827,438
Road Dist. No. 2	1,377,800	850,258	2,228,058
Road Dist. No. 3	458,659	159,240	617,899
Road Dist. No. 4	721,905	138,300	860,205
Road Dist. No. 5	599,895	157,729	757,604
Road Dist. No. 6	187,770	56,252	244,022
Road Dist. No. 7	613,835	135,841	749,676
Road Dist. No. 8	735,650	254,159	989,809
Road Dist. No. 9	372,515	100,210	472,725
Road Dist. No. 10..............	225,271	117,470	342,741
Road Dist. No. 11..............	97,685	49,285	146,970
Total	$ 6,058,320	$ 2,178,827	$ 8,237,147

VALUE OF PROPERTY IN SONOMA COUNTY.

The following table shows the assessed value of property in the several townships of the county of Sonoma:

Name of Township	Real Estate	Personal Property	Total
Petaluma,...................	$2,956,874	$1,185,223	$4,142,097
Santa Rosa,...............	2,584,509	971,688	3,556,197
Mendocino,...............	1,288,121	645,975	1,934,096
Sonoma,....................	1,779,058	617,120	2,396,178
Anally,......................	1,396,690	457,330	1,854,290
Bodega,....................	581,496	204,576	786,072
Cloverdale,................	316,041	169,348	485,390
Vallejo,.....................	1,465,160	305,081	1,770,241
Washington,...............	280,466	113,259	393,725
Salt Point,..................	147,821	124,636	272,457
Ocean,......................	164,314	57,269	221,583
Redwood,.................	59,405	23,414	82,819

Russian River,...........	761,734	286,251	1,047,985
S. F. & N. P. R. R....	58,225	885,995	944,220
Totals..............	$13,840,184	6,047,166	$19,887,350

(354)

TABLE OF TEMPERATURES.

Below we give the mean temperature of each month in the year, at Napa City and Calistoga, at 6 A. M., 12 M. and 6 P. M.

	Napa City.			Calistoga		
	6 A.M.	12 M.	6 P.M	6 A.M.	12 M.	6 P.M.
January................................	35^0	69^0	50^0	46^0	56^0	52^0
February.............................	46	59	55	50	59	36
March..................................	50	68	61	56	60	56
April....................................	45	69	57	52	70	60
May.....................................	50	73	62	68	77	76
June.....................................	56	77	67	68	90	68
July......................................	60	80	72	73	74	79
August.................................	52	84	70	60	86	77
September............................	55	81	72	55	82	68
October................................	43	88	76	52	81	72
November............................	46	72	55	48	64	61
December.............................	35	61	58	46	57	56

The observations at Napa were taken at Dr. Boynton's drug store; those at Calistoga at the Springs Hotel.

VALUE OF LAND IN MENDOCINO COUNTY.

In 1868-9, land and improvements are classed as land, except improvements on possessory claims, or on land of non-residents, which will account for the small valuation that year under the head of improvements, and large valuation in proportion:

	Land.	Improvements.	Personal.	Total.
1859-60...............	$492,457	$371,694	$1,728,754	$2,562,905
1868-9.................	472,678	164,501	1,372,666	2,009,845
1872-3.................	1,985,084	749,647	2,580,168	5,314,899

(355)

VINEYARDS OF NAPA

In addition to the vineyards already noticed in the body of this work, we here note a few more, and give some statistics connected with the business of viniculture.

J. H. McCord has a vineyard of 20,000 vines, three-fourths of which are foreign, near Pine Station, above Rutherford's. Mr. McCord is a pioneer of 1849; purchased this place in 1855. Besides his vineyard, he has an orchard and considerable fine farming land.

Next above Mr. McCord's place is the farm and vineyard of Mr. M. Vann. This gentleman came to California in 1852; purchased a tract of land of Mrs. Bale; now has a fine homestead, a large orchard, and a vineyard of 25,000 vines, about two-thirds of which are foreign.

Above the farm of Mr. Vann is that of Mr. Smith, who has thirty acres of vines, about half of which are foreign. Next and last, we notice the splendid premises of Mr. John Lewelling. This estimable citizen was born in North Carolina, in 1810; came to California in 1850; settled at San Jose Mission; planted an orchard of 80 acres in the years '53 and '54, and sold out. In 1858 he went to San Lorenzo, where he still owns 118 acres all in orchard and small fruits. In 1864 bought 163 acres near St. Helena, known as the Young Anderson place, on which he has set an orchard of 500 apple trees, besides plums, cherries and other fruits; also an almond orchard of 1,800 trees, and a vineyard of 35,000 vines, all foreign. In 1865 he bought 184 acres more of L. H. Moor on the opposite side of the road, and extending from the road to the foot of the mountains on the Western side of the valley. He has since bought a mountain tract back of the Moor place of 190 acres, which gives him fine pasture lands and splendid water privilege. In 1870 he erected a splendid house on the Moor place at a cost of $10,000; on this place he also has 1,600 almond trees and 50,000 vines, comprising about 24 varieties, the greater portion foreign.

In the district of country lying between Oakville and Calistoga there were 1,967 acres in vineyards, nearly two-thirds of which were foreign varieties. In 1871 only about one-half of this number were bearing vines, yet the yield of grapes was 25,320,000 pounds. Since (356) that date many new vineyards have been set, and the work still continues.

VINEYARDS OF SONOMA.

Sonoma Valley is the greatest wine-producing section in either of the counties. In this valley alone, and on the surrounding foot-hills, there are over 3,000 acres set in vines, all bearing; and in the whole county there are over 1,000 more acres. In 1867 the total number of vines was only 2,564,850; in 1872 there were 4,798,348.

The largest vineyard in the county is that of the Buena Vista Vinicultural Society, which covers nearly 400 acres, and contains nearly 400,000 vines. There are several other vineyards of over 100 acres, and over thirty more that have from 20 to 100 acres.

We had hoped to be able here to give tables showing the various vineyards, their extent, number of vines, and yield, but the statistics furnished us we find to be unreliable, and will not therefore present them.

SONOMA BARRACKS.

In our Frontispiece is seen the Plaza, old Barracks, and many of the buildings of the town of Sonoma. The building near the center, the end of which is propped up, is what is known as the Barracks. Around this building were enacted many of the most stirring scenes in the history of Sonoma. Here the Independent Party in 1846 hoisted the memorable Bear Flag, and here the Government forces were quartered. The view represents the town of Sonoma of to-day.

Index

To C. A. Menefee's
Historical and Descriptive
Sketchbook
of
Napa, Sonoma, Lake, and Mendocino

Copyright ^c 1993, James D. Stevenson, Jr.

Page numbers in this index refer to the number at the top of a page, not to C. A. Menefee's number on left margin in the text.